FEEDING HORSES & PONIES

David & Charles

TO BERNARD

A DAVID & CHARLES BOOK

First published 1995

A catalogue record for this book is available from the British Library.

ISBN 0 7153 0309 0

Typeset by Drum & Co
and printed in England by BPC Paulton Ltd
for David & Charles
Brunel House Newton Abbot Devon

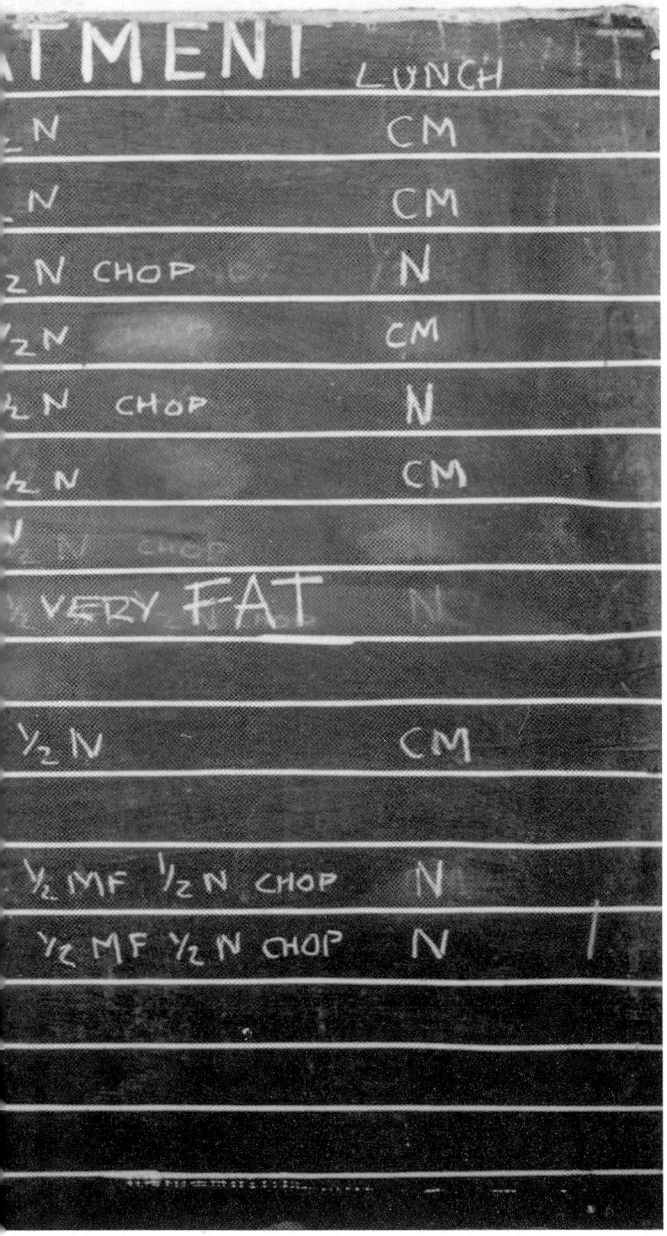
LUNCH
CM
CM
CHOP
N
CM
CHOP
N
CM
VERY FAT
½ N
CM
½ MF ½ N CHOP
N
½ MF ½ N CHOP
N

CONTENTS

INTRODUCTION

If you described a horse as a stomach on legs you would not be far wrong. In natural conditions, and left to themselves in domestic circumstances, horses will eat for sixteen to eighteen hours out of each twenty-four, night and day. They only sleep in short snatches for four or five hours, again night and day, and the number of hours left leaves very little time for doing anything else. As grazing and sometimes browsing herbivores, horses have evolved to live on vegetation which, by its very nature, is not a concentrated form of nourishment. Grass forms the bulk of the horse's food, and consists mainly of fibrous roughage and water, and so do most other plants at most times of year. Young growth is often 'richer' in nutrient content, but although vegetation can contain all a free living horse needs in the way of nourishment, generally he needs to eat an awful lot of it to obtain his requirements; this is why he needs to eat almost all the time, so there is a constant, steady, moderate stream of food passing through his digestive system.

It is not surprising, then, that horses and ponies think of food most of the time: this is what evolution has programmed them to do. They are not necessarily greedy, just doing what comes naturally. Most observant owners must have noticed the change in a horse or pony's physical state and mental attitude when he is living out at grass in good conditions, with enough keep on his field, and with water, shelter, adequate space and congenial companions. He has everything he could wish for, and is settled, content, confident and relaxed. This is the lifestyle he was meant to have.

When we stable horses and ponies, they can adapt to confinement very well if we take care of their needs and wants. Unfortunately, the subject which is probably the single most important one a horse owner or manager needs to understand, that of feeding, is still abused and misunderstood. Many horses are still fed according to human-devised rules and conveniences, which treat them as though they had digestive systems more like our own than the type they actually do have. They are very often given just two or three main feeds a day, with restricted amounts of hay or its equivalent night and morning. The main feeds (in our estimation) are those fed in buckets or mangers and consist normally of some sort of concentrated food aimed at giving horses the energy we feel they need to do our work. The concentrated foods themselves are almost never of a sort the horse would come across in the wild. Moreover the gaps between feeds are often very long, particularly overnight when stabled animals can be without any food at all for as long as a human's working day or even longer, and this practice positively encourages colic and other digestive disorders, not to mention extreme physical discomfort for the horse.

'Colic' is a horseman's term meaning some type of serious indigestion; to veterinary surgeons it means abdominal pain and it can, of course, kill a horse and is always extremely painful. Colic is an affliction of the domesticated horse, not the wild one. A great deal of research has been done on equine nutrition over the last decade or so, research which is fortunately continuing, but human nature being what it is, the general horse world is being slow to take on board much of the new knowledge it is bringing. Many people find it very hard to abandon pet theories and practices they have followed for years: old habits are comfortable and comforting, and they die hard! But surely the first responsibility of anyone caring for a horse is that horse's best interests and wellbeing. Very gradually, people are beginning to advocate a more natural way of life, a change in attitude which is becoming increasingly noticeable in the horse world, conservative though it usually is.

Feeding practices affect horses quickly and dramatically, and the safest and most effective way to feed them is to follow their natural needs as closely as domesticity

will allow. Fortunately, new knowledge and new feed products now make this not only possible but easy. This does not mean that all domesticated horses and ponies are recommended to be kept entirely at grass, although this sort of management practice is certainly important to them. What it does mean is getting to grips with truly appropriate feeding practices and products, understanding what horses and ponies really need and thrive on, and going along with that even if it means changing some of our long-held ideas. I do hope this book will help in that process, and that horses, ponies and their owners will all benefit from it.

I

WHY BOTHER TO EAT?

The whole point of providing a horse with food, or letting him find it himself by grazing grass or browsing on leaves, is to give him first, the fuel and raw materials so that he can actually build and repair all the body tissues from which he is made, and also the energy or fuel to maintain that body and to live.

Horses evolved to eat most of their time, round the clock; left to themselves, they spend sixteen to eighteen hours a day just eating and foraging for a variety of foodstuffs. In natural conditions, they will be grazing and living amongst other species of animals with whom they have complementary grazing and feeding practices. They may eat different grasses or different parts of the same grasses. For instance the zebra, a close relative of the horse, is known to eat mainly the fibrous stems of grasses, and their colleagues, the wildebeest, the flowering or seeding heads. In this way, the horse family has forged its own niche in the world of herbivores (vegetation-eating animals) and co-exists happily. It is, like other animals, free to migrate and wander to find fresh pastures, shelter and water. This pattern has been followed for many millions of years.

Left: These are feral horses living in the Camargue in the south of France. They are in good condition, and receive everything they need for a successful lifestyle from their environment

The Problems of Domestication

The domesticated horse faces a different life altogether. Particularly if he is mainly stabled, he has no freedom at all really to do anything. He eats only when and what his human attendants permit, he can only wander under human supervision, and even when turned out into a paddock he is severely restricted by the space and herbage available in that comparatively tiny area.

Under these conditions, feeding problems often occur and the horse's human attendants have to learn as much as possible about how to feed their charges if they are to get the best out of them, and also to avoid illness and possibly death.

The Purposes of Food

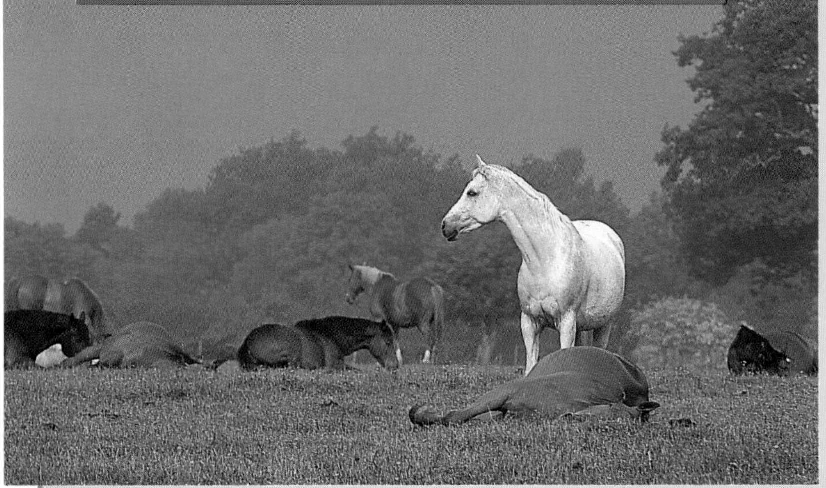

Even when lying flat out in a deep sleep, horses need energy from food to keep the mind and body working

Most mammals, unless they are hibernating, need to eat regularly and frequently in order to live. This is because energy is essential for all life processes; even when a horse is flat out, deeply asleep, his body uses energy to keep his systems going. Every twitch of a muscle, every heartbeat, flick of the tail, blink of an eyelid needs energy to fuel it, and obviously, the more movement or work that takes place the more energy is needed. Just as obviously, the only way that the horse is going to obtain energy (fuel) is from his food; and he can only get out what he can take in: in a domesticated state this is the key to his entire life, and it is completely up to us.

Allocating Priorities

The most important requirement of food is to maintain body temperature, which in the horse is about 38°C (100.5°F). The body has evolved to work optimally at that temperature, and very little variation is possible without problems.

The second requirement of food is the making of new body tissue (skin, horn, hair, organs, body fluids and so on) to permit growth and development in youngstock, and to replace that used daily in both young and old just by living.

Thirdly, food is used for the provision of energy for movement and life in general.

Fourthly, food is used to maintain bodily condition, to keep 'weight' on and store food in fat depots around the body, in the liver and in the muscles.

The maintenance of body temperature

This is the most important requirement of all: without the correct body temperature – which can only vary a very few degrees either side of the optimal if health, and even life, are to be sustained – everything else counts for nothing. Old horses, and horses which are very fit, have a lower body temperature than young or unfit horses. This is one of Nature's adaptations, so that hard-working horses can withstand the rise in temperature in the body which always occurs with activity. Ponies tend to have a higher temperature than horses.

Food is allocated by the body more or less in order of priority, and it is particularly noticeable that horses left out in cold, wet weather lose condition as the body calls on its reserves to keep its temperature up. If the situation is not relieved, the horse becomes thinner and thinner, feeling the cold more and more as the fat reserves beneath the skin are used up (fat being an excellent insulator); eventually it will be unable to keep up its temperature and will die.

Growth, development and tissue repair come next in importance. The very substance of the horse's physical structure has to be produced, from conception to death – the foetus, growth in youngstock and the repair of any body tissues which are damaged or come to the end of their life during everyday wear and tear.

These two pictures show a grossly malnourished pony restored to good condition by the Horses and Ponies Protection Association. It can take many months for good condition to be reached from as severe a start as this and when the animal concerned is a youngster the stunted development which results from lack of feed may never be fully made up

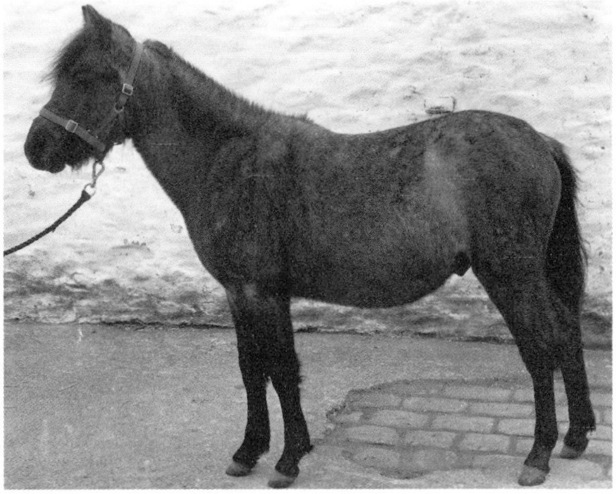

The work-related ration

The two requirements described above are the most important of the four we have identified. If a horse's ration is only just enough to satisfy these two needs, he will remain in reasonable condition, but he will not put on weight, and he will not have much energy for anything but light work. If we force him to work harder, his body will need extra energy but will not be able to generate it from such basic maintenance feed, and so will call on whatever fat reserves he has; and so the horse will lose weight. Moreover, if the forced work continues, the body will start using up its own tissues as fuel, and weight loss will be quick and marked. Ultimately the skin-and-bones stage will be reached, the body temperature will drop critically low, and the horse will die.

Conversely, if the horse receives more food than he needs for maintenance of temperature and for growth and repair, he will store much of the excess as fat, to be converted to energy when required. Thus he may well be bouncing with health, but if he is allowed to become obese he will find physical movement an effort and a strain, and over-fed horses are subject to all those familiar and distressing conditions such as laminitis, azoturia and breathlessness, as well as general over-stressing of their heart, tendons and bones.

Stud stallions, particularly those who are not working apart from their stud duties, are often kept overfat to counteract the tendency of some to 'run up light' (lose weight) later in the stud season. However, correct feeding and physical fitness produce higher fertility rates than obesity

Feeding the Mind

As well as maintaining the horse's physical wellbeing, the act of grazing grass, browsing leaves or munching hay (or its equivalent) for many hours a day is a programmed-in need in the horse. Many experts and experienced, sympathetic horse people feel that the horse has a deep psychological need to eat almost constantly.

Stable vices

It is certainly true that horses on a roughage-restricted diet frequently develop the stereotyped habits or abnormal behaviours that we commonly call stable vices, partly as a way to keep moving, a replacement for the movement involved in grazing and chewing, and partly because this sort of movement produces the body's own tranquillisers, endorphins and encephalins – or so it is currently and with good evidence believed; these calm down a troubled mind, troubled because it is being deprived of a natural need.

Providing a more or less constant supply of suitable roughage food goes a very long way towards ensuring that the horse's mind is kept busy and his digestive tract kept occupied and filled as nature intended; such food might be an appropriate grade of hay or hayage, or feeding straws, if suitable, such as oat straw or barley straw, or large roots left available for the horse to crunch on, or plenty of fibre in the manger, or 'short' feeds in the form of chop (chaff) or the short-cut forage feeds now available and discussed in Chapter 3. Providing such food leads to a more comfortable, contented and problem-free horse.

Ponies and cobs have evolved to live on very sparse keep or grazing and browsing. There is no point in letting them graze on rich, 'improved' pasture such as that found on most cultivated land; too much of that can give them serious health problems

Food and Freedom

Pasture is probably the most underrated facility and source of food, and one of the most neglected, in the horse world. Horses need occupation, nutrition and liberty, and being turned out to grass provides them with all of that.

Grass can, however, cause problems for certain categories of horse, or more usually, cob and pony. Our native cobs and ponies evolved to survive very adequately on extremely poor grazing and by browsing, but modern agriculture has killed off most of the type of keep on which they do best; farms have crept further and further up hillsides, and farmers have sown richer and richer varieties of grass so as to achieve better growth rates and greater weight on what are primarily meat animals, namely sheep and cattle.

Horse and ponies, however, are athletic animals needed for work far more than for food. But our native breeds now only find their natural keep in the higher lands of our country, or on the moors which are not conventionally farmed. When kept on 'improved' (enriched) grassland they easily become overweight, and this often triggers off mainly laminitis, but also other disorders.

It is important for the contentment and wellbeing of our horses and ponies that we pay more attention to the creation and management of suitable pasture for them. The value of turning out to grass for all equines should be appreciated, and the importance of providing the right type of pasture for them – not too difficult a task today, with suitable grass-seed mixes easily available – given due regard and practical action.

These feral horses in Kaimanawa, New Zealand, are mostly well-covered without being fat; in good condition for their lifestyle

Energy is the Key

Energy is the intangible but essential end result of the horse eating his food. It is produced as a result of the various nutrients being oxidised or 'burnt up' and used by the body. Most of the horse's energy comes from starches and sugars (carbohydrates), but it also comes from fats and oils, and finally from any excess protein.

The amount of protein in a food used to be regarded as the main factor in deciding what feed to give a horse, but research has now shown us that mature animals, even in hard work, require less protein than we had previously supposed; about 8.5 per cent contained in the entire diet, including grass and hay or its equivalent, should normally be adequate, and probably no more than 10 per cent. Stallions, broodmares, youngstock and elderly horses need more. Excess protein can cause various problems (discussed in the following section).

These Thoroughbreds racing almost neck-and-neck to the finish of their race show the lean condition and muscular development needed for the job

Constituents of Food

The main feed constituents are carbohydrates (starches and sugars), proteins, fats or oils (also called lipids and lipins), vitamins, minerals and trace elements (minerals needed in tiny amounts). Most feeds contain some or all of the above constituents, but in differing proportions.

Carbohydrates are used for the production of heat and energy. The body stores excess amounts as fat around the body and as glycogen in the liver and muscle cells. Glycogen is the main source of energy.

Proteins are the only foods which can make body tissue. Excess protein can be stored as fat, but it then loses its tissue-making qualities and simply provides extra, rather expensive energy when needed.

Fat is a heat and energy producer. It is good for helping to put weight on a horse and is energy-dense, providing one-and-a-half (some experts now maintain up to two-and-three-quarters) times more energy than carbohydrate. It is therefore useful for hard-working horses, particularly endurance horses and those doing sustained work (hunters, eventers and competitive carriage-driving horses, for example) at the limits of their appetite. It also helps condition skin, hair and horn.

Vitamins, minerals and trace elements are all needed as vital nutrients, but often in only very small amounts. All commonly given foods possess different amounts of different ones, all having an individual purpose. Serious physical and mental disturbances can occur due to deficiencies or overdoses of these substances, so expert advice on formulating a balanced ration, with or without a supplement, is essential. Even knowledgeable owners are sometimes reluctant to seek advice and may rely solely on the product's label when deciding whether or not to feed a supplement, even though it takes scientific knowledge, which they probably do not have, to understand the significance of the analysis.

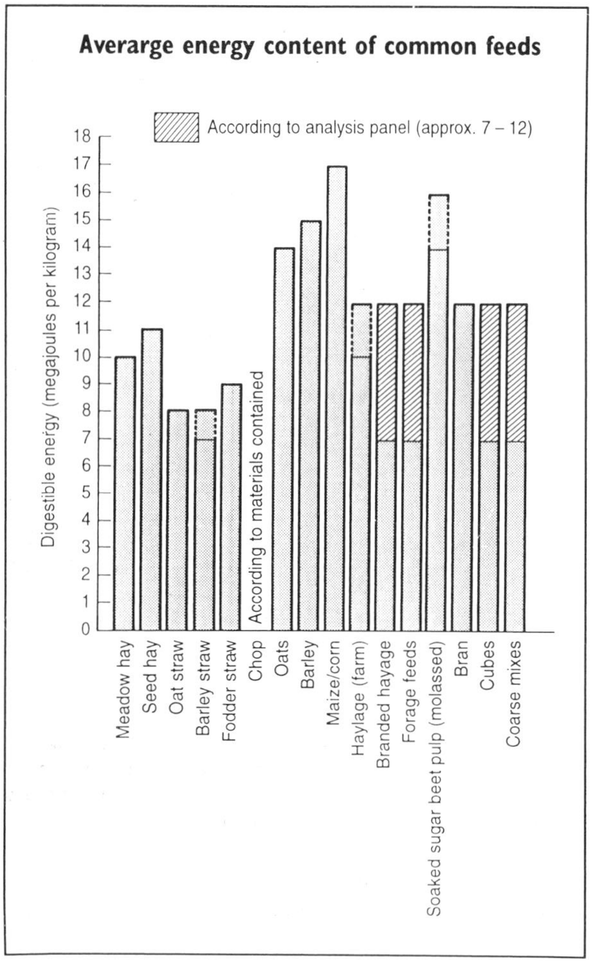

The energy content in feed

The factor you should use in deciding whether a feed is suitable for your horse is, firstly, the energy content. It is energy which fuels the horse's body, not protein; energy is actually used in making use of protein in the diet. It is the energy requirement which increases when the horse's work increases, not the protein requirement. Particularly with most commercially made feeds such as cubes, coarse mixes and pre-packed hayage and forage products, if you buy the right energy-level feed you can more or less assume that the rest of it will be suitable for your horse or pony's purposes.

Whilst protein is measured as a percentage of the diet, energy is measured in joules (a scientific measure) or megajoules of digestible energy, not all the energy in the diet being digestible or available to the horse's system. Branded products of a reputable make should state on their analysis labels the energy levels they contain. If they don't, ask the manufacturer.

For ponies, cobs and horses at rest or in light work, use feeds having an energy level of 8.5 (or less) to 10 MJ (megajoules) of DE (digestible energy) per kilogram; for horses in moderate to hard work, look for 10 to 12 MJ of DE. Rarely will more than 12 MJ of DE per kilogram be needed.

Although the horse's type and constitution must be taken into account when deciding on a suitable ration, you can basically work on the principle that if he remains skinny on what seems to be a suitable diet you should try increasing the energy level (assuming you have got the actual amount right). Of course, this also assumes that he is regularly and properly wormed, and that his teeth are not causing him eating problems.

Where does protein come in?

Having stressed the importance of using energy as a yardstick, it should also be emphasised that protein *is* a vital feed constituent: the body is largely made of proteins. There are various types of protein made up of amino acids, the 'building blocks' of the body. There are twenty-five amino acids, of which the horse needs twenty-two. Ten of these are called essential amino acids, as it is essential that they are provided in the diet, unlike the other twelve which the horse can make for himself in his body and are therefore called non-essential amino acids. The horse must also receive a nutritionally adequate diet so that he is able to make them. Most of the former are readily available in most of the feeds we give to horses; the three that are likely to be deficient (although not in a reputable branded compound feed such as horse cubes/nuts or coarse mix) are in particular lysine, also methionine and tryptophan. These are probably the first three a nutritionist would check when evaluating a horse's diet.

Protein requirements

Mature horses in light to moderate work should have no problems in getting adequate protein from a reasonable to good diet. It is those categories of animal which are under pressure – such as horses in hard work, breeding stock (mature and young) and elderly, sick or run-down horses or ponies – that may need more. The highest levels – 18 to 20 per cent – are needed by foals up to about three months of age; weanlings of six or seven months of age will need 16 per cent, reducing to 13.5 per cent as they become yearlings; and 10 per cent as two-year-olds (although possibly more if they are racing as well). Lactating mares in the first three months of their lactation need 14 per cent protein in their diet, reducing to 12 per cent from the fourth month to weaning. When in the last three months of a pregnancy, broodmares need 11 per cent protein in their diet.

Mature horses even in hard work need the least, 8.5 per cent in their total diet.

As with energy, not all the protein in the diet is available to (digestible by) the horse. The total protein content is usually expressed on analysis panels as a 'crude protein' percentage. A nutritionist would need to know the levels of the amino acids present and their balance before being able to assess whether the amount and, even more important, the quality (as shown by the amino acids present) were suitable. This is only one reason why it pays in both financial and health terms to buy the best brand that you can, and also, possibly, to get even that assessed for suitability by an independent nutritionist or veterinary surgeon interested in nutrition.

Breeding makes great demands on a mare and foal, and correct feeding is crucial for optimal health in both and for the development of the latter. This mare is in very poor condition. Her milk supply will be adversely affected and, therefore, the health and development of her foal. These are feral animals and will not be receiving supplementary feeds

Too much protein

It is not a good plan to feed extra protein in the hope that more of it will become available to the horse during digestion. Excess protein can actually cause health and performance problems: it takes a good deal of metabolising (processing) by the body, and uses energy in that process; it can make horses lethargic and ultimately put a strain on the kidneys which have to filter out and excrete the excess toxins produced. Too much protein can also cause excessive sweating (another means of excreting toxins) and the horse to break out (in a sweat) after work, as well as raised pulse and respiration rates – not the sort of thing you want in an athletic animal.

Concentrates

Concentrates are foods which contain higher levels of nutrients than a horse's natural food of grass or leaves; the nutrients are *concentrated* into a form which takes up comparatively much less space.

Cereal concentrates

The sorts of food which come to mind when we speak of concentrates are cereal grain foods such as oats and barley which are commonly fed to horses, and also maize/corn. Wheat grain is not normally a good food for horses as it is glutinous and can impact into a doughy, sticky mass in the stomach, causing colic. However, wheat by-products such as bran, breadmeal (sold as a commercial mix) and wheat feed can be obtained.

Other types of concentrate used more often by feed makers than by horse owners may include sorghum, rice products and other fairly unfamiliar seed or grain feeds, to us, anyway. Feed manufacturers have the scientifically qualified staff and the 'hardware' or laboratory facilities and equipment to analyse such cereal concentrates and to calculate the amounts of their different nutrients, so enabling them to make up a suitable mix (cubes or coarse feed) for different categories of horse or pony. No 'ordinary' horse owner can do this, and neither can those with even the highest equestrian (as opposed to scientific) qualifications.

What about dry matter?

The dry matter content of a particular feed means the value of that feed with all the water removed, so that one feed can be compared with another on a fair basis. Although it may not be obvious, most foods contain some water, and nutritionists use the dry matter basis for assessing feed content or value as it gives a truer picture.

Dressage is a discipline in which horses are often asked to go at a faster or slower pace within a given gait than they would naturally choose. In addition to carrying a rider, adjusting their weight backwards and performing taxing movements in a limited space, the mental concentration needed by the horse is demanding. This all adds up to hard work needing fit condition and careful feeding

Non-cereal concentrates

There are also 'non-cereal concentrates' which include sugar beet, dried grass and alfalfa/lucerne, 'old-timers' such as beans and peas, linseed, soya beans and meal and other feeds which are, again, more commonly used by feed manufacturers. Fats and oils such as corn oil, soya oil, cod-liver oil and animal grade linseed oil may also be considered as specialised concentrates.

Concentrate requirements

Concentrates are commonly known in the horse world by other names such as 'hard feed', 'shorts' and 'corn'. The expression 'hard feed' seems to have come about because it was said that horses doing hard work needed hard, or 'rich', concentrated feed; this may also have led to the fashion for feeding levels of concentrates which are far too high, some people believing (quite wrongly) that the more concentrates you feed, the fitter your horse will automatically become. While it may be true that most hard-working horses may need some concentrates, they seem to be generally overfed, and if the hay (or equivalent) portion of the horse's diet is nutritious enough, it is surprising how little concentrated feed a horse will need.

The expression 'shorts' implies – correctly – that this sort of food takes up comparatively little space and takes a much shorter time to eat than hay; also, the habit of calling concentrates in general 'corn', whether or not it is actually corn/maize which is being fed, has led to such expressions as 'corned-up' (meaning that the horse is being fed high levels of concentrates and is 'on his toes' or behaving excitedly as a result of the large amount of energy such feeds contain), and 'corn-sick' which, to horsemen if no one else, means that the horse has gone off his concentrates and is not 'cleaning up' (eating each feed right up). This may happen, whether or not the horse's human connections realise it, because the diet contains too many concentrates and not enough fibrous, bulky roughage without which concentrates cannot be efficiently digested anyway. These sorts of problem occur when horses are overfed with cereal concentrates, mainly because more waste products or poisons are produced during their metabolism, and these can have an adverse effect on the horse's wellbeing and temperament.

Roughage

Thankfully for the horse which is on the receiving end of all human theories and fancies about feeding, it is finally being realised that the equine system needs more fibrous, bulky roughage than it has, in many quarters, hitherto been 'fashionable' to feed. All sorts of reasons for keeping horses on low hay quotas have been put forward, the most common being that 'He mustn't fill himself up with hay or he won't have room for his corn and he won't get fit'; or, 'He'll get fat if he eats too much hay'; also 'He can't work if he's full of hay and he'll eat it all the time if I let him'; and, give us strength! 'It makes him cough'!

Racing demands a few minutes of supreme effort and top speed from horses, for which carefully integrated work and feeding is essential

Scientific research and advice

It may take a generation or so for current feeding practices to change significantly, but it is heartening that there is more interest among the general horse-owning public in equine research, science and scientifically based information on feeding and nutrition. Magazines now regularly publish reliable articles by equine nutritionists as well as by vets and writers with purely equestrian qualifications, and many top competitors employ nutritionists (and other specialists such as physiologists and physiotherapists) to help them get and keep their horses in peak health. A generation ago the only specialists who found their way on to a yard were the vet and the farrier.

Most equine nutritionists and vets with a specific interest in nutrition are now recommending that more good quality roughage (hay and suchlike) is fed as it is fast being realised how essential bulk is to the effective functioning of the equine digestive system, and also how important it is in keeping the horse feeling physically comfortable and, just as important, mentally occupied. The sound of horses munching hay is music to the ears of any horse owner concerned for his or her horse's physical wellbeing *and* his psychological contentment and health.

Insufficient roughage in the diet results in, at best, inefficient digestion, and at worst, colic – which can kill. It also results in anxiety, hunger, boredom and frustration in the horse, all of which can cause stable vices such as wood-chewing (partly due to hunger and lack of minerals), crib-biting, windsucking, box-walking, nasty temper and so on.

Types of roughage feed

These include hay, feeding straws, chop or chaff, hayage, coarse grass, and commercially packaged forage feeds which are basically grass, straw and alfalfa-based, sometimes cut up short and sometimes fed in long form. They also comprise two main sorts of fibre: woody lignin, which has no nutritional value but is needed to bulk out and stimulate the intestinal tract and to help physically break up other food; and cellulose, which can be broken down into mainly starches by bacterial action in the lower end of the digestive tract.

Roughages do contain other nutrients too, and at their best equate to good quality grazing minus the high water content of grass which has been dried out of them. They therefore represent a virtually complete, or a complete feed for horses and ponies on a maintenance or light-work ration, and on good roughages of fairly high feed value (for roughages), horses, cobs and ponies can certainly perform moderately hard work.

The value of roughage

Your horse's roughage is responsible for the following: 1) it helps keep him warm for long hours in winter; 2) it keeps him full and content; 3) it enables the concentrates you give him to be digested; and 4) it forms the most important part of his diet. Unfortunately, many people still think that concentrates are the most important dietary constituent, and treat hay as almost a throw-away, second-rate feed. Nothing could be further from the truth.

Yearlings at grass. Feeding is important at any age, but critical for youngsters. Deformities and stunted growth, or overstress from obesity, may never be fully corrected in later life, no matter how careful the management

Life in the Herd

Horses, as we know, are very much herd animals: there is safety in numbers when you are a prey animal. On your own you stand out for attack: in the herd you can hide, and the chances are that the predators will catch someone else. For this reason it is imperative to most horses that they are accepted within the herd. Most horses need company; true loners are very rare. But in a herd there is a very distinct hierarchy, with a leader (usually a mare) and a few high-ups, then the majority in a certain order down the middle line, and finally those at the bottom of the heap who come in for all the brickbats from the others.

This type of 'kicking-order' can be seen clearly in a domestic paddock, and even amongst stabled horses not allowed to mix freely with each other. There are friends, enemies and mere colleagues, and while things are ticking along normally the hierarchy rarely changes. However, when an animal becomes sick, injured or run down for whatever reason, things can change rapidly.

Horses feel secure when they know their place, and this state will continue as long as they are willing to co-operate in The System and not rock the boat. If a horse's physical or mental health suffers, however, even through no fault of its own, it often

Herd Leader or Whipping Boy?

Feeding obviously has a wide-ranging effect on a horse's physical wellbeing, and therefore on his mental state too, and it is this second factor – and maybe the first as well for all we know – which affects his standing with other horses and ponies. It also affects his behaviour with horses, humans and other animals, his learning ability, his physical and mental development, temperament, general attitude to life and, of course, his physical health.

happens that others previously subordinate to it, or not normally concerned with it, will suddenly start to pick on it. They see this as an opportunity to get rid of opposition, to move up in the hierarchy and therefore to improve their own status and position, and increase their security and safety. And it is certainly not only with horses that this happens!

The old and frail, the young, the sick, the injured and the timid are always near the bottom of the hierarchy, and this may upset their human connections; but keeping your horse in good condition, healthy, strong and well fed can, believe it or not, help him to rise in the crucial kicking-order, or at least to maintain his position. Healthy and strong, your horse will feel good and will have much more self-confidence in status struggles, as would any individual of any species; he will then have the strength and energy to fight if need be, or at least to push his way into his share of the grazing, water, shelter and favoured friendships and so enhance even further his health and security.

Conversely, if he is seen by herd members to be accepting bullying, to be weak, non-assertive and perhaps sorry for himself, they will, naturally, take advantage.

The qualities conferred by good feeding and health filter out to other areas of his life, too. He will learn better and more quickly, and will remember his lessons and experiences; his mind and body will develop optimally and he will have a much better chance of fulfilling his potential in life, whether it is to be the leader of a wild herd, an Olympic medal winner, a much loved family member or a safe, willing hunter.

Feeding affects every aspect of your horse's life, it is what he thinks about most of the time, it is what he *does* most of the time, given the chance, and it is the single most important topic of horse management to learn and understand.

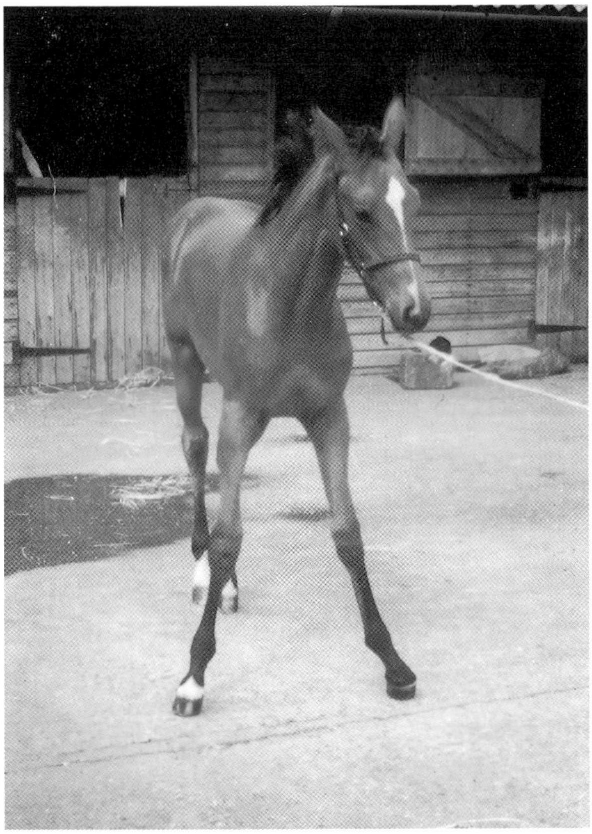

It may be understandable that people often overfeed foals as they want them to grow big and strong. However, overfeeding, or an unbalanced diet, can result in uneven growth and limb deformities such as in this case of so-called contracted tendons where the bones have grown faster than the tendons, which are now exerting a flexing pull on the feet and lower legs. In bad cases the hooves may actually turn right under and the foal be forced to walk on the fronts of the coronets

Key Facts

- **Feeding goes much further than affecting the horse's body. It also affects his mind, his temperament and his attitude to life.**
- **Do not underestimate the importance of roughage in the diet; it is the most important part of your horse's overall diet. A good roughage source can provide just about everything a horse or pony resting or in light to moderate work needs.**
- **Food obtained naturally, grazing and browsing at liberty, is just as valuable as that provided in the stable.**
- **Use energy levels as the yardstick by which to measure the suitability of a given food for your horse, not the level of protein.**

2

THE EQUINE DIGESTIVE SYSTEM AND ITS EVOLUTION

Probably the best-known and most widely published fact about the horse's digestive system is that it has a small stomach compared with the size of the animal and the stomach sizes of other animals. Also, the horse does not take its food, unchewed or prepared by crushing and soaking in saliva, into a rumen for fermentation before passing it into the stomach – unlike cattle with which, for some reason, it is often compared. In cattle and other cloven-hoofed animals, the rumen is like a large fermentation vat and comes before the true stomach; in the horse, fermentation – a vital part of digestion and the one which probably most defines its practical nutritional needs – takes place lower down the intestinal tract after the food has passed through the stomach and small intestine.

The horse's fermentation vat is the large intestine – the caecum and colon – where a population of billions of organisms (called, variously, gut micro-flora, micro-organisms, bacteria and protozoa) break down the cellulose in the diet. The vat is the equivalent of our tiny appendix.

Left: The equine digestive system evolved to thrive on a more or less *ad lib* supply of a varied but consistent diet. This pattern should be followed in domestic conditions

The Role of Lignin

The lignin or woody fibre in the diet is important, even though it has no nutritional content: it helps to fill out the intestine and encourages it to pummel and push the food along and to break it up. It can be seen in the droppings as tiny stiff fibres. It opens up the food to allow the digestive juices containing enzymes to get in and chemically break down the different nutrients, and this also facilitates the work of the essential gut micro-organisms. The food can then be turned into a liquid form, so its nutrients can be absorbed into the blood and carried round the body for use or storage, as needed.

A Natural Diet

The horse's digestive system therefore depends on a proper intake of his natural food, or something very like it. In a natural situation he would eat mainly grass and leaves and these consist largely of fibre and water with a fairly dilute nutritional content at most times of the year. Spring grass contains the highest levels of starch and sugar – the culprits in triggering laminitis – and also protein. At other times of year the nutritional content is lower and therefore safer for most categories of animal, except possibly ponies and cobs – it depends on circumstances such as the actual amount of grass, whether or not it is overgrazed, whether or not it is well cared for, or has been treated with high-nitrogen fertilisers (fatal for horses), and the level of rainfall, on which growth depends.

Grass and leaves can, obviously, provide enough nutrients for the horse, but because these are not sufficiently concentrated, large amounts have to be consumed fairly continuously; horses left to themselves with an adequate supply of foodstuffs will graze and browse for about sixteen to eighteen hours out of the twenty-four. In fact, in order to get enough nourishment from herbage such as grass and leaves, horses and ponies need to take in quite vast amounts of it (although we still do not know exactly how much grass a horse might eat) which accounts for the large capacity of the equine digestive system.

Cubes: a Complete Diet?

Some years ago, a new innovation arrived in the horse world in the form of 'complete' cubes which, it was claimed, removed the need to feed hay to horses. This was hailed with relief and wonder by many horse owners who, at that time, had gone through a particularly difficult winter trying to get even half-decent hay due to an appalling crop the previous summer. The more experienced may have been interested, but their interest was generally tempered with a degree of suspicion, knowing how important a horse's hay was to him.

The cubes were claimed to contain all the fibre the horse needed in his diet, as well as his other nutrients. It must be said that at that time, thirty years or so ago, we did not have the knowledge of equine nutrition that we have now and had no experience of 'hay-less' diets.

In practice the cubes may well have provided a consistent, *nutritionally* balanced diet as far as carbohydrate, protein, fats, vitamins and trace minerals were concerned, but the practical aspect of providing fibre in this form was a dismal failure. Not a few animals went down with colic due to the lack of bulky, fibrous roughage, and in general, horses were obviously very discontented, uncomfortable, bored and anxious: woodchewing became a problem, they started eating their own tails or those of other horses in their craving to get some bulk inside them, and crib-biting started in yards which had never known it before.

I personally could stand it no longer, and telephoned the manufacturers to see if I was 'doing it wrong'. No, I was told. Your horse will soon get used to it. He didn't, so I contacted my vet who advised feeding a small amount of hay at night. This helped, but was not enough, and after several weeks of misery on both my and my horse's part, I reverted to a normal ad lib hay-plus-concentrates diet.

I was not the only one, and most of my friends and contacts gave up the new cubes in despair. That was long ago; the so-called 'complete cubes' are still available, although they are improved; but even so, the manufacturers

The Importance of Fibre

Fibre (also called roughage, forage and bulk) is, as mentioned earlier, a still underrated yet vital part of the horse's feed requirements. Cellulose is a form of starch or carbohydrate and makes up part of the bulky, fibrous material in hay, hayage and grass. Grass is, of course, the horse's natural food so the importance of this digestive process is paramount and explains why the horse has such a capacious large intestine.

Grass is a highly underrated food: it is the horse's natural and major food source in the wild, and the one the equine digestive system is best suited to, having evolved on it over millions of years. The right type of grazing not only provides a completely adequate diet, but the action of cropping and chewing food, and being gently on the move most of the time, fulfils a vital physical and psychological need in the horse

themselves admit that it is advantageous to feed hay at night.

The main problem is that ingredients in all cubes are ground to a powder, then bound together with some type of syrup or molasses and finally pushed through a cylinder or dye to form a pencil shape which is cut to the lengths we are all familiar with. The horse can chew these up easily, and although they swell when in contact with his digestive juices, they do not, despite the original marketing claims, give that satisfied feeling so essential to him; they also pass through his digestive tract much more quickly than real roughage such as hay. So he is hungry again very soon, and also very bored. By all means use high-fibre complete cubes, but not alone; they are a good idea for horses which need fibre as a fibre supplement to hayage, say, or as part of a balanced concentrate ration.

Square or round?

The term horse 'cubes' comes from the earliest days of manufactured feeds for all farm animals. Older horse owners may remember when they were, indeed, cube-shaped, and some were marketed as horse 'nuggets' and also 'nuts'. Manufacturers then found it easier, for some reason unknown to me, to make them round rather than square, so the present-day shape came about although the terms 'cubes' and 'nuts' have remained.

Respect the Horse's Digestive Needs!

So, then, despite our efforts, the horse's digestive system is basically the same as it has been for millions of years, and if we are to manipulate his diet to suit our purposes – that is, getting the extra nutrients into him so that he can develop athletically and work for us – we must at least feed him those nutrients in a form his digestive system can cope with. On the whole this means providing high quality forage/roughage feeds and feeding concentrates – which constitute an 'artificial' feed for the horse even when fed as 'straights' (individual ingredients such as oats, barley and so on) – more or less as an extra, only if and when needed.

The Importance of 'Trickle-Feeding'

'Trickle-feeding' is one of the terms which has come into equine nutrition jargon over the last few years. It means that the horse's digestive system is designed to have a fairly constant *trickle* of food running through it most of the time. In a natural environment, horses, ponies, donkeys and zebras will feed for about sixteen to eighteen hours out of twenty-four, and sleep for about four to six hours. That doesn't leave much time for anything else, and in fact horses weren't 'designed' to do much else.

We have problems in domestication when we set out to get a high enough level of nutrients into our working horses to give them the energy they need for our work; to do this we cut down on their roughage in order to make more room for higher energy-containing concentrates. Thus the horse takes in his nutritional requirements, higher though they are, in much less time; and because in cutting his roughage we also cut down his time-passing, roughage-chewing periods, he is therefore left with many hours a day in which he has nothing to do; for a horse this is mind-numbing.

This situation provokes problems of both temperament and behaviour, partly because of the boredom, partly because of discomfort in the digestive tract from eating an unnatural diet, and partly as a result of being over-confined in the stable.

Why are Horses so Prone to Colic?

Horses are not susceptible to colic in the wild. It is the artificial feeding methods such as those described here which are the main cause of colic. With an erratic and inadequate supply of their natural foods, the gut micro-organisms are weakened or starved to death, and will therefore not be available to process or digest properly the next batch of food which arrives. The food may remain only partially digested, it may not move along the tract and may start to ferment producing gases and toxins, or it may literally clog up the works, all of which cause colic.

There is one very narrow point in the large intestine which is often the site of colic, when incompletely digested food blocks up and cannot pass through.

Other causes of colic

There are several other aspects of domesticated life which can cause colic – which is, after all, simply abdominal pain and does not *necessarily* originate in the digestive system. These are 1) **stress** which can upset the blood and entire body biochemistry; 2) **worms** which would not build up to dangerous numbers on land used naturally and in rotation by its varied inhabitants; 3) the **administration of antibiotics** sometimes, or other drugs and medicines; 4) prolonged **fast or hard work too soon after feeding**; 5) **erratic feeding methods**, such as feeding with too long a stretch of time between feeds (including hay), or not keeping to the same ingredients in each feed – the gut micro-organisms and enzymes are tuned to 'expecting' a certain supply, and find it difficult to cope with change; and 6) **poor quality** or even **tainted foodstuffs**, moulds being a prime offender, and also naturally occurring poisons (mycotoxins) on the feed. If the gut micro-organisms are upset, the horse will feel below par; in this situation he may have chronic indigestion all the time, and serious and painful digestive disturbance can certainly occur.

Transporting horses is a major and often unrecognised cause of stress; several experts believe it is often the reason that horses go down with colic or laminitis some hours or days after a journey, a fact not often recognised by their human connections.

The Real Meaning of 'Little and Often'

We all regularly hear that horses should be fed little and often, as they eat in nature, but where we go wrong is in our interpretation of it. Giving three concentrate feeds a day and hay only night and morning, which is a very common way of feeding stabled horses, does *not* imitate nature's way: it leaves horses for many hours out of the twenty-four with virtually no food passing through their digestive system, resulting in discomfort, digestive upset and boredom.

Again, we are told to give the largest (concentrate) feed and most of the hay ration at night – yet a quick check in almost any yard at midnight (except perhaps those with high performance horses on high levels of concentrates which may be at the limits of their appetites) will reveal that all the feed is gone; yet the horse may not be fed again until 7 or 8 o'clock the following morning. This means his digestive system will have seven or eight hours with virtually no food passing through it – a highly unnatural and dangerous situation for a trickle-feeder.

The Horse's Need for *Ad Lib* Feed

The digestive bacteria, as we have seen, need a constant supply of food if they are to thrive – some can even start to die off after as little as four hours without food. Without a healthy population of micro-organisms, digestion must be significantly impaired. I am sure that many puzzling cases of colic must be due to this erratic yet largely standard method of feeding horses.

In yards where horses are given four or five small feeds a day with roughage *ad lib*, digestive disorders are rare and the horses are visibly more content and mentally settled and relaxed (provided the feeds are correctly balanced for each individual's requirements). There is little wood-chewing, nervous tension or any other behavioural trouble, and the horse makes better use of the food he does receive – which must also make better economic sense.

NOTE: With an *ad lib* roughage system it is, of course, quite possible to remove food from the horse if he is going to be working hard. But even those in the hardest work need not have their food removed more than two hours before its commencement. Also, leaving such horses with little or no food during their day of hard work, whether it is hunting, eventing, an endurance ride or whatever, is also asking for a lot of trouble: it will result in many gut bacteria dying off, and increase the possibility of poor appetite, indigestion or colic some hours or days after the work.

Horses which are not fed according to a fairly natural pattern also eat their bedding when they can, although their attendants' answer to this is either to muzzle them so the unfortunate horses cannot appease their hunger, or to switch to inedible bedding, usually shavings. This, of course, does absolutely nothing to address the root of the problem, which is their bad feeding management.

Ad lib concentrates?

Perish the thought, you may well be thinking! But even this is possible, or at least you can trickle-feed concentrates. The horse gets no more than his allocation, but by feeding them thinly mixed in with his roughage ration in suitable containers – either in a corner hay-holder if the roughage is in long form, or in a large manger or similar container if it is chopped like chop itself or a short-cut branded forage feed – you can ensure that he gets just a little concentrate feed all the time with his roughage.

A corner hay-holder can be simply constructed by any competent handyman (or woman) by simply nailing a vertical runner down each wall in a corner, and then slotting a square of wood down them so that the top of the holder is about level with the horse's elbow; at this height he can easily reach down and in. To clean out the corner you simply lift out the wood – and do this every day!

In fact I find it a good plan to use a metal grille with perhaps only the bottom foot or so solid, as some horses will not put their heads down into a solid container which comes above the level of their eyes; this effectively blinds them, and frightens some animals. Having the bottom part solid just prevents bits falling out too readily on to the floor outside the container and into the bedding.

Natural Concentrates

In his natural state, the horse eats far more grass and leaves than he does grain. Obviously, horses wandering freely at all times of year over varying terrain will encounter different forages in different stages of development. Thus in the autumn they would certainly have come across grain 'on the stalk' and, having ripened, on the ground. In winter, often only the dried-up stems and leaves from the previous summer's growth would be available, the nearest to man-made hay that a feral or wild equid would get.

Horses can obviously cope with grain (concentrates), but feeding a lot, and erratically, does present problems; some horses can take only very small amounts at a time because of the high levels of natural waste products which result from the digestion and metabolism of this more concentrated food. Oats in particular seem to cause bad reactions in some horses; these come out in acidosis spots and itchy skin, and develop temperament problems, and become generally crabby.

Any concentrate fed to excess to an intolerant animal can lead to problems: these might be extreme nervousness and spookiness; behavioural problems ranging from restlessness to the developing of stable vices resulting from nervous tension and frustration; bad behaviour; azoturia; filled legs; poor skin and coat; laminitis; and digestive disturbances resulting perhaps in colic.

Although there are products on the market aimed at alleviating these symptoms in the relatively short-term, the real answer lies in adjusting the horse's diet so that he is fed more suitable food – perhaps a concentrate to which he does not react badly, and given in smaller amounts, and in particular, a higher-energy roughage source which will provide ample nutrients in a more natural and easily digested way.

The risk of 'hay belly'

Those who do wish to feed their horses more naturally by giving fewer concentrates and more forage-type feeds, and particularly if they choose to feed the latter, or hay, almost exclusively, may feel that their horses will develop what is popularly called a 'hay belly', where geldings have the appearance of being in foal! However, this will not necessarily happen. It may occur if the forage, or hay, or whatever roughage is used, is of poor feeding value, containing a good deal of fibre without the nutrient content, perhaps due to bad harvesting or storage; but as long as the feed is of good nutrient content and quality, in practice you should notice no difference in your horse's waistline!

The Digestive Process

The digestive process obviously starts with the muzzle. The horse's sense of smell is extremely important, and is much more effective than ours. He uses it and his important antennae-type whiskers around his muzzle (which some people are so fond of clipping off, 'for neatness'!) to select his food, and his lips gather it up – and even at this stage it may be rejected, as the horse seems almost to have taste buds in his lips. If he approves the food, the lips manoeuvre it into his mouth and he grasps it with his front or incisor teeth. The tongue manipulates it fully into the mouth, and with the cheek muscles, moves it around between the back or cheek teeth (molars) which grind it up and mix it with saliva. This chewing action is a very important preliminary operation, as the horse does not produce saliva at the mere sight and smell of food: it is the chewing action which produces the alkaline saliva which initially prepares the food for further action by the acid stomach juices. Thus the cheek teeth grind up the hard cellulose cell walls of the plant material and break up the food into small particles so the saliva can reach most parts of it and turn it into a soggy pulp.

Teeth

The teeth obviously play a major role. Wild or feral animals usually die, if not subject to predation, from starvation due to dental problems or just to worn out teeth, as it is impossible for them to feed. I was particularly impressed to hear of an American dentist (the kind who treats humans) who capped all the worn out teeth of his thirty-year-old family pony, giving it an extra ten years of life!

If the teeth are sharp or jagged, the food could well be imperfectly masticated and the more sensitive parts of the mouth (the tongue and cheeks) could be cut, causing pain and reluctance to chew.

Like other mammals, the horse has both 'baby' or 'milk' teeth, and permanent teeth. Apart from decayed or broken teeth at any age, the first problem likely to occur with age and time is that the first teeth can become jammed on top of the second teeth erupting underneath. This makes for an irregular 'fit' or articulation between the teeth, which adversely affects eating and chewing.

The second teeth continue growing throughout the horse's normal lifespan, initially meeting at more or less right-angles, but in the case of the front or incisor teeth becoming more and more slanted forwards as the horse ages

The horse's lower jaw is narrower than its upper jaw, so the chewing motion causes the insides of the lower cheek teeth and the outsides of the upper cheek teeth to become sharp. Hooks can also form on the front and back cheek teeth if the rows of teeth do not meet fully at the ends during chewing.

Small rudimentary teeth can appear on the bars of the jaw – the toothless part so conveniently placed to take the bit, in front of the cheek teeth – and these can cause soreness and bitting problems. Also, the tushes or canine teeth that are present in a male horse (occurring only occasionally in the female), growing near the corner incisors, can sometimes appear further back and, again, cause bitting problems. Anything which causes a sore mouth, including incompetent use of the bit, can result in difficulty in eating, of course.

Care of the teeth

All horses, but particularly the young and the old, should have their teeth checked every six months by a veteri-

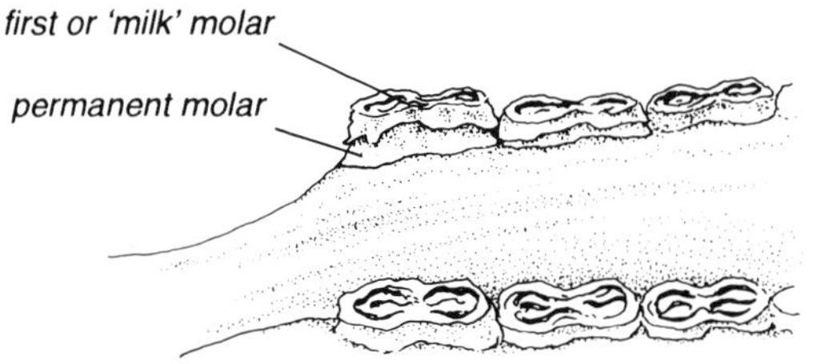

The first or 'milk' molars can become jammed on top of the permanent molars

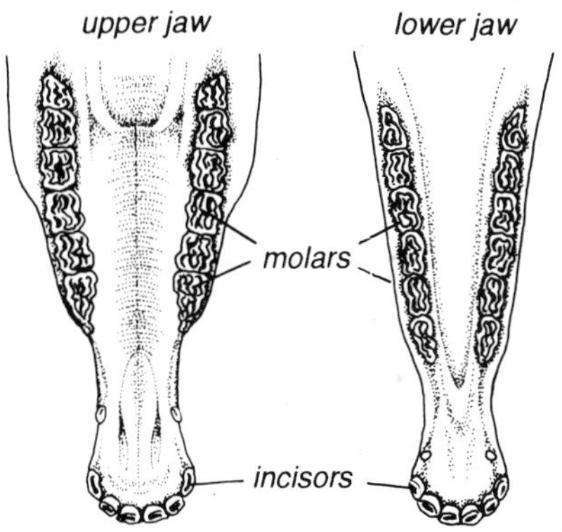

The molars are the grinding teeth and their surfaces are ridged

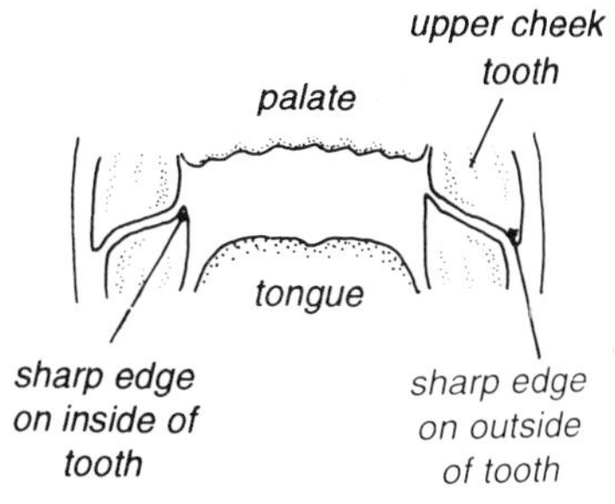

As the horse gets older the cheek teeth can wear and form sharp edges

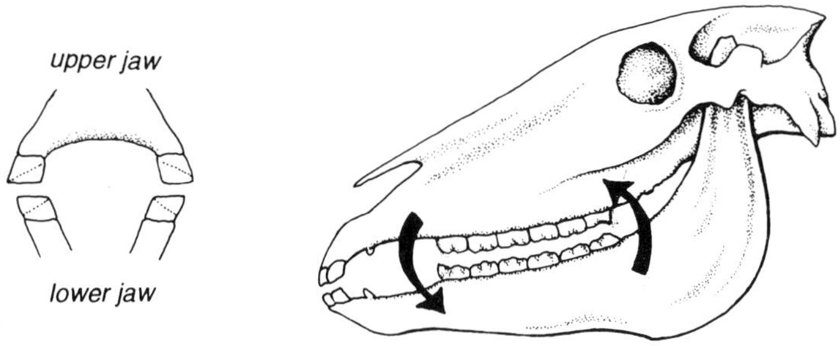

a) The edges of the teeth in constant contact are worn back progressively; in time this process will leave sharp, painful edges. Hooks can form on the front and back cheek teeth (b) due to the chewing motion

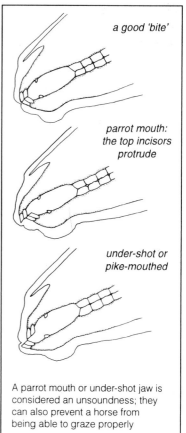

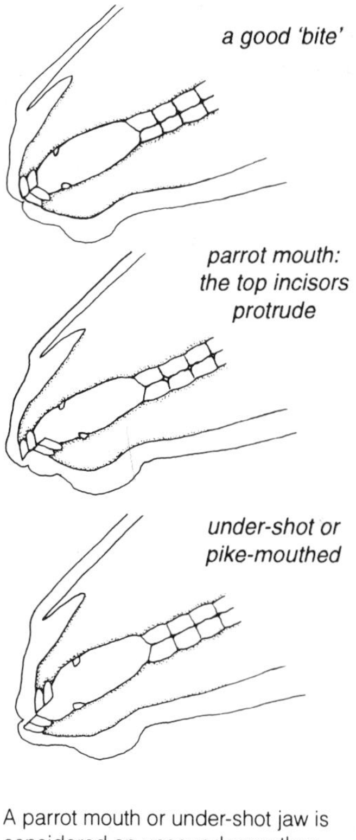

A parrot mouth or under-shot jaw is considered an unsoundness; they can also prevent a horse from being able to graze properly

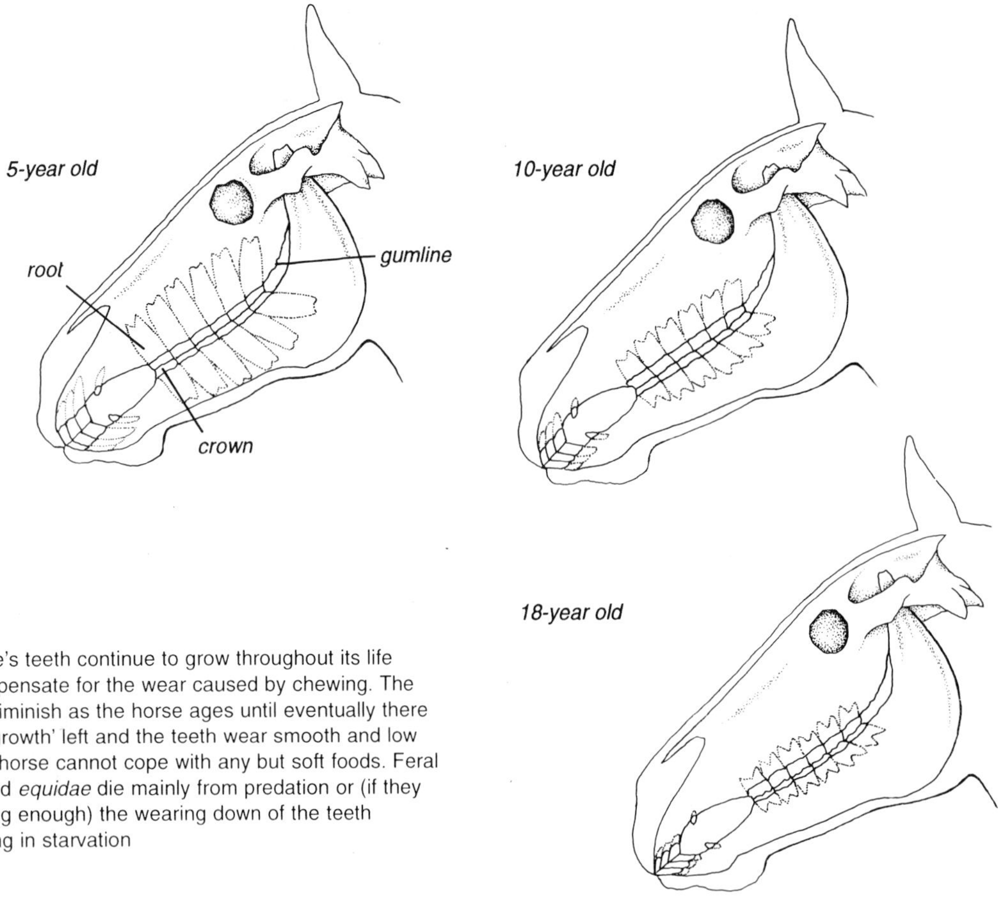

A horse's teeth continue to grow throughout its life to compensate for the wear caused by chewing. The roots diminish as the horse ages until eventually there is no 'growth' left and the teeth wear smooth and low so the horse cannot cope with any but soft foods. Feral and wild *equidae* die mainly from predation or (if they live long enough) the wearing down of the teeth resulting in starvation

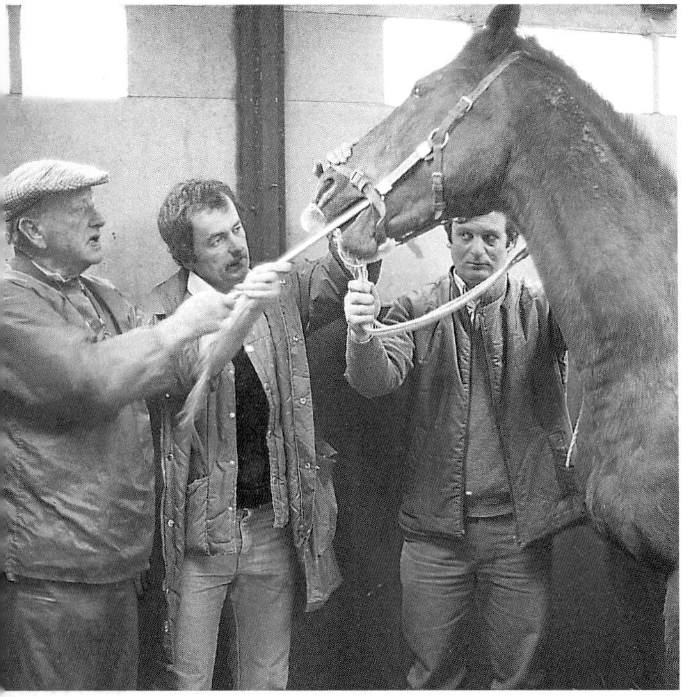

nary surgeon or equine dentist; any sharp edges or hooks should be rasped off, 'milk caps' removed, and also wolf teeth if they are causing problems, and the teeth generally checked for disease, loss or breaks.

If a tooth is lost or removed, the one growing above or below it will not be worn down by its now missing opposite number, so it will have to be regularly rasped down to prevent it growing to the extent that chewing becomes difficult or impossible, or even so that the horse finds it impossible to close his mouth – and that is not an unknown situation!

Many horses find having their teeth rasped uncomfortable, and a twitch is needed for some individuals. The most effective way to rasp or check a horse's teeth is to fit a special device which keeps the mouth open and prevents severe injury from a bite, as well as giving easier access to the back teeth. If a gag is not used, one person should gently but firmly hold the horse's tongue out of one side of his mouth so he cannot close it, whilst another person works on the teeth

Into the Stomach

Once chewed, the food is swallowed down the gullet or oesophagus and into the stomach, where it is pummelled about and mixed with digestive juices to further break it down. Food swells when in contact with saliva and digestive juices, and it will, by now, have doubled in volume; about 4 to 5lb of food (up to 2.5kg) at any one time is therefore plenty for the stomach to handle effectively in view of this feature. If more (concentrate) food is given, which the horse eats more quickly than roughage, the first food taken in may not have been fully dealt with by the time more arrives, and it may be pushed on into the narrow small intestine before it is ready, causing incomplete digestion. With roughage, which is eaten more slowly and chewed more thoroughly, this problem does not arise.

If the horse is given a large feed which it eats too quickly (perhaps because it is hungry due to our standard feeding practices), or if it gorges itself on concentrates to which it has accidentally gained access somehow, the stomach can become much too full and swollen. The pressure then interferes with blood circulation in the stomach wall, and also with the normal nervous activity which controls the release of food into the small intestine when the stomach becomes full; nor can the usual movements of the stomach take place. The contents may start to ferment too much, and gases may form, distending the stomach even further. Discomfort, pain and maybe even rupture of the stomach and subsequent death can then occur. If the horse survives, laminitis may occur.

The Small Intestine

Food may stay in the stomach for as little as twenty minutes, although usually it is there somewhat longer; it is then released down the tract, the first 'department' blood capillaries or thread-like vessels in the intestinal wall.

The food is pushed along by wave-like muscular contractions of the wall, a process called 'peristalsis'. Proteins are digested here and broken down into their component 'building blocks', the amino acids, which are also absorbed into the blood and carried, like the glucose, wherever they are needed; if they are present to excess they are stored as fat.

The role of the liver

Pancreatic juices and bile from the liver are secreted into the small intestine to enable fats and oils to be broken down into tiny globules of glycerol and various fatty acids which are transported in the lymphatic system and bloodstream, again for use or storage. The liver could be considered the 'food factory' of the body. One of its most important tasks is to filter out of the bloodstream the toxins present in it, and to detoxify them; it also breaks down metabolic waste products; stores glycogen and iron; carries out many important steps in the metabolism of carbohydrates, proteins and fats; and it makes the essential clotting and, conversely, anticoagulant properties of blood. In the foetus it forms red blood cells and produces blood plasma proteins. It also makes vitamin A and stores other vitamins. It is clear, therefore, that any liver disorder can very seriously adversely affect the horse's digestion and metabolism, in fact its entire health.

Helping digestion

The food will remain in the small intestine for about an hour, and the more food there is, the less time per given amount there is for the juices to work on it. The fibre simply passes through for digestion in the large intestine, but the rest is dealt with here. It is obvious, therefore, that small concentrate feeds get more efficient digestion in that hour than large ones – just one reason why we should keep horses' short feeds small.

After about an hour, all that should be left will be fibre, digestible and indigestible, and this passes on to the large intestine where the all-important micro-organisms break down the cellulose and obtain energy and other nutrients from it.

The Large Intestine

As the micro-organisms work, they also produce B vitamins and make available energy from the cellulose, both of which are essential to the horse. However some horses, particularly youngstock and those in hard work, may not get all their B vitamins this way and may need extra. The micro-organisms, like everything else, have only a certain lifespan, and when they die the horse can absorb the nutrients, mainly a small amount of protein, from their bodies, so 'recycling' the bugs he has kept alive in a symbiotic relationship.

The fermentation process in the large intestine produces a good deal of heat and the 'slow-release' type of energy produces equally 'slow-release' warmth, keeping the horse supplied with a good deal of his body warmth round the clock provided he has a virtually *ad lib* supply. This is an important function at any time but particularly in cold, wet, windy conditions which really drain the heat out of a horse.

The horse's viscera

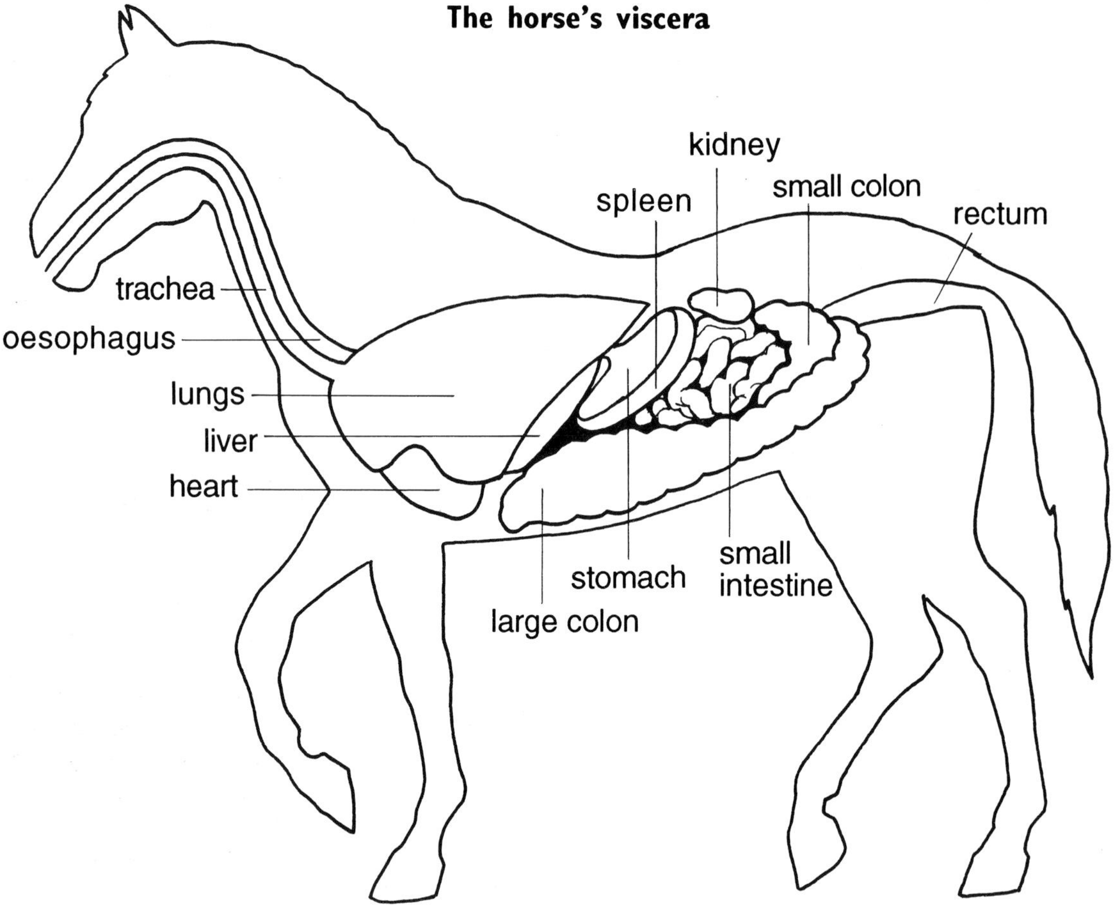

The digestive system of the horse

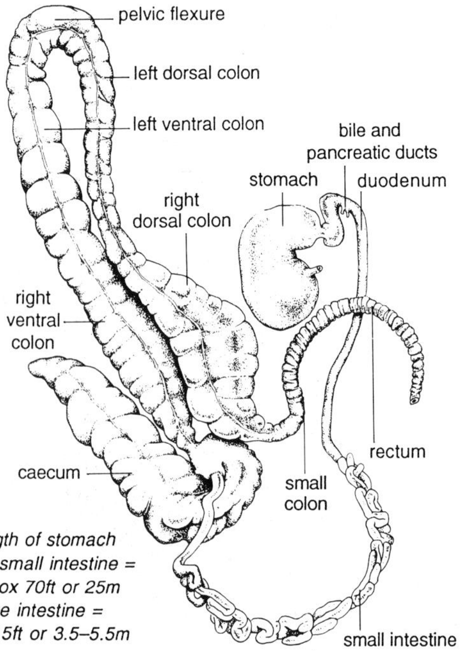

Length of stomach and small intestine = approx 70ft or 25m
Large intestine = 10–15ft or 3.5–5.5m

The large colon and caecum

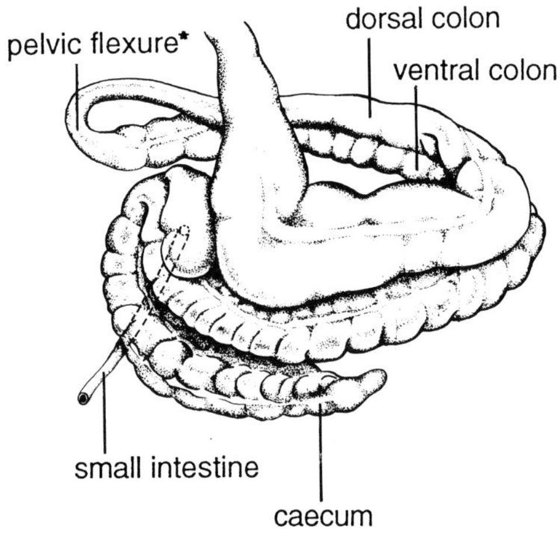

**Note the sharp, narrow bend at this point. As food travels through, the 'bottle neck' effect makes blockages more likely.*

The large colon

This part of the large intestine is where trouble sometimes occurs in the form of blockages. It forms two U-shaped loops joined together at a narrow point called the pelvic flexure, and it is often here that impaction colic occurs due to imperfectly digested material blocking it. This may be because of some disturbance to the bacterial population, as discussed earlier; or if the horse is on a low quality, too high lignin diet (poor hay, too much straw or nothing but dried-up grass) then impaction can occur because of the physical nature of the food.

Nutrients are absorbed from the food as it becomes more and more liquid in nature as it passes along the gut. One of the functions of the large colon is to reabsorb some of this liquid back into the body to avoid too much water loss. However, if the food is travelling too slowly through the colon, too much water may be reabsorbed, so making the contents too dry and impaction even more likely.

Blockages can occur elsewhere, but this pelvic flexure is more susceptible because it is so narrow compared with the rest of the large colon.

The small colon and the rectum

From the large colon, food passes on into the small colon and then to the rectum for evacuation as droppings. What remains now is largely undigested lignin and the waste products of metabolism which have been carried there in the bloodstream from various parts of the body for passing out with the droppings. Other waste products are passed out in the urine (as the kidneys also filter the blood of waste and toxins), in sweat and from the lungs as water vapour when the horse breathes out.

Droppings

The condition of the horse's droppings is a good indicator as to the state of his digestive system, his management and his health. Basically, the droppings of a 'corn'-fed, stabled horse should be a khaki colour, formed into largeish balls about the size of an average eating apple, containing mostly tiny 'splinters' of lignin, and of such a consistency that they just break on hitting the ground (or your clean bedding!).

Horses on a good deal of grass will have looser, greener droppings, to what degree depending on how much they are out. A horse normally passes about eight to twelve piles of droppings in twenty-four hours: too few can mean too little food. The more natural (that is cellulose-containing) his diet, the more droppings he will produce. This is a good sign, and not something to be manipulated in the form of cutting down the hay to reduce the droppings and the mucking-out, as I have known done!

If the droppings are small and hard this can indicate too little fibre and water, or that they are passing through the large intestine too slowly. Droppings of a very pale or very dark colour can indicate digestive disturbance (yellow often indicating liver trouble), and mucous-coated droppings indicate inflamed intestines. There should never be blood, either purplish, near-black or red, in the droppings as this obviously indicates bleeding, perhaps due to severe inflammation, worm damage or injury, or some other cause.

The smell and taste of food

Horses can be very finicky feeders. Even the greediest little pony will not eat food which, to him, smells or tastes unpleasant, and no matter how excellent in theory a feed might be, it is no use at all if your horse will not eat it. Food tainted in any way – by moulds, exhaust fumes if it is stored near the garage or a road, or by rat droppings and urine or dust if it is stored around or near a schooling area – is very bad for horses, even if they *will* eat it. Paddocks, too, may seem full of greenery which to the horse is nevertheless objectionable because it is tainted by droppings, even many months after these have been cleared up (although horses generally do not find cattle and sheep droppings unacceptable), by urine or by fertiliser, or simply because it is in a late stage of growth or of a type he does not like. Mixing feed with dirty or smelly hands can also put horses off eating, as can dirty, soured containers.

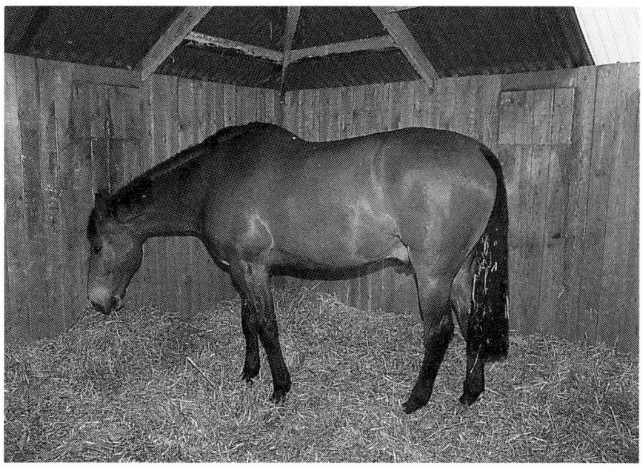

Key Facts

- The most important part of a horse or pony's diet is his roughage, not his concentrates. Cereal concentrates, in particular, are generally over-fed and over-estimated in both importance and quantity.

- The best way to supply a horse with a permanent supply of body warmth and non-exciting energy is to give him a more or less constant supply of high quality hay, or its equivalent such as suitable grazing, hayage, forage feed or chop.

- Sugar beet is probably under-used in most stables. It is an excellent, palatable and well balanced non-cereal concentrate and could receive the status of a significant portion of the horse's diet, not simply be seen as a means of damping feeds.

- The horse needs only small, if any concentrate feeds: no more than 4–5lb (about 2kg) should be fed to a full-size horse at once, and less to ponies; in fact ponies are generally better without cereal concentrates. Too large a concentrate feed can result in incomplete digestion; not only is this a waste of money, but even more important, it may cause digestive disturbance or even potentially fatal colic in the horse.

- Saliva prepares the food for further action by digestive juices. Do everything you can to encourage a horse to chew his short feeds so they are thoroughly broken up and soaked in saliva – for example, give plenty of good quality chop (chaff), say a couple of large double handfuls in each feed; or trickle-feed concentrates by mixing them in with the roughage, as described earlier.

- Get your vet or an equine dentist to check your horses' teeth thoroughly once or twice a year; giving them just a cursory look aided by guesswork is not enough. Also, worm your animals just as thoroughly; in the UK, most horse paddocks are overcrowded and grazed by just horses, allowing considerable build-up of worms.

3

TYPES OF FEED

The range of feedstuffs available for the horse owner to feed his or her horse or pony is very wide and varied today, and owners have a right to feel overwhelmed and confused in spite of information leaflets being available from most feed manufacturers. Advertising is very persuasive, and each proprietary or branded feed seems to have its own unique claim to fame, some quality possessed by no other feed on the market. Most feeds from known makers are very good for the category of horse or pony they are aimed at, and are probably the most reliable way for novice owners to feed their animals without problems, provided they feed the correct amount.

In addition to named feeds from the large national and even international firms, there are regional and local firms making their own feeds for the lucrative horse market. Some of these are good, and they are invariably cheaper than those of the big firms. And then there is the bewildering range of vitamin and mineral supplements on the market, again all marketed persuasively and many of them excellent for their purpose – but you have to know which, if any, your horse needs in order to get the best from them and to avoid trouble, for vitamins and minerals are potent nutrients quite capable of causing problems if fed incorrectly.

A Wide Choice

Horse owners are generally familiar with the types of feed given to horses today: oats, barley, flaked maize/ corn, also compound feeds such as coarse mixes (also called sweet feeds), cubes/nuts/pellets (all the same type of product) and roots or succulents such as carrots (a great favourite with most horses), apples, mangolds, swedes and turnips, parsnips, fodder beet and, probably the most popular today at least in Britain, sugar beet. There are also hays of various sorts, feeding straws, hayage (also called haylage), occasionally silage, and forage feeds which are the biggest improvement for decades in equine nutrition.

Basically, the purpose of any feed is to provide fuel for the body to live and work on; but no feed is of any use at all if the horse won't eat it. Fortunately, from the wide range available today we are most unlikely to be unable to find something suitable for our horse or pony which is also popular with him.

Hay

Hay is made from long grass, cut, dried (outdoors or in a barn) and baled. Its nutrient content and quality as far as being 'clean' and safe to feed (virtually free from moulds, dust and weeds) depends on the types of grasses and other plants contained in it, and the standards of harvesting and storage.

The most familiar types of hay are what horsemen call **seed hay** (specially sown leys or crops of grass) and **meadow hay**. In the past, meadow hay consisted of grasses and herbs growing naturally in hay meadows. This type of meadow is now extremely rare but meadow-type hay is still grown from varied seed mixes.

Seed hay can consist of several types of grass, usually including both ryegrass and timothy perhaps with others as well, or even only one type. Seed hay containing different grasses may be called **mixture hay**. The most nutritious grasses are usually used when a high nutrient content is required, such as for racehorses (or, indeed, any hard-working horses) and such hay is often called **racehorse hay**. Some owners or trainers who have a preference for a single type of grass in their hay will look for, say, ryegrass hay or timothy hay.

Horses, however, like variety (with, of course, no sudden changes!) and mixture or meadow hay may be more popular with them. Meadow hay will have a wide variety of grasses and other herbage and is usually fed to ponies and horses doing little or no work.

Clover hay and hay containing other legume plants such as vetches is high in protein but inclined to be dusty, and is hard to harvest well due to the differing nature of parts of the plants, which tend to dry at different rates. **Lucerne/alfalfa hay** also comes into this category, as does **sainfoin hay** which was very popular generations ago and is slowly making something of a comeback. Well harvested samples of these hays are very nutritious and particularly good for breeding stock.

Hayage

Hayage, or haylage, is commonly fed to horses now: this is a cross between hay and silage; it is moist but not wet, and like bag silage, is vacuum packed and so 'pickled' in its own juices, a process which preserves it. It comes in vacuum-packed, polythene-wrapped bales which can usually be stored outdoors, thus saving valuable under-cover space. Once opened, a bale has to be used within three or four days (sooner in hot weather, so try to keep it in the shade) or it goes 'off'; this can also happen if the polythene is pierced, so some care is needed in storage and handling. From a reputable maker hayage has the advantages of being consistent in quality, with its analysis available, and free from the moulds and dust which can be present even on a good, 'clean' sample of hay, and to which some horses react very badly, developing disabling respiratory allergies.

Hayage marketed to the horse world comes in differing grades, so the purchaser can choose the appropriate energy grade for the work his or her horses are doing; hayage is good for any horse even if it does not have respiratory problems, because of its known feed content and consistent quality. Early problems concerning variable quality have now been largely overcome.

Sources of Roughage

The importance of adequate roughage in a horse or pony's diet has been discussed, and most horses' main roughage source is still hay. If fed correctly and of suitable quality (nutrient content) it is often also a horse's, and particularly a pony's, staple feed. Nowadays, however, there are many alternative sources of roughage for horses.

Above: Different types of hay

(Left) Highly nutritious seed hay, used for animals on a high plane of nutrition such as racehorses (seed hay is often called 'racehorse' hay), hunters doing at least three or four days a fortnight in galloping country, eventers, endurance horses and so on. It may also be used for breeding stock and for thin horses being built up in condition
(Centre) Mixture hay
(Right) Meadow hay which is finer and softer than seed hay and most mixture hays. Meadow hay is nowadays mostly specially sown (as opposed to natural meadow grass which barely exists from a practical point of view). It contains a fairly wide variety of grasses and other plants such as herbs and, provided it is a good, clean sample, is safe to feed to almost any horse or pony

Right: Hayage is a moist, preserved long-forage product halfway between hay and silage; this example is the branded product HorseHage. The main advantage of hayage is that it is non-dusty and so is suitable for animals on a clean-air régime. It is also more nutritious than most hays (there are different grades available), and it is usually possible to greatly reduce the amount of concentrates fed. The disadvantages are that it is expensive and it can cause serious illness if not fed within a very few days of opening a bale (as air gets in and bacteria can start to breed) or, for the same reason, if the vacuum packing is punctured. Never feed any hayage which smells at all 'off'

Another excellent reason for using hayage is to conserve your horse's bodily resources which, even if he does not actually show symptoms of allergy or adverse reaction, will be used up in fighting off attacks on his health from moulds and dust – and why let valuable resources be used up which could go into other areas, such as working for you as well as maintaining general health? This point is particularly important for hard-working horses or those under any kind of stress, such as breeding stock, the elderly, the sick, or those out in adverse weather.

One complaint about these usually excellent products is that they cannot be fed *ad lib* because the recommended amount is too small to satisfy the horse; and most horses simply get through their ration faster than hay because they like hayage so much. This can be overcome by feeding more hayage but of a lower energy grade; also by adding oat or barley straw well mixed in with the ration; and by feeding in a special net or rack with small holes so the horse cannot get out so much at once.

Branded hayage products are expensive, but this extra cost can be saved by the reduction in concentrates which should normally take place, most hayages being of higher nutrient content than the hay commonly used by horse owners.

Silage

Silage is not, in my experience, a very satisfactory, safe or practical feed for horses. It is wet and messy, not marketed well to the horse industry, and although horses at the Irish National Stud were kept satisfactorily on it some years ago, there have been problems with botulism from contaminated big bale silage. If the bales are pierced (as also with hayage) and oxygen gets into the crop, bacteria multiply very rapidly indeed and this can result in fatal illness in the animals that eat it. I feel silage is much riskier than hayage in this respect, and not worth bothering with as there are so many preferable feeds.

Forage Feeds

The term 'forage feeds' has come into horsey jargon fairly recently, introduced by equine nutritionists. 'Forage' is any herbage that a horse would forage or search out for himself in the wild, and forages may simply equate to a nutritionally controlled version of excellent meadow hay. They come in long form, looking like hay and hayage; or short form, looking like chop/chaff, the short form being most common at the time of writing.

Forage feeds are not moist like hayage, and they keep better – up to six months if stored in dry, cool, shady conditions. They, too, have the advantage of being mould- and dust-free and of known nutritional content, again coming in different grades for different categories of horse or pony.

They can be fed as the sole dietary ingredient, or supplemented with (a small amount of) concentrates. Some brands consist of a wide variety of grasses and herbs. Furthermore at least one reputable brand markets an alfalfa (lucerne) forage which is high in feeding value – lower in energy than cereal concentrates, but high in calcium, protein and energy-giving fibre. In nutrient value, alfalfa is nearer to concentrates than to hays or hayages, so you can really improve the digestibility of your horse's diet by cutting down on cereal concentrates, which is better for your horse; probably only hard-working horses, breeding stock, old or debilitated animals and those out in winter will need concentrates as well. Alfalfa is also proving to be an ideal feed for laminitic horses and ponies: these should *not* be 'starved', but have special nutritional needs, a part of which involves getting their energy from cellulose/fibre rather than from the soluble carbohydrates (starches and sugars) in cereal concentrates.

Feed Straw

Most owners are familiar with wheat straw as a bedding, but comparatively few currently consider straw as a feed. Horses, of course, readily consume straw when bored or dissatisfied with their diet – usually their wheat straw bedding, a habit which often leads to their complaining owners either changing to an inedible bedding, or muzzling the horse at least part of the time.

This is not, however, the answer to the problem. If the horse is bored, he needs more interest and activity, and if he is dissatisfied with his diet it needs adjusting. It is pointless to take away his own method of relief. Horses normally eat straw due to hunger or lack of fibre, and may accompany it with chewing wood, or even their own or other horses' manes and tails if the problem is bad enough. They often adopt this practice when their owners reduce their hay rations beyond a reasonable level – below a third, or certainly a quarter of the total daily food ration – in an attempt to get them to eat more concentrates in preparation for hard work instead of filling themselves up on hay. In fact if the hay is of good enough quality and feed value, and the horse finds it palatable, he will obtain considerable nourishment from it, and there is no need to reduce it unreasonably.

Another situation when the practice often arises is when the horse is switched from hay to hayage which may need to be fed in smaller quantities in accordance with the maker's advice.

In all these situations, the horse is telling us as plainly as he can that he feels hungry, uncomfortable inside which makes for mental anxiety, and maybe also bored, as he is lacking the mental entertainment of munching on his hay. Feeding straw can very often be a satisfactory answer to all these situations.

The best straws to use are, first choice, **oat straw** and, second choice, **barley straw**, provided it has no prickly awns – and it is unlikely to have these nowadays due to modern harvesting methods. (The prickly awns were a valid objection to the use of barley straw for either feeding or bedding years ago, because the awns scratched the outside of the horse, and caused colic inside it.)

Both oat and barley straw are easier to eat and more digestible and nutritious for the horse than wheat straw; they can be used to bulk out a hayage ration, to eke out the hay ration, and for feeding to such animals as very good doers which need something filling inside them but without too much nourishment, and those prone to obesity or laminitis.

Another good feeding straw is known in agricultural circles as **fodder straw**: this is oat or barley straw with some dried grasses in it, and it can be used very satisfactorily in place of other roughage sources if you are having problems of supply.

Your normal feed merchant should be able to supply you with feeding straws as well as your other feeds.

Chop

Chop is commonly but incorrectly called 'chaff'. Chop is hay and/or straw chopped small (hence its name) – usually about $1^1/_2$in (4cm) in length – on a hand- or electrically operated machine; years ago this was an essential part of any good yard when the value of adding chop to feeds was more appreciated and understood than it is today.

Chop *has* made a comeback now. Some owners have managed to get small machines, either having the old wheel-type manual ones restored or finding the rather scarce, small, electrically operated ones, and chopping up their own hay and straw at home.

Commercial firms now also supply dust-extracted chop, often mixed with molasses (which is obviously very sugary) for palatability. Most horses love molasses, but some experts feel that this constant intake of sugar cannot be any better for a horse's health than it is for ours; because of this some firms now also provide 'plain' (unmolassed) chop, so owners can feed chop in plenty and just add molasses if and when they feel it necessary.

The point about chop is that it is essentially the same product as hay and straw: thus if it is made from dusty, mouldy hay and straw, it, too, will be dusty and mouldy and will create allergic respiratory problems in susceptible horses and not be very good for those which are not. Be sure that any chop you buy is stated as being 'dust-extracted' or 'vacuum-cleaned' or some such, as unscrupulous dealers (and foolish owners) may make chop from bad hay and straw as a way of using it up and getting rid of it.

Technically speaking, a nutritionist would probably tell you to deduct the weight of chop you add to feeds from the horse's roughage ration. In practice, as you will probably add a good double handful or two to a feed, you will find this weighs very little and is not worth worrying about. The horse will, in any case, deduct the amount himself if he is being fed *ad lib* hay/roughage. It is good to be careful and reasonably precise, but being pedantic and nit-picking about comparatively tiny amounts of roughage is, for most horses, a waste of time and effort.

Chop: an excellent addition

Chop is an excellent medium for opening up a feed of any type: mix all the ingredients with it very thoroughly so the horse finds it impossible to wheedle out the tastier parts, and you will find he eats more slowly, thus soaking his feed more in saliva and better preparing it for further action by the digestive juices; he will probably find his feeds more satisfying, too. Thus the addition of chop virtually puts a stop to the horse bolting his feeds, and makes them more digestible.

Forage feeds

Short-cut forage feed (1). This type of forage feed is most conveniently fed in a large tub in the corner of the stable, if of the type meant to replace hay
Alfalfa (lucerne)(2 long cut) This can be fed in a net, but a tub would be better as it tends to break up
3 (dried) Dried short-cut alfalfa can supplement forage feeds and be used in place of cereal concentrates for light to medium work

Different types of straw

Oat straw (4). This is the best feeding straw to use and can be used to bulk out both hay and hayage where supplies are short or the energy content of the diet needs to be reduced
Barley straw (5). This is a good product to use as bedding or feed. The old arguments about awns causing colic or skin irritation no longer apply since modern harvesting methods remove them
Fodder straw. Fodder straw is oat or barley straw with dried grasses in it. Normally used for farm animals, is also useful for horses and the same quality standards apply
Wheat straw (6). This is best used for bedding, being too fibrous for feeding. Horses will eat it, however, if short of roughage or hungry, or just as a plain change if on a 'rich' diet. It can be used in small quantities when making chop

Chop (7) and molassed chop (8). Chop is hay and/or straw chopped short for adding to concentrate feeds to make horses take their time and chew properly. It can be fed alone or with non-cereal concentrates such as sugar beet pulp. The addition of molasses to chop makes it more palatable although there is a school of thought which feels the constant addition of sugar to the diet is not good for the horse's general health, not to mention his teeth

Different types of oats

Whole oats (9). A traditional grain for horses and one still in widespread use, it is better fed bruised, rolled or crushed as many horses will not chew whole grains properly and they simply pass through
the horse whole and undigested, and therefore wasted
Rolled oats (10) are lightly crushed, just breaking the husk enough to allow for easier chewing
Crushed oats (11) are crushed more heavily, more of the kernel being

1

2

3

4

▲5

▲6

▼7

▼8

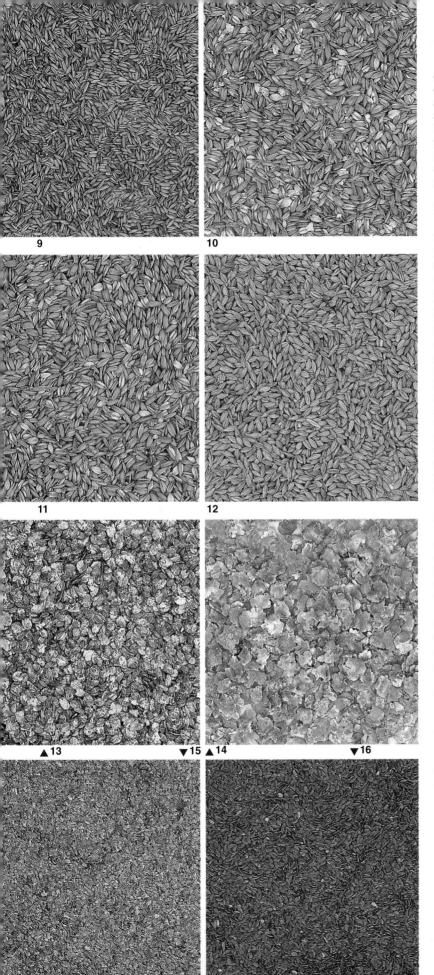

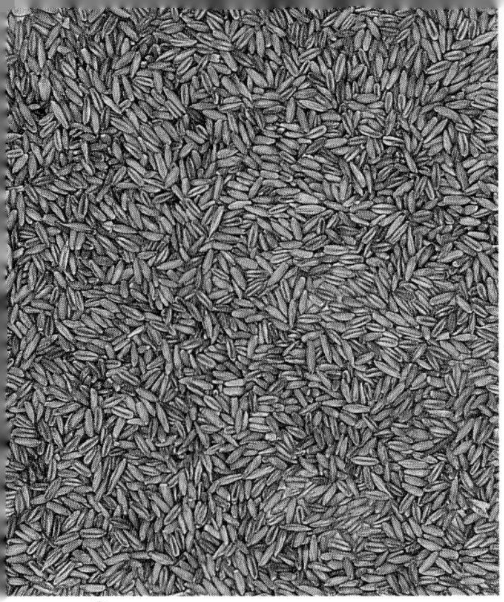

9

10

11

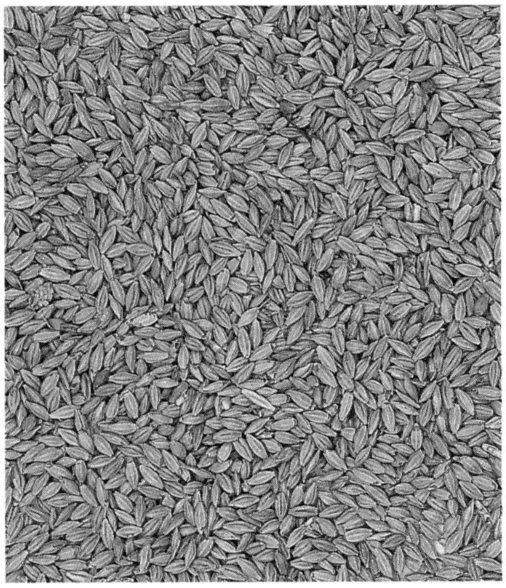

12

▲13

▲14

▼15

▼16

exposed. Crushed, rolled or just bruised oats are all easier for the horse to chew, and therefore the inside grain is more accessible to saliva and digestive juices. However, as these processes kill the grain, they should be used within a week or so to be sure they are fresh enough to eat, otherwise they start to rot and become mouldy as part of the process of decay

Different types of barley

Whole barley (12). Suitable for boiling (if you really wish to do this), whole barley is a very hard grain, difficult for horses to chew, and not recommended to be fed. Barley, like oats, should be fed crushed, rolled or bruised. It can also be fed pre-cooked and flaked

Bruised barley (13). Barley is best fed crushed, bruised or rolled (different stages of the same process) as it is easier for the horse to eat

Boiled barley is still a standby in old-fashioned yards. Boiling feeds makes them easier to chew but kills off various vitamins. With today's pre-cooked and supplemented feeds there is no need to cook your own feed like this. If the horse likes cooked feeds, however, and has the relevant grain in each feed, there is no harm in feeding them for a treat

Flaked maize (14)

Corn off the cob, cooked and flaked. This is a high-energy feed which is not sufficiently well balanced to form a staple grain. It is low in protein and (unless fed on the cob as in the USA) is deficient in fibre. It is a good ingredient as part of a ration, however

Bran (15)

Once an essential ingredient in horses' diets, modern-day bran is nothing like the product it used to be. Of low feeding value, its small flakes carry little flour and resemble sawdust. Bran is very poorly balanced nutritionally, and too much of it can cause bone disease. It is also expensive, and can well be dispensed with in a modern yard

Linseed (16)

The grains are small, shiny, hard and a warm chestnut-brown colour

Boiled linseed. Linseed must be fed boiled as otherwise it can be poisonous. When boiled, and particularly once cooled, it resembles brown frogspawn and is the same consistency

Linseed tea. Linseed tea is simply a more dilute form of boiled linseed

Straights

'Straights' is the term for individual ingredients such as oats, barley, maize/corn and also bran which is often regarded as a bulk/roughage feed but which is nearer to concentrates in type.

Oats

Oats are the cereal grain traditionally fed to horses in the western hemisphere and in Australasia, and are the most popular because they appear to be very suitable for horses: they have a reasonable proportion of fibre because of their husk; they are palatable and digestible; and because they have the lowest weight for their volume of other cereals, variations in quantity in those yards which feed by the scoop instead of weighing their feed can result in less serious anomalies than with other grains. Barley, for instance, weighs 'heavy' compared to the same volume of oats.

Oats are often said to be the safest grain to feed to horses because of their high proportion of fibrous husk to actual grain: however, in practice many experienced owners treat oats with great respect because they are justifiably noted for having an almost intoxicating effect on some animals, causing 'fizzy' behaviour; a few actually seem to be allergic to them, developing itchy, spotty skin problems. These symptoms, as also the over-energetic behaviour, seem to disappear when oats are changed for barley as the staple cereal grain. Where ponies in particular are concerned, I feel oats are best avoided: if they need cereal concentrates at all, they will do better on barley.

Oats also have an undesirably high content of a chemical called phytin or phytic acid which can prevent calcium in the diet being absorbed by the horse's digestive and circulatory systems. Cereal grains in general are low in calcium and high in phosphorus (the reverse applies with hay and similar roughages), and the high phytin content of oats just makes matters worse.

Barley

Barley can be a much better feed for many horses and ponies than oats. Roughly, $^{3}/_{4}$lb (0.3kg) of barley equals 1lb (0.4kg) of oats, and many horses become less idiotic on barley and lose the minor skin problems such as dull coat, scaliness and itching mentioned above. Barley has, like all cereals, a poor calcium : phosphorus ratio, being low in calcium and high in phosphorus, but it does not appear to contain as much phytin as oats. It has very little husk and should be fed crushed or bruised or cooked, never whole (see section on Commercial Feed Production, p47); it is best fed with a good helping of chop to make up for the lack of fibre.

The old wives' tales about barley being unduly fattening and causing cirrhosis of the liver can be ignored: barley is more energy-dense than oats, so you simply feed a quarter less for the same amount of energy. As for liver problems, this fairytale may have come about because when a horse is first fed on barley the droppings may appear yellowish and a little looser if the changeover is made too quickly. Take a good three or four weeks, or even longer depending on the amount in the final ration, to make the change and you should have no problems.

Maize/Corn

In the UK and Ireland maize is usually fed cooked and flaked. In the USA and some other countries it is commonly fed on the cob which significantly increases its fibre/roughage content. Basically it is a starchy food suitable for putting weight on thin animals or providing extra energy. However, it contains little protein and this is of low quality, and the fibre content of the grain is low. It must not form the staple grain ration but be simply part of a ration, say up to a quarter, to which some form of fibrous roughage has been added.

Bran

Bran is a bulky food which used to be – and still is, in some quarters – considered an essential part of the feeding routine of any stabled, sick, convalescent, recently-brought-up/soon-to-be-turned-out or box-bound horse. Moreover bran mashes were – and sometimes still are – considered to be easily digested, palatable and bland. In practice, however, they are the exact opposite.

Bran is part of the husk of the wheat grain, and although in the old days floury 'broad' bran, as it was called, with flakes 'as big as snowflakes', may have been worth using, today's bran has little goodness in it due to the efficiency of modern processing, and need play little or no part in the modern stable yard.

Bran does contain a moderate amount of energy and is high in low quality and not very digestible protein. It is fibrous and very high in phosphorus but very low

Weighing feed

It is inaccurate to feed any food, particularly concentrates, by the scoop; you should always take the trouble to weigh everything to make sure you are feeding the correct amount. Feeding by the scoop without weighing can result in either deficiencies, or 'overdosing' of that particular food; it is uneconomic, and could be wasteful.

in calcium, like cereals; also, like them, it contains some phytin which can prevent the absorption and metabolism of much of what calcium there is in the diet. It is certainly not, therefore, a bland, harmless food suitable for horses on little or no work.

The disadvantages of bran

The poor calcium : phosphorus ratio can cause 'Big Head' or 'Miller's Disease' where the bones become weak, porous and sometimes enlarged, making the horse prone to bone stresses such as splints, fractures and general 'soreness' from concussion that normally it would be well able to withstand. In adult horses the process may not become immediately apparent, but a diet with a consistently reversed calcium : phosphorus ratio will cause trouble in the long run.

In youngstock and broodmares carrying foals and with foals at foot it can quickly cause problems, as its effects are accelerated because bone is still being formed. There should always be more calcium than phosphorus present; at present a ratio of 1.5:1 seems about right according to current research.

Bran is also an expensive food and likely to become more so as its popularity as an ingredient in human foodstuffs and high fibre diets increases. I am sure some merchants play on the fact that horse-owners of the old school feel they cannot run a 'proper' yard without bran, and are less likely to take scientifically qualified advice than farmers and their other customers, so do not know any better than to keep pumping in the bran!

Being so high in fibre and nowadays virtually akin to sawdust in texture and taste, it is neither palatable nor easily digested, and certainly not the sort of food you want to offer to a sick horse! It irritates the intestine, which partially accounts for its famous laxative effect, something increased by its high absorptive capabilities: it absorbs a lot of water when you make a bran mash. Furthermore, unless you feed bran in significant amounts regularly (which you shouldn't), every time you give a horse his traditional weekly bran mash before his rest day you upset considerably the bacterial balance in his gut and kill off or seriously incapacitate a high proportion of the gut micro-organisms, seriously disrupting digestion. As it can take the micro-organisms up to a fortnight to recover, a weekly (or more frequent in the case of a sick horse) mash can mean that the unfortunate animal is constantly working under par. His digestion will be permanently less efficient than it could be if he were fed correctly, he will doubtless not be feeling at his best, and his metabolism will be compromised – hardly the sort of treatment you intend to give a sick or an athletically working horse.

The possible advantages of bran

Having pulled bran to pieces, I should say that it can be useful to feed in cases where the gut needs clearing out, say if the horse has managed to overload himself by gorging on concentrates, spring grass, been poisoned in the field or elsewhere or is suffering from any kind of overload in his system of toxins or unfriendly bacteria. It can be recommended to 'mash a horse down' during the first twenty-four hours of an attack of laminitis, for instance. You would naturally be advised to take a vet's advice on this first.

How to make a bran mash

If you do have to mash a horse on veterinary advice, this is one way to do it. Fill a feed bucket half full of the best bran you can get, and pour a kettleful of boiling water on it. Mix it thoroughly with a clean stick or other utensil, add a little salt (say a teaspoonful) to give it a bit of taste, put a $^1/_2$in (6mm) layer of dry bran on the top to help keep in the heat, and thoroughly wrap the bucket round with old rugs, hay or whatever you can find for insulation. (A friend of mind who insists on feeding bran mashes, despite all advice to the contrary from various quarters, swears by bubble wrap.) Let the mixture cook for a few hours until it is cool enough to mix with your hand, then you can give it to your horse. You can add all sorts of goodies to get him to eat it, such as thinly sliced carrots, apples or other roots or fruit, black treacle, honey and even essence of peppermint (seriously) – but don't be surprised if he won't!

The alternatives to bran

Instead of a bran mash you can use a mixture of dried grass, purchased as pellets, a coarse powder or easily crushed wafers; or a short-cut forage feed (as described earlier) mixed with soaked sugar-beet pulp, molassed or not. This is nutritionally balanced, unlike a bran mash, and provided you feed a little of these ingredients in each feed so the digestive micro-organisms are used to them, it will not upset your horse's digestive system and set him back instead of helping him.

The linseed mash

An even more upsetting mash was – and still is – the linseed mash. Linseed is the seed of the flax plant and is poisonous unless thoroughly boiled. Horses not used to high-fat foods were even more adversely affected by being given a linseed than by a bran mash and would take even longer to recover.

To summarise

Basically, bran as a regular feed item is unnecessary, and even in amounts regarded as normal by its fans, it can be harmful in the long term, even if not seriously so.

What's in a cube?

A common and not very well thought out objection to using cubes or pellets, which still persists decades after they have proved their worth, is: 'I don't like using cubes because I can't see what's in them'. Presumably those who use this objection mean they cannot see what ingredients are in the cubes. This is not important: what does matter is the nutritional balance. You cannot see what is in oats, barley, maize or anything else for that matter. You can only tell the nutritional content of any feedstuff by having it analysed in a laboratory or by reading the analysis panel on a branded product or on a sample of straights which comes with its analysis from a high quality feed merchant.
All you can test is a feedstuff's quality, by looking, smelling, tasting and feeling; this will tell you if it is fit to feed, or whether you should reject it – and cubes, like other feedstuffs, *can* go 'off' if kept in warm, damp conditions. But you cannot tell the nutritional content by these means.

Compound Feeds

By 'compound feeds' we mean cubes/nuts/pellets and coarse mixes/sweet feeds. They are called compounds because they consist of several or many ingredients mixed or compounded together, as opposed to 'straights', which are single ingredients.

Cubes/Pellets

Cubes were the first compounds to come on to the market several decades ago, and there is now a wide range to suit all categories of horse and pony: these include cubes for the average family-type horses and ponies; for those doing moderate, 'riding club'-type work; for those out of work and resting, on invalid or convalescent diets; for those in strenuous work; for breeding stock, including youngstock of various ages to take account of their changing nutritional needs. The latest addition to the market are special 'cool' cubes for native ponies and cobs, those horses and ponies needed for 'quiet' work, and those which seem unable to take other concentrates (this last eventuality is probably because they contain too much starchy/sugary energy which gives a sudden boost of energy rather than the slow-release sort which comes from fibrous cellulose and is found primarily in good hay and hayage).

An objection to cubes was, and occasionally is, that they consist of sweepings off the feed warehouse floor. In the earlier days this did actually happen to my certain knowledge, but with today's stricter consumer laws and increased knowledge of feeding, plus a more aware and demanding attitude on the part of owners and yard managers, this sort of thing must be very rare, if indeed it still exists.

Cubes today, from any reputable maker, national, regional or local, consist of ingredients carefully checked for quality, and carefully formulated for nutritional balance. Palatability is also important, and horses almost without exception eat most sorts of cubes.

Cubes are an excellent way of providing an animal with a properly balanced, safe diet for its purpose, provided the owner or manager chooses the right cube.

Roots and Succulents

Carrots are loved by most horses. It is usually recommended that they be fed in long thin slices to prevent choking, which can result if they are cut across in chunks. Coarsely grated carrots, however, mix better with other feeds and are perfectly safe

Apples are popular with most horses. It is usually recommended that they be fed cut in quarters to prevent choking, even though the resultant chunks are ideally suited to do just that! It is far safer to grate them coarsely, as shown here

Molassed sugar-beet cubes
Sugar-beet cubes should not be confused with ordinary horse and pony cubes as they can be fatal if fed dry, swelling up once eaten and choking the horse or causing impaction. They must be soaked for 3 hours in three times their own volume of cold water and must be thoroughly soggy before use. The latest research seems to be showing that 3 hours soaking will probably be enough but check with a nutritionist. Sugar beet is also available in shredded form, this should only need to be soaked for one hour. The picture shows (clockwise from top right) soaked cubes; dry cubes; dry shreds

Coarse Mixes/Sweet Feed

Coarse mixes are justifiably popular these days, particularly for novice owners who do not want the responsibility of balancing a ration themselves, as well as for expert horse people who recognise that this is, in any case, a job for a scientifically qualified nutritionist. Those mixes available are usually of high, reliable quality and are a definite boon to the modern horsekeeper. In my experience, they have the added advantage of not losing popularity with horses, which often seem to go 'off' cubes after a few weeks or months.

Like cubes, coarse mixes consist of a variety of ingredients and are properly balanced, the analysis being on the sack or label. Again like cubes, they have a binding agent added such as molasses or syrup, which takes out the dryness and makes damping unnecessary; thus most coarse mixes are moist and *slightly* sticky, but 'not so's you'd notice', as they say. Horses do seem to love them, although, as ever, some are choosy as to which brand they prefer. However, the binding agent does mean that they do not keep as well as cubes, particularly in warm weather, so small yards should not buy large batches to last over several months.

In the summer months it could be worth having an old, large fridge, minus shelves, in the feed room in which to keep the currently opened sack of coarse mix.

With coarse mixes/sweet feeds, as with cubes/pellets, the analysis is worked out by the feed company, and differing grades of energy level are available according to the type of animal you have and his work. All an owner has to do is feed the required amount since the ingredients are all present – and visible! – and the vitamins and minerals all in balance in a good brand.

Roots and Succulents

Roots and succulents are welcomed by just about every horse, particularly those denied much grass, as they help satisfy his natural craving for juicy, fibrous, natural food. The most popular seem to be carrots. Apples are also favoured, and some horses like to crunch on a whole turnip left in their mangers overnight.

Carrots should be thinly sliced lengthways or, even better, coarsely grated; apples and parsnips can be fed this way too. The reason for not cutting carrots and parsnips across in chunks or feeding apples in quarters is to help avoid lumps becoming stuck in the horse's gullet or oesophagus (food pipe) and causing choke. Choke in horses is not connected with the trachea (windpipe), as in humans – it represents a blockage of the oesophagus which is extremely uncomfortable for the horse.

Food comes back down the nostrils with saliva, and the horse makes frequent attempts to swallow. The lump can often be seen on the underneath of his neck. If your horse is affected, remove all food and water and call the vet at once. Do not attempt to dislodge the lump yourself: this is not a first-aid situation.

Amounts of Succulents to Feed: Most roots consist mainly of fibre and water with varying amounts of different vitamins. In the past, people were advised to feed not more than about 4lb (1.8kg) per day, but it is actually quite acceptable to feed up to about 10lb (4.5kg) per day split evenly between feeds with the rest of the ration.

With soaked sugar beet, a useful guide is to give equal amounts by volume of sugar beet plus chop or a short-cut forage feed, adding any other minor ingredients as required, so that the total volume of the feed fills a normal three-gallon feeding bucket up to about half, but to *no more* than three-quarters full; remember the small size of the horse's stomach, but also that such a feed will be largely fibre. If you need to feed more than this, increase the number of feeds daily so you don't have to feed too much in one go. If this is not possible, discuss the matter with a vet or nutritionist, who should be able to give you more precise advice.

Sugar Beet

This is probably fed in larger quantities to more horses in the UK than any other succulent. It is a good food in its own right, but is subject to some misunderstanding, being much more than a wet succulent used for damping feeds.

As it is grown for sugar for the human market, the remains are largely fibre, but there is still some sugar left. The pulp, which is what is left after processing out most of the sugar, is dried and marketed for animal feeding either as shreds, or compressed – very hard – into cubes. These, like the shreds or pulp, are dark grey in colour, darker if molasses has been added as is usual, and are *not* to be confused with ordinary cubes which are usually greenish or sometimes mid-brownish in colour.

Soaking sugar beet

Feeding sugar-beet *cubes* in their dry state is almost certain to cause serious colic, blockage and death in your horse, as they expand greatly once in contact with saliva or digestive juices. They **must** always be soaked for about three hours in cold water so they are thoroughly soft and soggy before feeding. Opinions vary as to the exact amount of water, but a safe guide is to use three times their volume of water; so if you fill a stable bucket one third full of dry cubes, fill it up to the top with cold water and don't use it until the same time the next day.

A word of warning: for many years I soaked sugar-beet cubes in hot water and found they had swelled to their maximum in about two hours; this proved a good way of giving the horses a warm feed on a cold night. Then came the advice never to soak sugar beet in hot water as it caused it to ferment very quickly, which could cause serious colic and poisoning. I have never used hot water since, but must have been exceptionally lucky to have used it for so long with no problems.

Also, in freezing weather it is particularly important to soak your sugar-beet cubes in an area not subject to freezing, perhaps a well insulated tack room or feed room or indoors at home, because if the water freezes the cubes will not soak through. Some owners may not realise this, and simply tip the cubes into the horse's feed whilst they are still dry and unswollen inside, with serious consequences for the horse.

Use plenty of water to soak sugar beet. Squeeze it with your hand to check it is thoroughly soft all the way through before feeding. The rule is: if it's thoroughly soggy you can feed it. In warm weather, the longer you leave it the more chance there is that it will ferment so check for this before use

The latest information coming from the field of equine nutrition research is that the shreds or pulp – as opposed to the cubes – do not need soaking. Some years ago one of Britain's leading agricultural colleges running high level and scientifically based exam courses on equine studies ran tests on soaking sugar beet as a student project, feeding large amounts of dry material to the college horses and ponies – with no problems. Even so, the results were not widely publicised to the horse world, which is still advised to soak all sugar-beet products. Being fibrous, the shreds can in fact be used as a partial hay replacer for horses with respiratory problems; however, as we are advised not to feed more than about 4lb (1.8kg) dry weight per day, this would not fully satisfy the horse.

Most people would wish to play safe and soak the shreds anyway. If you do want to feed dry shreds it is probably advisable to mix them thoroughly with chop and damp the feed thoroughly to stop the ingredients separating out. Also, the shreds could be mixed with a coarse mix or other damped feed.

If you wish to feed dry shreds, it is advisable to discuss the matter fully with an equine nutritionist or vet first. Otherwise you do so at your own – and your horse's – risk!

The content and properties of sugar beet

Although sugar beet contains some sugar, most of its energy is of the slow-release sort, coming from its fibre. It also has a high calcium and low phosphorus ratio, quite the opposite to cereal grains, and so balances them, and bran if you are using it, very well. For horses resting or in light work, you can mix it with chop or forage feeds at every meal and use it as a major source of your horse's energy requirements.

It is ideal as a feed in both hot or cold weather. It has the quality of helping the horse store water in his large intestine so helping delay or prevent dehydration during endurance-type work or if his water supply is frozen in winter (although this should *never* be used as an excuse not to break the ice several times a day for outdoor animals). Also, as its energy is of the slow-release sort, it is, again, excellent for endurance work and as in-built 'central heating' during cold weather, particularly for animals living out.

Hydroponically Produced Grass

A popular way of producing grass for stabled horses or for those on frozen or dried-up paddocks is by means of a hydroponic unit. These units enable you to grow a nutritious mat of grass or green cereal with just water and sometimes added nutrients, plus warmth and light, but with no soil, and there are commercial units available ranging from ones to suit very small yards to ones suitable for large establishments. Many owners are finding this an excellent way of providing nutritious succulents for stabled horses, especially in winter, and claim that feed and veterinary bills are reduced because of the increased wellbeing of their horses.

Using a home-made system

Even the smallest units can be expensive, but if you are prepared to put up with some slight inconvenience in your home, or if you have a heated greenhouse or conservatory, you can grow your own grass or cereal fairly simply. You will need trays for the seeds – seed trays with no drainage holes will do, or supermarket vegetable containers, old roasting tins, empty large-size ice-cream containers or any other fairly shallow container which will hold a little water. You will also need a set of open bookshelves or unlimited window-sill space.

You can buy seed from any seed merchant or provider of hydroponic supplies (see the equestrian press for advertisements). The most suitable seed seems to be barley, but you can use pasture-grass seed, wheat (also very popular), oats or maize.

You can feed the resulting growth in every feed, either in the manger or mixed in with the hay, so you can safely give one 'mat' of greenery (for want of a better word) in each feed, if you wish. (As ever, if you are concerned about amounts, consult a vet or nutritionist.)

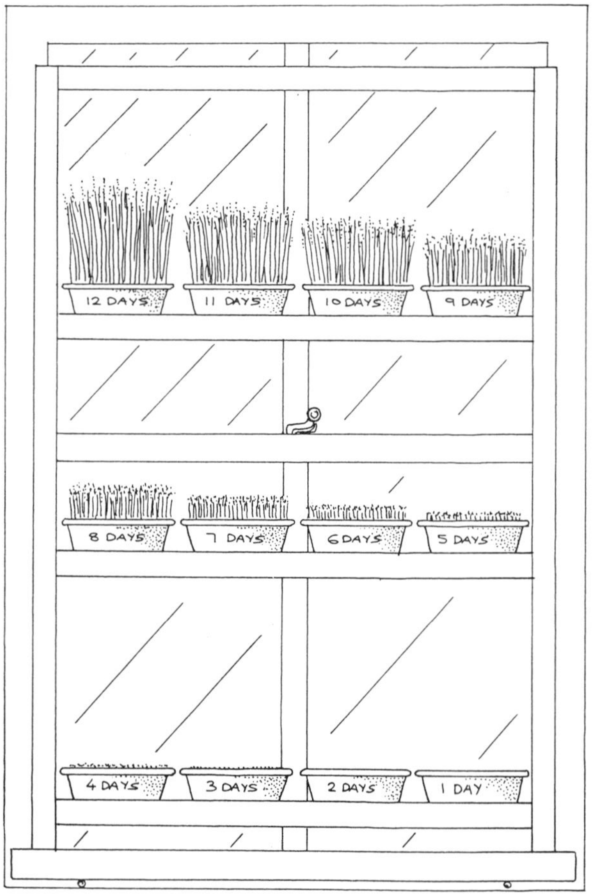

Home-made 'one-horse' hydroponic unit

Method of cultivation

Set out your trays, scatter your chosen seed in a thin layer on the bottom, sprinkle about a quarter to a half cup of water evenly on it, remembering never to let it dry out, and wait. Do one batch per day and in ten days your first batch should be about ready for feeding, depending on the species you have chosen.

Carry on doing one batch a day and harvesting one batch a day for as long as you wish, to keep a constant supply going. You can feed grass and roots together: simply lift the whole lot out of the container and give it to your horse.

If you wish to buy a commercial unit, you will receive full instructions with your equipment and may well find the initial outlay and small amount of daily labour well worth it to provide your horses with nutritious, cheap, welcome, natural food every day.

(Left) A small hydroponic growing unit, the Natrafeed Hydroponic Feed System from Aquacrop. These units are ideal for the one- or two-horse owner

Commercial Feed Production

Most owners don't care how their horses' feeds are produced as long as they are suitable, safe and not too expensive! However, a little knowledge concerning this subject may not come amiss.

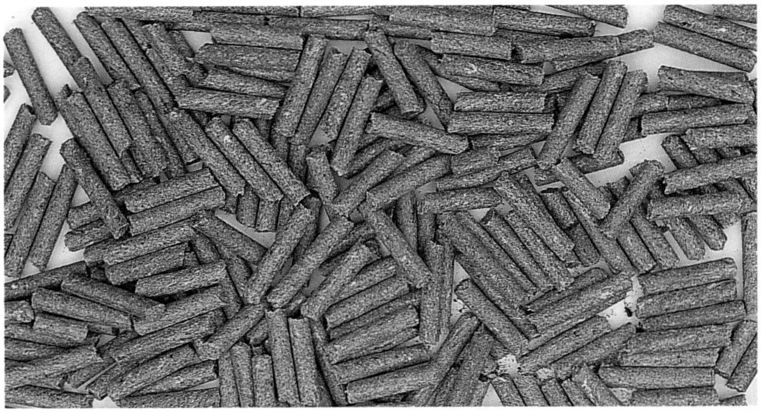

Horse and pony nuts are brownish to greenish in colour. They come in many different guises, and under names intended for various categories of horse and pony doing different jobs. They are well balanced nutritionally, if of a reputable brand, keep well and are convenient and easy to feed. However, some horses soon tire of them

Cubes

Cubes are basically made by having the ingredients ground down to a coarse powder, mixed with a syrup-type binder to keep them together, and the resulting mixture forced through tubes, then dried and cut to a convenient length for the horse to chew. The resulting cylindrical-shaped pellets are easily broken up by any horse with normal teeth, although those with sore mouths or worn, missing or broken teeth may have problems. As a concentrate, they are usually eaten quickly and I find it advantageous to mix them with soaked sugar beet and chop to make the horse take his time and masticate them thoroughly.

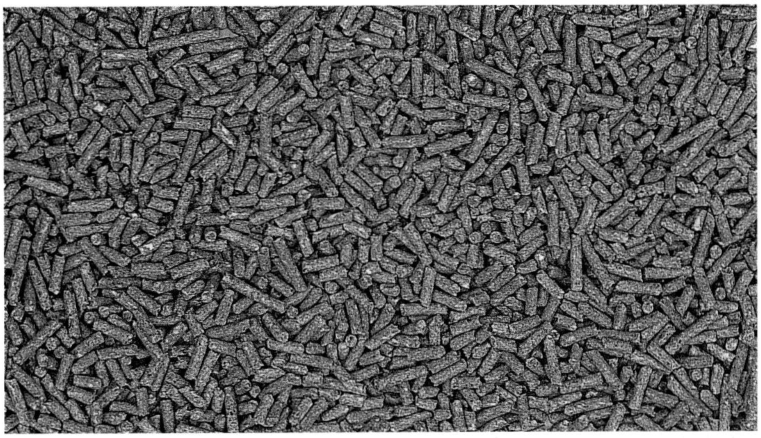

Foal and yearling pellets, normally smaller than cubes for adult horses, are specially balanced for growing youngstock

Coarse Mixes

Coarse mixes consist of similar ingredients to cubes, but they are not ground to a powder. They may consist of crushed or cooked dried grains, perhaps something juicy such as locust beans, legumes such as peas and beans, vitamins and minerals usually in the form of little cubes, with the whole lot being thoroughly mixed with molasses or, again, some type of syrup. They do not usually contain chop, but you can only improve them by adding some.

Coarse mixes (called sweet feeds in the USA) are composed of a variety of grains and other ingredients and small pellets. They are 'bound' with some sort of syrup to make them slightly moist, such as a molasses or honey product, and so are sweet to the taste. Most horses love them and do not tire of them as some do with cubes. Because of the syrup content, they must be kept cool and used within a few days of opening a sack. Ideally, they should be kept in an old fridge in the feed room. As with any product, it is essential to follow the feeding and storage instructions on the sack

Boiling linseed

Many nutritionists nowadays would say that giving boiled linseed is a waste of time and effort, as linseed is probably not as good for horses as adding oil to the diet in the form of a tablespoon of soya, corn or cod-liver oil. The fact is, though, that many horses do like linseed, and it is also believed by some experts to have a soothing effect on the intestines, although in a normal healthy horse this should not be necessary. As cooked linseed forms a high fat, sloppy jelly, it has the benefit (provided it is fed daily so as not to upset the digestion) of the concentrated energy which comes from fats plus the texture of sloppy, slimy jelly rather than straightforward oil, so there may be something in that theory.

If you do wish to cook linseed, be sure to boil it properly. It contains two substances which, when the seed is wet (from water, digestive juices or whatever), can react together and result in cyanide poisoning. Boiling hard for ten to twenty minutes is sufficient to prevent this reaction, although most nutritionists would recommend that the linseed is boiled for between four and six hours as the shorter boiling period does not produce the jelly-like quality for which linseed is favoured.

You have to keep adding water during the boiling process (put one cupful of seed straight into the boiling water) – and be warned that it boils over *very* easily, making a terrible mess of cookers. This tendency can, however, be considerably reduced if you also add a handful or more of whole barley seed, or packet pearl barley. Adding black treacle during the end stages of the boiling makes the brew even more appealing, as this is absorbed by the barley and incorporated into the jelly.

The resulting mixture is then used whilst still piping hot and liquid to make a mash instead of plain boiling water, or it can simply be added to a normal feed, although remember that the energy content of that feed will be considerably raised by its addition.

Feeding a little of such a (fresh) concoction every day will increase the nutritional level of the diet; however, if you only do it as a mash once a week (as is traditional) you will upset the horse's digestion (hence the acrid, sloppy droppings the following morning) with all the disadvantages already discussed.

Cooked Feeds

Grains have been boiled or steamed for generations of horses in the belief that they are easier to digest that way, and that the horse gets more goodness from them and will 'do better' on them; hence the tradition that boiled barley is fed to poor doers, run-down, thin or sick horses. But giving boiled feeds does add a lot of water to a concentrated grain and inevitably dilutes it, so some experts would recommend that the grain be steamed (in a sieve over a pan or tank of boiling water) instead. However, exposing the feed to such high temperatures also destroys many vitamins, which rather defeats the object. You could always add a supplement to restore the vitamin content, but do this after the feed has cooled or the heat will damage the vitamins in the supplement – it's a vicious circle! In fact, with today's ready-cooked feeds (although they are not warm) there is no need to boil barley or linseed for your horse.

Larger yards wishing to feed boiled linseed or linseed tea will find it more practical to use a boiler like this. Nutritionally, there is no need to feed boiled linseed with today's improved feeds, but some nutritionists feel that the demulcent nature of the resulting jelly helps soothe intestines possibly irritated by too many cereal concentrates. A little should be fed daily rather than weekly

Extruded feeds

Extrusion is a method of cooking grain at high pressure which breaks up starch molecules, making the resulting feed easier to digest. Extruded feeds tend to look like a cross between popcorn and dog-mixer.

Micronised feeds

The grain is flaked and cooked dry, again with the object of breaking up the starch molecules for easier digestion. The most obvious example is flaked maize.

Crushing, Rolling and Bruising

These are all different stages of the same process. Oats are often fed whole in their husks – particularly in more traditionalist establishments such as some racing and hunting yards and military and police yards (although by no means always) – but not all horses chew them up adequately, and undigested (wasted, in other words) whole oats can be clearly seen in their droppings.

Crushing, rolling and bruising crack the husk and damage the grain somewhat to open it up to the saliva and digestive juices. Crushed oats are considerably flattened, bruised oats just have the husk cracked, and rolled oats come in between. It is a matter of preference which you choose.

Barley should never be fed whole: its grains are much smaller and harder than oats, and so are even less likely to be crushed by the horse's teeth; they have just a thin, papery husk. Again, you can get it crushed, rolled or bruised, but more commonly these days it is bought cooked (extruded or micronised) and flaked, as is maize.

Disadvantages of crushing

Although different grades of crushing open up the grain for the horse, the process also kills the seed which is alive before treatment. This means it immediately starts to decay, and in quite a short time, as little as two weeks, the grain can become unfit to eat. Therefore never buy more crushed grain than you can use in a week or two, and then only if you know it has been freshly crushed. You have to trust your merchant here, even if you buy your grain whole and then tell him to crush it for you, which he won't want to do with a single sack for one horse. Ask him which day he crushes oats, or whatever you want, and ask for some of that day's grain. Even so, you may not get it unless you stand and watch!

To be fair, most merchants need to maintain a good reputation and should try to co-operate, so shop around until you find one who will.

> ## What do we mean by a 'heating' feed?
>
> The expression 'heating' or 'non-heating' when related to feed means, to horse people, the effect a feed has on a horse's behaviour, whether it makes him uncontrollably 'giddy' or not; nutritionists, however, seem to be taking it to mean whether a feed is warming to a horse in cold weather.
>
> Most people in the horse world, including nutritionists and vets who also ride or drive (and not all do so by any means), would embrace the first meaning – but it would be as well to check with your own specialist as to what he or she understands by the expression, so you both know what you are talking about!

Molassine Meal

Molassine meal is simply molasses (a type of black treacle and, obviously, very high in sugar) mixed with peat. It is like a sticky powder and more convenient to feed than pure molasses, but it does not keep at all well in warm weather and neither does anything to which it has been added, such as sugar-beet pulp, coarse mix or molassed chop. Such feeds must always be kept in a cool place in warm weather (such as an old fridge) otherwise they will become sour and unfit to feed very quickly. It is extremely difficult to find nowadays.

Particularly in summer, it is probably safer to melt and dilute molasses with hot water, and use that for damping feeds.

The water in which sugar-beet pulp has been soaked, particularly the molassed sort, is rich in energy and minerals and is almost equivalent to an electrolyte drink, although it, too, must be given to the horse to drink whilst fresh. Offer it perhaps after a hard ride or training session, before his feed; most horses love it.

There is some difference of opinion over the advisability of giving horses regular feeds containing molasses. Some people say horses get sick of it, others maintain that once used to molassed feeds they won't eat normal ones. As ever, it is probably best to play it by ear and feed molasses and other sugary products only in moderation.

Judging Quality or Fitness to Feed

Although you can only be sure of a feed's nutritional content by having it professionally analysed or by checking the analysis panel on it, you can judge practical quality yourself.

Most feeds are significantly affected by storage (discussed in Chapter 10), and as a general rule should be kept in dry conditions in vermin-proof containers. Most feeds benefit from being kept cool, too, although this is less important with *whole* cereal grains.

Hay and straw are still very commonly kept under cover, but in open-sided structures euphemistically called barns. True barns provide cover plus walls to keep destructive rain off the crop. Old barns would have four walls with ventilation holes in them as air is also needed, particularly while a crop is still 'making' itself after harvesting.

Hay

Generally, hay should not be fed before it is six months old, to allow time for all the chemical processes to have completed. However, it is another old wives' tale that the older hay is, up to two years, the more mature and better for horses. Hay this old will have lost much of its feed value, no matter how well it has been stored and will, in fact, be rotting away slowly but surely, so do not let anyone try to palm you off with it.

If you are really desperate and have to feed 'new' hay less than six months old, you can safely get away with it if you open up the bale a day or two before you will need it and thoroughly toss it and air it under cover. Try to feed it mixed with your

Hay is best stored in well ventilated storage where it has adequate protection from rain which washes out nutrients and ruins the bales exposed to it. Open-sided storage areas which have only overhead coverage are inadequate and wasteful

Shaking out hay before feeding was always recommended to 'remove dust'. Hay with any noticeable dust should not be used at all, especially for horses with a hint of respiratory problems

old batch or with straw if you possibly can to avoid sudden changes in feeding.

All hay should smell sweet, be lively and 'bouncy' when you open the bale, and have no sign of dust or of white, green or black mould. It should be greenish to golden in colour, and bright, not dull yellow or brown. If it smells a bit like tobacco it has been baled whilst too wet and is slightly mow-burnt, as it is called, having heated up in storage. Whilst some horses may like this, it will nevertheless be of lower feed value than had it not become mow-burnt. Provided it is not dusty (and it often is) it should do no harm.

When assessing hay, be sure to look for extraneous material such as weeds and poisonous plants, many of which are even more toxic dead in hay than alive in the field. Nor should hay and straw contain lumps of soil, as this indicates that it was harvested in wet weather and probably baled before it was dry enough, so it may also be dusty and mouldy.

Straw and Chop

When assessing quality, these are subject to exactly the same criteria: look for sweet-smelling, bright, clean products with no mould, dust, dirt, dull appearance or unpleasant, musty or sour smell. They must also be dry and not 'clingy' with damp. Hay, straw or chop which is dusty or mouldy is not even fit for bedding, as your horse will still be exposed to the mould and irritating dust; it is only fit for making compost, if that.

If chop has molasses added it will, of course, be moist, slightly tacky maybe and smell of treacle. Good makers do not use molasses just to disguise poor quality.

Concentrates

All concentrates should look and feel clean and bright, and smell either sweet, slightly pleasant or of nothing at all. Any 'offish' or sour smell, visible dullness, dampness, or fungi and moulds, plus any dirt or dust in the feed, not to mention vermin excreta, mean it is unfit to feed.

Hayage and Forage Feeds

As branded products these should be in good condition when you buy them. Again, although hayage does smell rather sickly to us, it should not actually smell unpleasant or sour, and there should certainly be no sign of slime, mould or dirt in it. Forage feeds can be judged in the same way as hay, straw and chop.

Bran

If you do buy bran it, too, should smell and taste sweet and be free and loose, and quite dry; moreover any clumping together means it has been damp and spoiled at some time. Obviously, if it is actually damp reject it, also if it smells musty or sour.

Roots

All roots bought in their natural condition such as carrots, mangolds, turnips, apples or whatever should be hard, firm and crisp. Roots may have soil on them which is fine; they keep better if you leave the soil on. However, there should certainly be no softened, slimy or brown patches on them which indicates they are rotting. Some sellers regularly try to palm off such material to animal owners, but do not accept it for your horse.

Sugar-beet shreds or cubes may seem difficult to judge. The cubes should be quite dry and firm with, as ever, no unpleasant smell. The shreds are naturally dull and grey, but experience – and particularly your nose – will soon teach you whether they are normal, or dirty and going sour. The usual molassed sort does not keep as well as the plain, and in summer it may be as well to buy the plain type if you can find it and add your own diluted black treacle to feeds, if required.

Swedes and turnips are not so popular with horses, but if yours likes them they are worth leaving in the manger overnight for him to chomp

A whole fodder beet. These are high in energy and fibre, for a root feed, and can prove a valuable addition to feeds where available

What is best for you and your horse?

- You don't need to feel as though your back is against the wall when suppliers tell you they can't get or don't sell a particular product you want to try. With today's variety of feeds available to horse owners you can always find something suitable, or ring the firm whose feed you want.
- Whatever you try, just remember to introduce it very gradually and buy the smallest quantity you can at first so you don't waste money on something which turns out not to suit your horse or which he doesn't like.
- Horses can be finicky, even greedy ones often showing suspicion of anything new. Be patient and give a feed a fair trial before rejecting it so that your horse has time to get used to it and make up his own mind. If he doesn't like it, there's always something else to try.
- Never buy what you don't really want just because it is cheap and someone is trying to sell it off. Economy is important, but most people spend too much on their horses' diets simply because they overfeed expensive concentrates or supplements! Be sure, perhaps by taking advice, that you get what is best for you and your horse.

Key Facts

- **The hay or main roughage element in a horse or pony's diet (hayage, straw or forage feed) is the most important, not the concentrates. If fed correctly, and as long as it is of suitable quality and nutrient content, good hay is often a perfectly adequate feed on its own for cobs and ponies and for horses in light to moderate work.**
- **Hayage is a good and increasingly popular alternative to hay, particularly for animals which have respiratory problems. The main objection to it is that horses finish their recommended rations too quickly, leaving them bored and hungry. This can be overcome by feeding a larger amount of a lower energy grade of hayage, as well as by feeding it in small-mesh nets or hayracks.**
- **Do not overlook fodder straw or oat or barley straw as a roughage source for your horse or pony, particularly when good hay or hayage is hard to come by or you want a low-energy source of roughage.**
- **Also important is good quality chop, the value of which is now being appreciated by a new generation of horse owners. A generous double handful can be added to each concentrate feed. It is far better as roughage and for bulk than bran.**
- **The easiest way to feed your horse or pony a balanced diet of the right energy grade is to use a reputable branded product specifically formulated for your type of animal. This is far more certain than trying to make up your own ration on a hit-and-miss or wait-and-see basis.**
- **Succulents should be included in each feed as an important ingredient, not just a tasty treat or extra.**
- **Never use grain which has been crushed, rolled or bruised more than two weeks previously, as it will have started to deteriorate too much.**
- **You cannot judge the nutrient content of any feed by traditional quality-testing methods of appearance, taste, smell and feel, only its fitness to feed. To obtain certain knowledge of a feed's nutrient content it has to be professionally analysed in a laboratory.**

4

A LITTLE BIT EXTRA

Vitamin and mineral supplements have been on the market for several decades now. Only a very few human generations ago commercially and scientifically formulated products were unheard of, but most horse owners and trainers had their own pet items they swore by (and many still do) which they added to feeds, sometimes not even letting their staff know what they were. There would be secret concoctions passed down from stud groom to stud groom, father to son, and sometimes, out of sheer spite or selfishness, taken to the grave, never to be revealed to anyone!

Feeding has always been an art, and these days it is a science as well, the ability to blend the best of those two aspects being the real road to success. The art is still very much in evidence, and the science helps us evaluate old and new feeding practices and theories. The main advantage of scientifically formulated supplements is – provided they are fed strictly in accordance with instructions from the maker, a vet or a nutritionist – their safety as well as their suitability. By all means use older substances or recipes, but take advice first so you are sure what is in them.

Favourite 'Secret Ingredients'

These include eggs, honey, beer (particularly stout) and specific plants and herbs, even spices. Some old favourites have been analysed, sometimes for human medicine, and beneficial ingredients found in them which account for their popularity and apparent effectiveness.

Most such ingredients contained vitamins and minerals, protein, energy, oils or particular chemicals or enzymes which were unknown to the old-timers who swore by them but which have since been discovered and evaluated. In some cases, their benefits have been confirmed, in others their undeniable effects have been shown to be possibly due to substances of dubious safety.

Old-fashioned and still-popular feed supplements – black treacle (molasses), eggs and honey. They all contain various nutrients which your horse may or may not need, and he may like them anyway. For that reason alone, there would be no harm feeding them in moderate amounts. Molasses is probably the most popular of these three

Does my Horse Need a Supplement?

This depends on the horse's condition and health, his diet, work and the grazing available. The horses or ponies most likely to need supplements are those on a low plane of nutrition – on poor pasture, for example, with no regular feed (a large self-feed block would help these); hard-working performance horses; broodmares in the last three months of pregnancy or the first three months of lactation; horses which have little or no significant access to grazing or sunshine; run-down or sick animals; and older animals whose digestion and metabolism may have deteriorated with age.

The owners of such animals should certainly discuss the matter of supplementation with a veterinary surgeon or nutritionist.

Analyse the Diet

The only way to discover whether or not your horse does need a supplement is to obtain an assessment of his full diet (including concentrates, roughage and grazing), discuss it with a specialist and then decide if anything needs to be added or taken away; finally you should arrive at the optimum diet for the horse's circumstances. Buying blindly simply because the product sounds good in the advertising material will not do your horse any good: he may become ill due to an overdose of a certain product or nutrient, and you could also waste money – most supplements are quite expensive, and some of their contents may simply pass through the horse as the body recognises that it does not need them, to be excreted in the droppings or urine and so wasted; their presence in excess may even do actual harm.

What is the Difference between a Supplement and an Additive?

The basic difference between a supplement and an additive is this: a **supplement** forms part of the nutritional content of the feed and helps to balance it according to a particular animal's needs. This depends on his condition and health, the feedstuffs he is receiving and their amounts and proportions, his work and environment, and his grazing and the content of the soil it grows on.

An **additive** is something which is 'added' to a diet which is, we hope, already balanced. It may not even be a nutrient, and may even *un*balance the diet. Worming pellets can be described as a non-nutritional additive, for example.

Broad-spectrum vitamin, mineral and trace element feed blocks help outdoor horses make the best of their grazing. They are best placed in specially made holders for some protection

Types of Supplement

There are supplements aimed at all categories of horse and pony – every imaginable job or lifestyle is covered to take advantage of a niche in the market. Many supplements are excellent products, properly and carefully formulated and manufactured. Of course their manufacturers want to make money; that is why they are in business. But it is not in their interests for their products to be fed in inappropriate circumstances – to animals which do not need them and which may be adversely affected by them – because their reputations and livelihoods depend on their products being successful and beneficial. No reputable manufacturer would advise you to feed one of their products simply to make money without due regard to your animal's needs.

As well as being able to select a supplement (if you need to at all) suitable for your animal's circumstances, you can also choose between broad-spectrum supplements which contain a wide range of vitamins and minerals, specific ones which may contain only one vitamin or mineral and those which contain a select few. The specific ones are the ones likely to cause most trouble if fed wrongly, as it is easy to overdose them and give your horse a large helping of something he does not need.

REMEMBER: **Vitamins and minerals can be potent nutrients capable of causing serious problems if wrongly fed.**

Forms of Presentation

Supplements come as pellets, powders, liquids, syrups, licking blocks (ordinary salt licks are supplements) and pastes. Most have been made to be appealing to horses and ponies as they are normally added to feeds or, more rarely, water. Horses are particularly fussy about their drinking water and there are often problems getting horses doing endurance work to drink water containing electrolyte (mineral salt) supplements to counteract the dehydration caused by sweating for prolonged periods. This is why it is always advised that plain water be available in addition to the 'doctored' sort. Horses in need of electrolytes normally sense what they need and drink the separate product fairly willingly.

Feed blocks and salt licks

With most supplements, you can be sure that the horse is getting the correct amount simply by putting it in his feed and checking whether or not he is eating up. With feed blocks which the horse has to lick on a self-feed basis you cannot be so sure, because some of these products give horses a sore tongue which can affect their willingness to eat other food. Also, they may simply not like the taste of the block and not use it.

It is advisable to spend time watching your horse or pony to check whether or not he seems happy using the block; make a point of looking at the block to see if it is worn down gradually from use. Check, too, inside your horse's mouth to see if there is any sign of a sore tongue.

Do not site blocks over the water source, because if the horse bites a lump off and it falls in the water it will probably affect its taste and put him off drinking. This can be serious or even fatal for animals which are not checked regularly, or if it is simply not noticed by their attendants.

Horses on Compound Feeds

One of the advantages of compound feeds is that normally they are already properly balanced. This is a great plus in their favour, as not only can you see the energy and protein levels but also the levels of vitamins and minerals. You will hardly ever find a sack of oats, barley or maize with this information available unless you pay to have each sack analysed, which is inconvenient and prohibitively expensive.

Normally, therefore, you should not add supplements to compound feeds except on scientifically qualified advice. The only time supplementation might be necessary is if your roughage source is low in nutrients, for example if you are feeding poor hay, or straw, or your grazing is poor. Otherwise it is probably best to avoid supplements when using good compound feeds.

Horses on a Grass, Hay and Cereal Diet

Horses on a conventional diet of grass, hay, cereal and some bran are most likely to need calcium (probably in the form of ground limestone) and salt; they will probably need roughly 1oz/28mg of salt a day, depending on the weather and work – horses working hard in hot, humid weather will sweat more and so lose more body salt. In winter, fat-soluble vitamins A, D, E and probably K will have been depleted from the body stores by about Christmas and will probably need supplementing. In fact on this sort of diet, also bearing in mind that the vitamin D levels in grass hay over six months old will be very low, supplementation could be needed for fully stabled horses at any time, and for those out but wearing clothing and so shielded from sunshine which helps the body make vitamin D.

Horses on a High Concentrate/ Low Roughage Diet

Some owners persist in feeding this sort of diet despite modern knowledge and advice to the contrary, and it could well be deficient in two important amino acids (protein 'building blocks'), namely lysine and methionine; so look for these in the analysis table of any supplement you consider when feeding such a diet.

Treat your supplement as a normal feed ingredient, feeding a little in each feed rather than the whole advised amount in one feed.

If giving a supplement in a home-cooked, warm feed, allow it to cool to eating temperature before adding the supplement, as the heat could otherwise kill off valuable nutrients, making the whole operation pointless and a waste of money.

How to Use Supplements

Where supplements are concerned, 'more' is not necessarily good. Stick to the recommended dose and do not mix supplements, particularly broad-spectrum ones, unless advised to do so by a specialist. It is all too easy for the non-scientifically minded to think that because something *sounds* good it must do their particular horse good, and also that this can apply to several products. In fact a little bit of this and a little bit of that given indiscriminately or on the feeder's whim or mood can do a great deal of *harm*, and the horse may be better off with no supplement at all.

Supplements come in powder, syrup, liquid, granule, pellet and paste form and there are many different brands. Making the right choice can be extremely difficult and it is best to consult a vet or nutritionist on this matter

What Others Do

Never use a supplement because you know someone else does, no matter who they are; their horses' needs may be quite different from yours, as might the rest of their diet. Certainly be suspicious of anyone whose normal policy is to give regular booster injections of vitamins: if this sort of supplementation is necessary, their horses must be on permanently unbalanced or deficient diets. The only animals who might need this sort of treatment are sick or debilitated animals of any age, or perhaps those on moorland or range-type grazing of very poor quality where fat-soluble vitamins could be deficient, or where the soil might be deficient in certain minerals. Injections as a solution to a temporary need may be used for youngstock on an unbalanced diet, but the diet should be subsequently corrected.

Salt and mineral licks of various sorts are available for fixing in the stable or field shelter. Plastic-covered holders are best as they resist the corrosive effect of salt which causes metal to contaminate the lick

Herbs

Herbs as ingredients in feeds, and in particular as vitamin and mineral supplements, are receiving more and more interest. Obviously as vegetation they are eaten readily by horses, and they used to form a normal part of any grazing and hay meadow until 'improved' agricultural methods during and since World War II classed them as worthless weeds and promoted their eradication in favour of what conservationists, with some justification, termed 'green deserts' – monocultures of one sort of grass or single crop. Wild flowers which were normally found in wheat and oat crops, for example, were eradicated (with some justification in certain cases, such as the corncockle which is poisonous), and for decades both herbs and wild flowers have had to find a living on spare land and verges only.

Now matters are turning full circle – as they tend to – and herbs are making a return to both agriculture and gardening. In cooking, herbs have always been used, if less so in Britain than in Mediterranean countries for example. The fact is that, in general, herbs are natural foods which contain valuable nutrients and healing/health-promoting agents. They are also particularly rich in minerals, and probably contain many substances not yet scientifically identified. Scientifically qualified people usually point out that there is no scientific proof that the substances in herbs have any healing properties, but herbalists and many human patients and animal owners can testify to their efficacy in many cases. Although this 'evidence' is subjective, the truth is that herbal remedies have been successful for thousands of years, both inside and outside the bodies of humans and animals, and were almost the only medicines available before the advent of synthetic medicines.

A short list is given on pages 59 and 60 of some herbs, their purported effects and their medicinal uses. However, the most important fact to remember is that herbalists usually treat the whole body and the mind, rather than taking one disorder and its remedy in isolation. Self- or home-treatment may well work, but the most effective method of using herbs in either health maintenance or the treatment of disorders is to consult a herbalist, as you would consult a vet, so that your horse or pony receives an overall assessment before treatment is prescribed. Some veterinary surgeons are now qualified herbalists too (and homoeopathists) and may well prescribe any single type of treatment or maybe a combination to achieve effective treatment.

If you wish to use a herbal feed supplement, look for a reputable firm which has at least one qualified herbalist on its staff or as a consultant. You can also buy feed mixes containing herbs but again, ensure you use a reputable make and ask the firm about the qualifications of the staff formulating its rations.

As for including herbs in pasture, herbs usually thrive best in a separate strip on dry, not-too-fertile soil rather than as part of the overall seed mix. It is most noticeable that horses do graze these strips, and it is interesting to note which plants and herbs they select to graze when allowed to eat on spare land and verges; also that they choose a far wider variety of vegetation than just grasses, as they would in the wild. Perhaps they know instinctively what they need, or maybe they just like the taste. Whatever the case, herbs contain valuable nutrients (and remember that many disorders can be caused by nutrient deficiencies) which can treat deficiency disorders. Some are also known for acting as actual germicides, treating diseases caused by an invasion of bacteria, viruses or whatever.

It is sensible, not cranky, to investigate the properties and uses of herbs, to take expert advice, and to use supplements, feeds and remedies wisely.

Herbal Supplements

Herbal remedies and supplements which until only a decade or so ago were regarded as 'cranky' are now quite well accepted as having definite benefits. They are nothing new, of course. Remedies and health boosters from various plant and animal sources have been used for many thousands of years, and many drugs used in modern medicine derive from plants, penicillin which comes from a mould being the most obvious example. Until the advent of synthetic drugs a few generations ago they were, along with various substances from animal sources, the only medicines available.

Some Common Herbs and their Uses

Agrimony Constricts the blood vessels and is used to staunch bleeding. Mildly anti-inflammatory.

Alfalfa/lucerne Said to increase a horse's speed! Helps kidneys secrete poisons and waste products. High in calcium.

borage

camomile

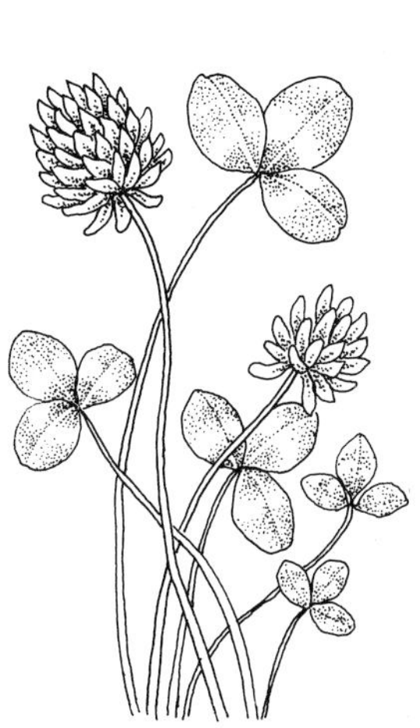
clover

comfrey

elder

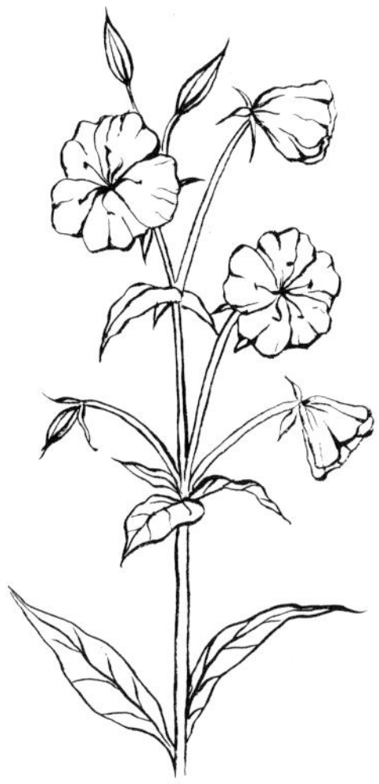
evening primrose

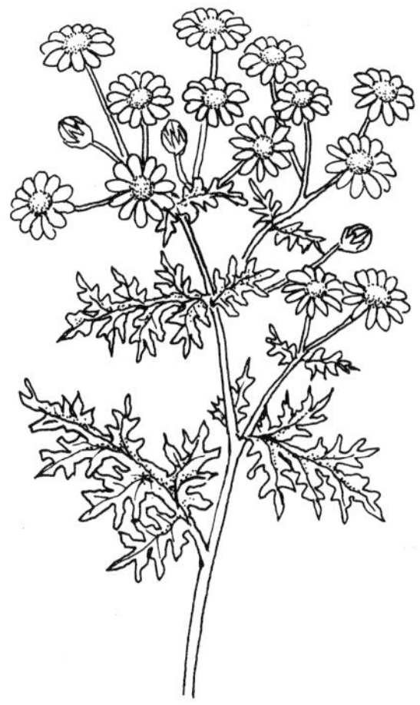
feverfew

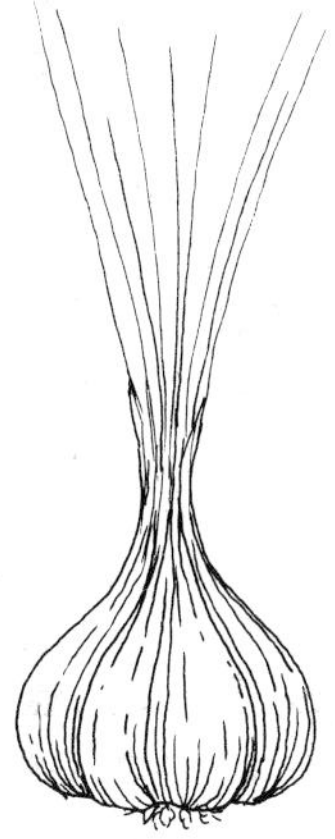
garlic

golden rod

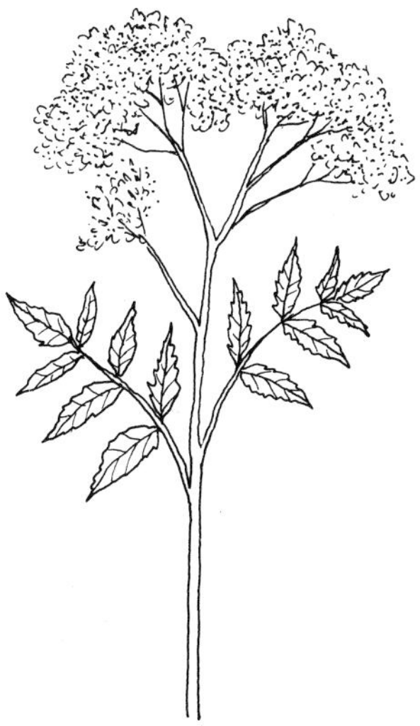
meadowsweet

plantain

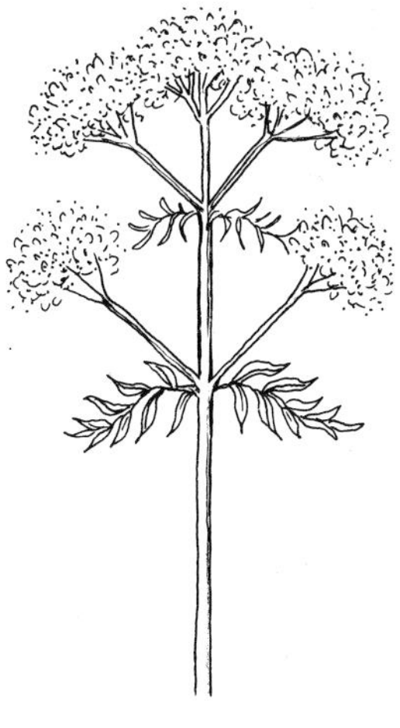
valerian

Arnica Used for joint stiffness, wounds, swellings and the relief of pain; mildly anti-inflammatory.

Balm Used for retained afterbirths and general uterine disorders, including the prevention of abortion. Said to help with heart disorders and nervous system disorders. Antispasmodic and good for the digestive system.

Borage Used as a remedy for eye ailments and ringworm, rickets and heart/chest problems.

Burdock Used for skin irritations, respiratory disorders, rheumatism and blood disorders.

Camomile Mildly sedative (without any 'drugging' effects), and helps to relieve pain.

Celandine, greater Used for eye ailments, particularly cataracts, and for warts.

Chickweed Used for all digestive disorders, skin problems, muscle cramps, arthritis and rheumatism.

Chicory For general weakness, poor appetite, liver problems.

Clover, red Sedative. Used to treat debility, nervousness, sore throat.

Clover, white Used to help blood disorders and chronic skin problems, especially persistent ulcers and infected wounds.

Comfrey Probably one of the most familiar herbs, comfrey is used to treat both bone and soft tissue injuries (its old name being 'knitbone') and diseases such as arthritis. In large quantities over prolonged periods of use (probably years) it *may* cause cancer, but in normal doses, used with expert advice, many people find it effective and prefer it in mild cases to, for example, corticosteroids which are often prescribed for inflammatory bone conditions.

Daisy Used to help skin problems – infections, inflammation and bruising.

Dandelion Used as a diuretic (encouraging urination), mild laxative and general 'tonic' – whatever that is.

Dock Used to treat skin infections and inflammations, stings and bites, nettlerash and in fever conditions.

Elder Insecticidal wipe. Helps digestive problems and chest disorders, and in inflammation of the uterus and vagina.

Evening primrose oil Used to ease arthritis, skin ailments, to relieve coughs and to help heal wounds; evening primrose oil also helps to regulate the breeding cycle in mares.

Fennel Colds and 'flu are said to be helped, as fennel is a mild expectorant. It is also mildly diuretic and antispasmodic.

Feverfew Said to help in all fever conditions and with digestive problems.

Garlic Described as a natural antibiotic and antiseptic, it is popular as a general healer and health maintainer. It is said to be effective at keeping flies away, helping sterility and poor fertility problems in breeding stock, as a digestion promoter and for treating respiratory diseases.

Golden rod Old herbals claim it helps to heal gangrene! Used to help digestive problems, also liver and kidney disorders. Helps to stop bleeding.

Ground ivy The 'gardener's curse': said to help with coughs and tuberculosis. Also helps to heal ulcers and abscesses, and to expel retained afterbirth.

Horse chestnut Said to improve the general efficacy of the lungs and to help in respiratory diseases and allergies.

Lavender Calming, antispasmodic, antiseptic.

Linseed (flax) Used to help soothe inflamed intestines and airways, and to help heal soft tissue injuries.

Marigold Used to treat fever, internal ulcers, circulatory disorders, skin ailments.

Meadowsweet Used to treat fever, blood disorders and also digestive problems.

Mistletoe Said to help with nervous ailments, uterine and vaginal haemorrhage, arthritis and panic attacks.

Mullein Used for chest diseases in general, also diarrhoea and digestive disorders, and as a poultice for muscle cramps.

Nettle When cut and wilted, horses will eat these readily; they are said

The value of science?

Very many people have experienced success for themselves and their animals using herbal remedies and health aids, including horse owners. And just because there is no scientific proof that something is effective, it does not mean that it doesn't work. Scientific proof may be highly desirable, but it should not, I feel, be used as an exclusive parameter by which to judge everything. For many years people strongly suspected smoking to be a cause of cancer and other serious respiratory disorders, but because for a long time there was no scientific proof that it was, smoking remained fashionable and vested interests continued to make a lot of money out of the habit. Some people, however, stuck to their beliefs and did not smoke. Now we do have scientific proof of the dangers of smoking, and its denigrators have been proved right.

to help with poor condition and appetite, heart and lung disorders, parasite infestation and many other conditions. Used as a brew and applied externally, the nettle is said to give a high gloss and bloom to horses' coats.

Plantain To treat dysentery, bleeding, ulcers and fever, also wounds and skin diseases and injuries including insect bites. Helps eye diseases and injuries.

Rosehip Mildly astringent, diuretic and laxative. High in vitamin C.

Valerian Sedative and anti-depressant.

There are many more herbs and other plants, and many more uses for those I have listed: I am *not* a qualified herbalist, and advise readers always to consult such an expert before trying to treat any living creature with herbs. Like synthetic medicines, they can be very potent, and even fatal if used incorrectly. However, I am greatly in favour of their use, indeed of anything, natural or synthetic, which helps promote health and wellbeing, ideally without distressing side-effects. Many roads lead to Rome.

Herbal Remedies

These are fast regaining their status as medicines and health aids, part of the apparently general worldwide swing back to a more natural and less harmful way of life: but they are not all harmless or 'safe' by any means, and must be used with care and according to the instructions of a skilled, qualified herbalist for the best results. Despite the many thousands of years of evidence, accumulated through usage, that herbal remedies and aids can and do work, scientific research aimed at proving this – or otherwise – has only very recently started to be done. If you buy a herbal remedy over the counter from a chemist or herbalist you will not find on it any claim as to actual curative properties, as this is unlawful: the label is carefully worded to give buyers a guide as to the product's uses and properties. However, if you consult a herbalist and ask what products seem successful for treating specific conditions, you will usually be given a straight answer.

Very many people who have used herbal vitamin and mineral supplements for themselves and their animals are very satisfied with the results. Herbs, of course, were at one time a natural part of every grazing or hay meadow, every roadside verge and every spare patch where they could get a hold. Then modern agricultural methods developed during and since World War II in response to the demand for ever more productivity, managed to exclude them to the point where many are now rare. But they are being rediscovered and specially cultivated, and herbal supplements are readily available to the horse owner now.

It is also encouraging that more veterinary surgeons are interested in herbal products, both supplements and remedies, and if you want to take this route towards treating or creating a balanced diet for your horse or pony, then by all means do so. There are several reputable suppliers of herbal products advertising regularly in equestrian magazines, so owners should have no problems finding sources. If you use firms having at least one qualified herbalist on their staff to whom you can speak about your requirements, and provided you follow the advice given, you may well experience considerable success.

Yeasts, Enzymes and Probiotics

These supplements may be considered as aids to digestion, and should be regarded as additives rather than as supplements. If your horse experiences problems digesting his food, your vet or nutritionist may, after consultation and investigation of the problem, recommend one of these to help him

Enzymes

These are part of the horse's digestive 'equipment' and it may be that the horse is simply not producing particular enzymes in the right amounts, or at all.

Yeasts

Yeasts have been the subject of much scientific work, and they can definitely be effective in creating a micro-organism-friendly environment in the horse's intestines. Because of this, the essential micro-organisms thrive and reproduce and enable the horse to digest more fibre better, which is all to his good. Fed as recommended by the makers, yeast supplements and feeds containing yeasts can be very beneficial to many horses, even if they do not appear to be having digestive problems.

Protein and Carbohydrate Supplements

Protein supplements may be recommended in cases where the diet is deficient in protein (although an increase in actual dietary protein would be better); where animals are in very poor condition, to help build up flesh; in stunted youngsters; and for young racehorses or old animals. Like most supplements, they should not be fed without correct advice, as too much protein can cause health problems.

Carbohydrate boosters are often used to boost the energy levels of hard-working horses before a hard day and sometimes after, depending on advice received, and are excellent for giving the horse extra energy without increasing his other feed ingredients (specifically concentrates), particularly if he is around the limits of his appetite.

Probiotics

Probiotics are actually the bacteria themselves, and in the same way as yeasts, probiotic products are recommended when the digestive system does not seem to be working properly. A rather cynical colleague of mine described them scathingly as 'processed droppings' (although he didn't use the word droppings), and in a way, he could be right. Horses' droppings inevitably contain large amounts of gut micro-organisms, and, for example, eating their dams' droppings is how foals build up a population of these essential creatures in their own intestines.

However, other horses which eat droppings (a practice known as *coprophagia*) are probably experiencing digestive disorder and indulge in this habit so as to satisfy a natural craving for what will put it right.

Probiotics do seem to be successful in remedying certain digestive malfunctions, and certainly have a place in maintaining equine health in appropriate cases; but they are not intended to be fed permanently. They can help restore gut harmony, but the root cause, as ever, should be sought out and put right. Probiotics are usually fed in a course, and may be used after 1) administering antibiotics (which kill off both bad and good bacteria); 2) after any stressful situation which also causes the loss of good bacteria; and 3) in animals with gut damage possibly due to worms or other causes.

Getting Help and Advice

Because feeding is more and more science based, and feeds are better because of it, it can be difficult for owners without a scientific background to assess what is best for their horse even with the help of informative literature produced by the feed and supplement manufacturers. In fact, reading too many of their leaflets sometimes leaves one feeling highly confused: which brand is best? Which method of feeding? I use yeasts, do I need probiotics? If I use a carbohydrate booster do I also need to increase my horse's feed, or can I actually decrease it?

Questions like these often arise and need the help of someone with a scientific background, either an equine nutritionist or a vet who has a specific interest in nutrition, to help you sort out the most likely answer for your horse and circumstances.

Branded Feeds

Where branded goods are concerned your task is easy, as all reputable firms employ at least one nutritionist who is available free of charge to answer queries or help you formulate a complete dietary management scheme for your horse using that firm's products.

Unbiased Advice

It is when you want truly independent, unbiased information that problems arise, because truly freelance nutritionists are a very rare species. For economic reasons, they usually need to have at least a part-time contract with one or more feed companies, and under those circumstances would be bound to lean towards their products – although in practice there would be nothing to stop them advising the use of other firms' ranges. Ideally you should get information and advice concerning the products of several firms, and get the nutritionist to recommend those products which are best for your horse, irrespective of commercial connections.

Prohibited Substances

If you compete with your horse or pony you may find that the ruling bodies controlling your particular discipline will have strict rules concerning substances which can affect your animal's performance, substances which can stimulate him to super-performance, or make him perform below standard. The whole area of prohibited substances or non-normal nutrients is still not satisfactory, because the science of detection has reached such heady levels that the tiniest traces can now be discovered – so tiny that, in the words of management consultant Gillian McCarthy, 'they wouldn't even stimulate a mouse, let alone a horse' – yet the ruling bodies may still ban them completely. Some substances may be allowed in 'safe' quantities.

On the other hand, suppliers and users can be equally adept at avoiding detection. Furthermore, there are not a few cases in the horse world where tested and banned horses have been found to be naturally manufacturing certain prohibited substances in their own bodies. There seems to be no end to the permutations of circumstances and it is a saga which will doubtless continue to run.

But where does this leave you as a competitor? Fortunately, most branded feeds and supplements which are 'safe' to use from a competition point of view (that is, they will, or should, not get you banned for 'doping' your horse will clearly state on their labels or in their literature that they contain no prohibited substances or non-normal nutrients. If something you want to use does not state this, write to the manufacturers and get a written reply back stating the situation, and keep it safe should you ever need it. It is also advised that you keep a sealed sample, even just a cupful, of any product you are using whilst training for or performing in competitions, so it can be tested in the event of any drugs test on your horse proving positive.

There are instances where medications advised and administered by a vet can also cause problems, perhaps simply because of the way your horse's body has metabolised them, so you need to keep careful records yourself, as well as those your vet keeps, of everything given to your horse.

Unfortunately favourite titbits may also be banned – for instance anything containing caffeine (all chocolate products) will produce a positive test. Fortunately the favourite treat of most horses in Britain, Polo mints, at least seems safe, unless the manufacturer adds something to the recipe at a future date!

The best advice is to keep as up to date as you can through your ruling organisation, your vet, your nutritionist and the equestrian press.

The main problem occurs because, at present, there is no regulatory or even organising body to which equine nutritionists can belong or which will govern their practice. Efforts were made in the recent past to set one up, but it fell by the wayside, although I understand it is hoped to rectify this in the future.

Another significant problem is that there is no specific qualification for equine nutritionists, although the various degree courses, and those approaching degree level, can contain a major element of nutritional science and practice. With actual veterinary qualifications, vets qualify in general veterinary practice and only specialise if they want to, once they have qualified. There is, for example, no specific qualification for a vet specialising in horses; although there is, at least, a British Equine Veterinary Association whose members will probably treat mainly, or only, equines, and are quite likely to make a personal specialisation in the species.

When looking for an equine nutritionist (if you don't want to use one employed solely by a particular firm), or a vet specially interested in nutrition, simply ask them where their interests and specialities lie. Tell them you are looking for unbiased, qualified advice on nutrition and ask if they are able to give it. No ethical, concerned vet or nutritionist will mind you asking such questions, and some may well refer you elsewhere if they feel unable to help you themselves.

Key Facts

- **If you are thinking of adding items to your animal's diet, get expert advice on what is in them before you risk unbalancing it. Branded supplements of reputable make are safest *provided* you have been advised your animal does need a supplement and that you use the type recommended.**

- **It is very unlikely your horse will need a supplement if you are using a good make of compound feed (a coarse mix/sweet feed or cubes/nuts) or certain forage feeds as these are fully balanced regarding vitamins and minerals during manufacture. Using a supplement with such a feed could detrimentally unbalance your horse's diet.**

- **Never use a supplement just because someone you know does so, or because some equestrian personality appears in a company's advertising. The produce may well be excellent, but not only may your animal not need it, he could also actually be harmed by a product which is not suitable for him or her.**
- **Always take the advice of an equine nutritionist or a veterinary surgeon interested in nutrition before using a supplement.**
- **Herbal supplements may be 'natural' but again, this does not mean they are mild or harmless. As always, seek expert advice before using them.**

5

'DR GREEN'

For 'Dr Green' simply read 'grass': well, grass plus leaves plus herbs plus a modicum of roots, in fact, anything the horse would naturally eat if on free range, natural pasture. He is a herbivore or vegetarian and, in theory, can eat any member of the plant world. In practice, horses are quite particular about what they eat, even down to individual preferences. It is not unknown for them to poison themselves through developing an acquired taste for some bitter-tasting poisonous plant or tree.

Natural grazing and browsing offers the horse a very wide variety of plant material to eat, with a corresponding wide variety of nutrients, many of which we can safely say have not even been discovered yet, as research work is showing, and particularly at present in work on rain-forest vegetation which is revealing many substances not hitherto known and proving invaluable in medicine.

Above: Land is said to be 'horse-sick' when it shows patches of very short grass with some longer ones, littered with droppings. This is a sad waste of a priceless resource. Well managed grassland is a much cheaper feed source than any bought-in feed. Right: Much good grass-growing space is taken up by weeds, most of which are vigorous growers. It is a waste of a vital resource not to remove weeds (as opposed to herbs). The feed value of the paddock is greatly reduced and its main use may be as an exercise area

The Advantages of Natural Pasture

Until fairly recently, 'improved' pasture offered horses (and other animals) a sadly restricted range of plants and therefore nutrients. Before such 'improvement' became fashionable, the cure offered by 'Dr Green' – for almost any ailment – was highly effective because natural meadow pasture contained a wide variety of nutrients in grasses, herbs and many plants; most of these, however, came to be regarded as useless weeds and were eradicated to make more room for 'real' grass.

Now, however, it is being realised again that not only is a wider variety of grasses beneficial, but so are herbs and other plants. Horses allowed to graze at will on, say, a roadside or bridleway verge, or on 'spare' uncultivated land, neglected patches and so on, can be seen to select many different plants in addition to grass, and to leave things we might feel they would want. I well remember once spending an hour breaking my back pulling grass to fill a haynet for my box-bound horse, which refused to eat a single blade! When subsequently led out to graze he happily grazed in the very same area I had pulled the grass from, obviously knowing much better than his frustrated owner what he wanted, liked and needed.

The Horse's Grazing Habits

Although choosy and seeming to waste much material, horses are very efficient grazers when they find something they like, and their incisor teeth can easily crop grass right down to the soil, like sheep; cattle, on the other hand, can only go so far as they have to grasp a fair length of grass with their tongues to tear it off. Like most animals, horses are generally revolted by their own droppings (although there are sometimes exceptions); they designate certain areas of their paddocks for grazing and others for lavatories, and the latter they never really graze even if the 'dining' or 'lawn' areas (as they are called) have become virtually bare. When they wish to defecate, they will wander over to a 'loo' area (there may be a few in each field, depending on its size) and, rather than pick their way through existing droppings, will dung on the edge of the area, which grows larger and larger, thereby decreasing the eating areas more and more. The grass in the loo areas grows long and rank and is constantly fed by the droppings, while the eating grass is constantly cropped, sometimes down to the bare earth, and is never fertilised, losing its nutrients all the time as the horses take off more and more grass.

In this sort of situation thistles, nettles, ragwort, docks and other useless and poisonous things will also tend to proliferate, particularly round the hedges and fences, and eventually the land is good for little other than exercising. What a waste of a priceless resource!

Turn Him Out!

Unfortunately for many horses, particularly those on controlled diets and in hard work, some owners have a phobia against turning them out, for all sorts of fanciful reasons, many of them quite invalid. From the point of view of pasture, the main objection is that the horse will get fat or fill himself up with grass (which he cannot possibly work on!) instead of with 'proper' food such as oats and hay.

Actually, it is grass which is his proper food, not the

other sort, and these days there is no excuse for denying a fit, hard-working horse a generous daily ration of grass taken at liberty, because there are pasture formulations for all sorts of horse and pony available for the asking from seed merchants, fertiliser companies, and in the UK, the Equine Services Department of the local office of ADAS, the Agricultural Development Advisory Service which is part of the Ministry of Agriculture. In the USA, contact the County extension agent. Independent, freelance management consultants and nutritionists should also be able to help you create the right sort of pasture for your horses and ponies.

Different Types of Pasture

Anyone who travels around the country will appreciate the vastly different types of soil there are, from red clays to rich loams, the shallow, poor soils of uplands, sandy soils, plus the variations which can occur in any region even from field to field.

Soil type largely governs what can grow best on your land, together with the climate in that area. Herbs in particular can be regarded as indicator species: in other words, the presence of a particular plant indicates what kind of soil it is growing on, and thus an expert will already have a good idea of the chemical and mineral analysis of the land.

Rented Grazing

Those renting grazing usually have a choice of thoroughly overgrazed, overstocked, worm-ridden horse-only paddocks or, if they are more fortunate, grazing also or usually used for sheep, dry cows or store cattle. The type of nitrogen-rich, lush sward used for dairy cattle is not usually offered to them, which is all to the good because horses, even young Thoroughbreds, cannot take this sort of pasture without the risk of developing bone disorders due to an unbalanced – for them – diet. Horses are not cattle and do not have the same nutritional requirements or digestive and metabolic capabilities.

Mixed Stock Grazing

The natural way of using grass is for different species of animal to graze together. The old way of putting oxen, sheep, goats and horses all together in the same field produced a much safer system and was better for the land which was eaten over fully and evenly, and fertilised by the animals' excreta fully and evenly; it was also a much better method of controlling the various animals' different species of internal parasites as they would be killed off when eaten by the wrong host animal.

Some years ago I was fascinated to be able to visit the permanent winter quarters of one of Britain's best-known circus families and see giraffes, zebras, camels, horses, yaks, llamas and ponies all grazing peaceably together in large, healthy-looking fields. Stupidly, I had not taken my camera with me!

Different Horse Paddocks

The type of pasture offered to, say, Thoroughbred bloodstock will – or should – be quite different (more nutritious) to that offered to native ponies. Youngstock and breeding bloodstock can and need to take higher levels of nutrients, including protein and the natural sugars in grass. Studs breeding performance horses with a good deal of Thoroughbred blood in them can use the same sort of pasture.

Native ponies and cobs need the lowest nutrient-content grass compatible with healthy growth; such animals are very prone to laminitis and the general problems that come with obesity.

Mature working horses can also have suitable swards created just for them, with plenty of the fibre-based energy they need as equine athletes. Modern seed mixes can take account of virtually any requirement.

Analysis of Herbage and Soil

To know more exactly what your horse is eating you need to know not only what is in his 'stable' feeds but also the nutrient content of the grass he eats. We can never really know, or probably need to, exactly what his intake is due to some inevitable wastage, also because analysing and assessing what he leaves would be so impractical, and because we do not know precisely how much grass, and what plants, he eats; however, we can get quite near to finding out by having the whole diet assessed, including grazing.

A specialist (again, probably a nutritionist up to date

with current research) can put all the information together and tell you if anything is much amiss, and also put it right. A once-a-year consultation – perhaps even a little less often – is not unreasonably expensive, and can be formulated to take into account changes in your horse's workload and management, including his access to grazing and its variances throughout the year, so you don't have to re-consult every time circumstances change.

An analysis should be made of the soil and also an assessment of what herbage is currently growing. From this starting-point, changes and improvements can be made if necessary. It may be that, in view of your horse's current workload, diet and management, things can be left as they are. You are also, of course, free to act on advice or not, or perhaps only on part of it, depending on your circumstances: just because you have an initial consultation does not automatically mean great outlay.

Grazing for Horses

As mentioned, horse pastures are ideally not the same as those for cattle. Whilst it may well be fine for native ponies and cobs to be put on pastures meant for sheep, and indeed family horses meant for light to moderate work, you may want something more fine-tuned for breeding stock or for maintaining performance horses.

Generally, good grasses for horse paddocks are meadow fescue, ryegrasses, cocksfoot and timothy. Wild white clover is also advantageous but not, it is usually advised, as more than 10 per cent of the pasture. It is a legume and has the useful ability to fix nitrogen in the soil, but it can take over on overgrazed, badly managed land. A healthy sward with grasses which tiller (spread well) and recover quickly from grazing can control it.

As horses tend to damage land, being more liable to gallop about than cattle, some hard-wearing grasses – perhaps bent, or grasses of the *agrostis* species – are advisable even if they are not very useful as food, to protect the soil surface. A 'spread' of grass types is also necessary to provide early growth, summer growth and sustained growth through to late autumn. In mild winters, grass may keep growing a little throughout the season.

You should include a herb strip in every paddock, too, as this will provide horses with all 'magical' nutrients and special tastes they cannot get from grass. Herbs seem to do better when grown separately in a strip, rather than being incorporated into the general seed mix when grasses can overpower them.

Poisonous Vegetation

One of the hazards of grazing horses at all is that they may come across poisonous things which can certainly kill them; despite an apparently bitter taste, some animals do acquire a taste for these, with often tragic results – yet another reason for taking time to watch what your animals like to eat. Good pasture management dictates that poisonous things be removed from paddocks, but

The Importance of Land and Herbage Care

It is still not sufficiently widely recognised that it is much more effective, from the point of view of horse wellbeing and health, and more economic to improve and take care of horse paddocks, and to permit horses to obtain most of their nutritional requirements from grazing.

This is still alien thinking in most quarters where grass, even more than hay, is regarded as a throw-away feed. In some instances when horses, and particularly ponies, are put on half-decent grazing, the owners are surprised that they put on weight, having apparently completely disregarded the possible feeding value in grass. How much money could be saved on bought-in feeds, and how much happier and healthier horses would be, if they all had ample access to the right sort of grazing for them!

It has been proved in practice time and again that it is much more economical to spend money on improving and maintaining land and letting horses and ponies get all or most of their nutritional requirements from grazing than to pay for bought-in feeds, possibly plus supplements.

it is impractical to check every square metre of ground every day for something poisonous appearing – and if it does, the horses will probably find it before we do. Fortunately, most horses only try out poisonous plants when they are very hungry, and the nasty taste of most of them will otherwise be a deterrent. One way to dissuade them from experimenting is to make sure they do not become so hungry that they will try almost anything; keeping the land productive with grass will serve its purpose of providing freedom, exercise and enough food at least to keep hunger at bay. On bare paddocks, feed the animals before turning them out and/or give hay in the field.

Many horse and pony owners cannot recognise many poisonous plants. It is imperative, however, that *some* effort is made to learn what they look like in order to safeguard horses' safety and health. Short of a practical lesson from an expert, in the UK an excellent booklet from any branch of Her Majesty's Stationery Office (see your phone book) called *British Poisonous Plants*, Book 161, ISBN 0-11-240461-8, is probably the most comprehensive one available and will really help you recognise dangerous vegetation. Meanwhile, here is a list of some of the more likely ones you may come across:

aconite
box
bracken (ferns)
bryony
buttercup
charlock
dodder
foxglove
giant hogweed
hemlock
horse/mare's tails
ivy
laburnum
marsh marigolds
nightshades
oak
privet
ragwort
rhododendron
rushes
thorn apple
yew

Sadly, some trees are poisonous. Oak trees look beautiful but can kill animals which eat them or their acorns. It is not uncommon for ponies, in particular, to acquire a taste for acorns for some reason

(Left) Lush, rich grass, particularly in spring, is bad for horses, even Thoroughbred breeding stock. Once the spring flush is over the sugar content will not be so high and the grazing will be safer, although there is an autumn flush of growth which is, however, not so rich as in springtime.

The most dangerous time to turn out any animal, from a point of view of grazing, is on a spring morning when the sugar content will be highest of all; in the afternoon and evening it drops

Good and bad grasses

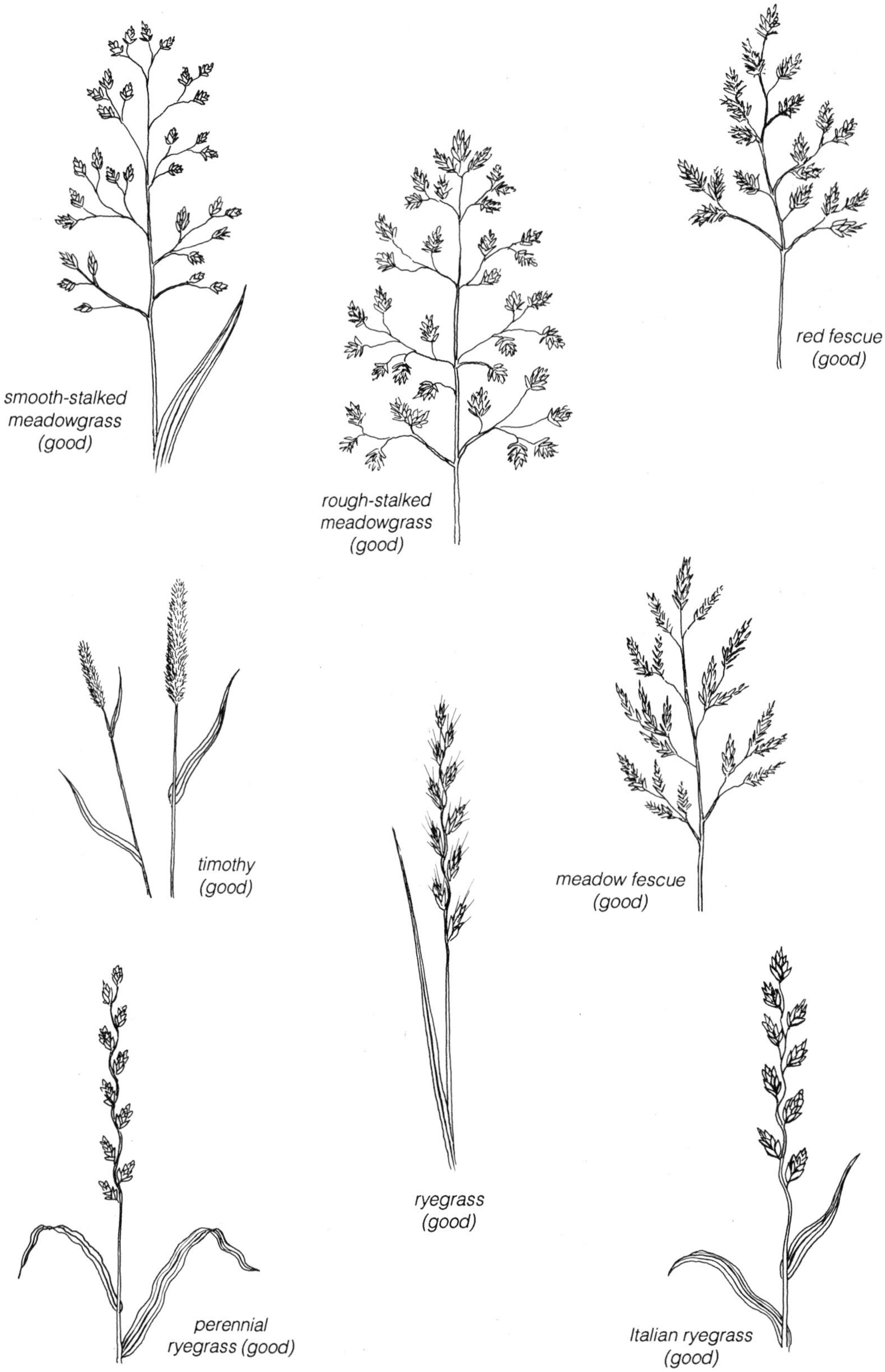

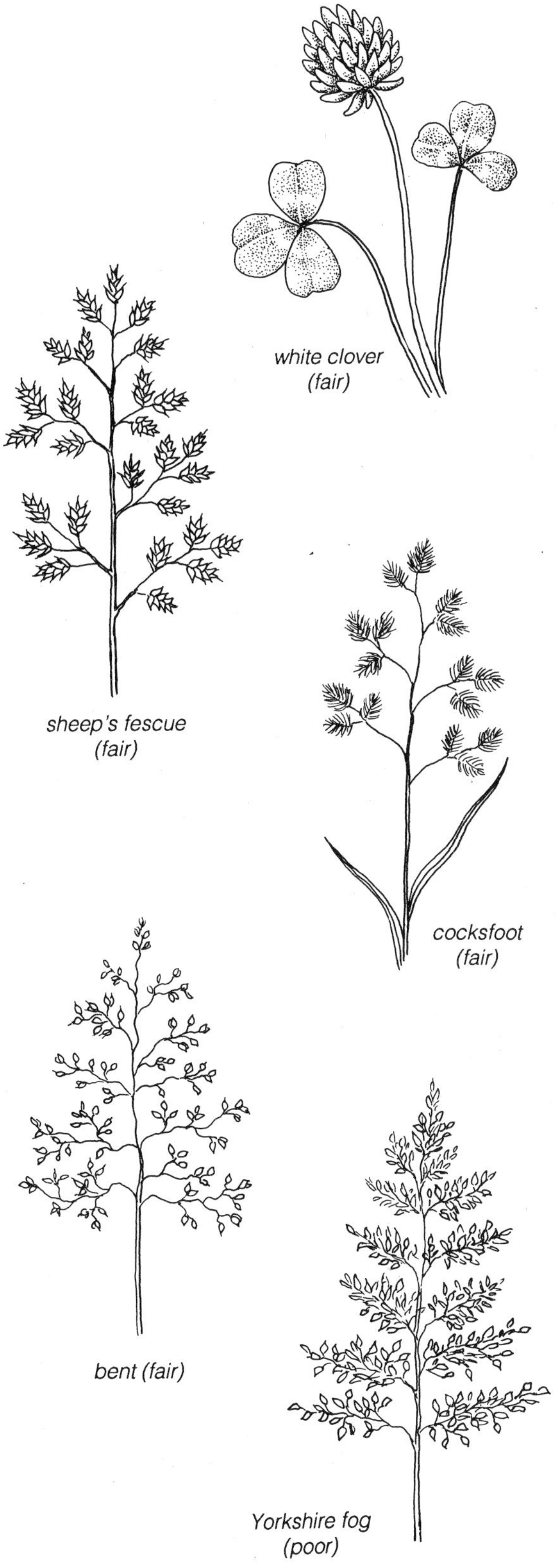

Poisonous vegetation

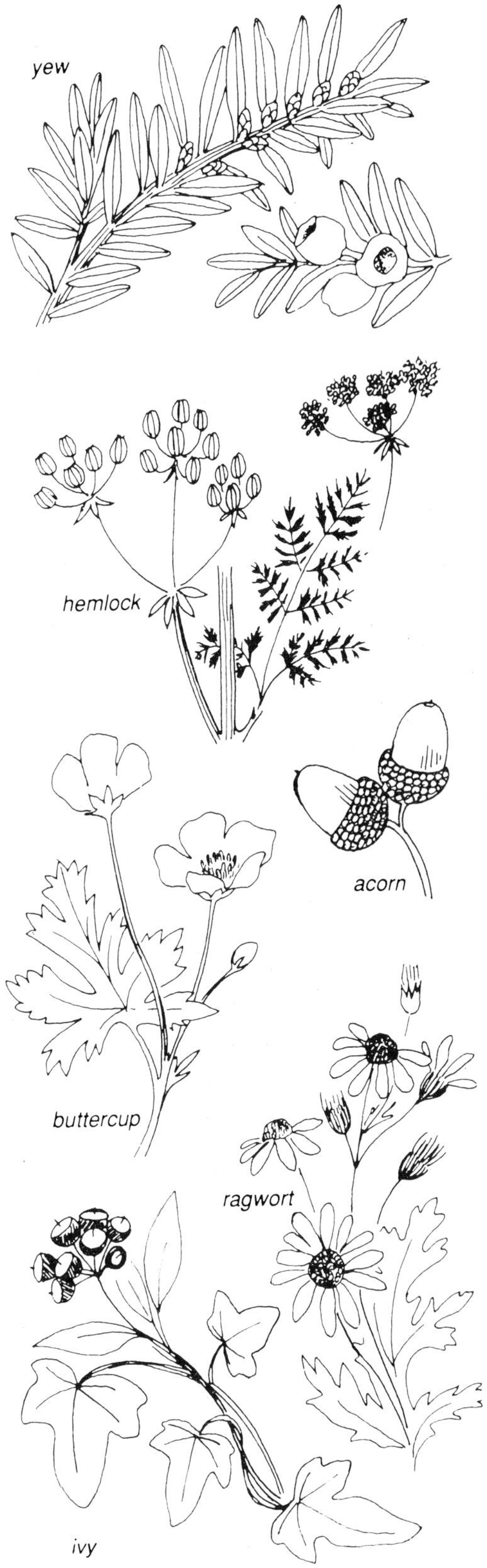

Where trees or shrubs cannot be safely removed, they should be fenced round so that horses cannot reach them. Many garden plants are poisonous, so check the individual geography of the area and fence the horses away from gardens. Take the trouble to ask neighbouring householders not to throw garden rubbish into your field, and explain why.

Methods of removal

These vary from spraying, hand pulling, forking or digging up, to constantly cutting down, particularly before they go to seed. Many are more palatable dead than alive, so they should be taken right out of the field and burnt in case the horses eat the wilted plants. For the same reason, watch for them in hay.

Ragwort seems to be proliferating alarmingly and is now seen everywhere. With its bright yellow, daisy-like clusters of flowers and ragged leaves, it is now a familiar sight on roadsides and motorway embankments and in the more poorly managed pony paddocks abounding in 'Equiburbia'. Although local councils do have the authority to make landowners remove it from infested land, they do not have the *duty* to do so, and because many do not bother to do anything about it, it is becoming increasingly well established all over Britain.

Ragwort. Increasingly familiar in Britain, ragwort is lethally poisonous and very difficult to eradicate. Although the advice must always be not to graze horses in reach of it, its bitter taste (as with many poisonous things) usually means that animals do not eat it unless desperately hungry, or by accident, when they usually spit it out very quickly. Well fed horses do not normally eat ragwort. When dead or wilted (on the ground or in hay) it loses its bitter taste and may be readily eaten, with fatal results

If a horse does eat ragwort, it has a progressive, cumulative effect on the liver and is ultimately fatal. Once ragwort gets a hold in a paddock it can reproduce from its root and is very difficult indeed to eradicate permanently.

Expert, up-to-date advice is available from your consultant concerning the removal of all poisonous things, whether from an independent nutritionist or the firm whose land-care products you use. Remind them that your land is for horses, as certain products are more toxic to some species of animal than others. Many products, these days, are being made safer for use and do not leave dangerous residues indefinitely in the land and on surrounding vegetation; but do check on this, and follow any advice and the product instructions faithfully if using chemical means of removal.

For those who prefer organic methods, it is well worth consulting the Soil Association (UK) to discover organic methods of removal. In the USA the local state authorities need to be consulted to find out the nearest organic farming association.

Parasites and Paddocks

Multi-species grazing – putting different species of animal to graze together – is an old and natural method, and as already mentioned, is making a comeback. One of the reasons for putting cattle on horse paddocks is so that they will eat the worm larvae in the horses' loo areas and help to decrease significantly the population of equine parasites on the land. This is also a reason for picking up droppings daily – something of a bind but a valuable way of really keeping infestation down. Worm larvae will migrate from the droppings into the surrounding grass within twenty-four hours, so unless they can be picked up daily it is a pointless exercise.

The worm larvae of the most infective and dangerous species crawl up the blades of grass and stay around the top, hoping to be eaten so that they can fulfil their life-cycles and mature. If cattle eat them the parasites will die; but if horses eat them they will cause trouble, so it is one of nature's safety mechanisms that horses decline to eat the long grass (which will contain larvae) in the loo areas of their paddocks. In overcrowded paddocks, however, there is a good chance that many worm larvae will be eaten, an excellent reason for not overstocking paddocks, for picking up droppings if at all possible, and for grazing with cattle or sheep, too.

Self-Fertilisation!

Many owners spread their own muck heaps on their paddocks, so providing a free source of natural fertiliser. If this is done make sure the muck used is really old and well rotted (at least a year old) as otherwise the smell will make the paddocks unpalatable to horses. The heat in the pile should have killed off any worm larvae left in that time, and owners who follow this practice report that their paddocks grow healthy grass which their horses appear to relish.

The muck should be spread in the autumn on paddocks resting for the winter, and in the spring on the winter paddocks which will not be used until much later in the year.

The problem of pasture and worms can be greatly minimised if horses and ponies are methodically and frequently wormed *all year round* to be on the safe side. If horses and ponies are wormed every four to eight weeks throughout the year, the numbers of infective larvae passed out in droppings will be minimal. Some present-day wormers will destroy worms in their immature form as they migrate through the horse's body – and some even in the stage where they form tiny cysts in the intestinal walls – as well as killing off mature, egg-laying parasites in the intestines. As the new drugs are so effective, you may be able to get away with administering them only every twelve weeks or so, depending on your circumstances (how overstocked, or otherwise, your paddocks are) and according to veterinary advice on the latest drugs and recommendations.

The Risks of Alternative Grazing

There are obviously dangers in grazing on 'spare' land. If it is not fenced, you run the risk of letting go of your horse and seeing him disappear into the wide blue yonder should something frighten him and you simply cannot hold him. Grazing in a bridle and bit is far from ideal for the horse, but you should at least hold him in such situations in a well fitting lungeing cavesson with your lead rope clipped to the front ring, for reasonable control – and wear strong, protective gloves for a stronger, painless grip, with a knot in the end of the rope to lessen the chances of it being pulled through your hand.

Alternative Grazing Areas

Many owners are so short of somewhere to turn their horses out that they are tempted to use any spare land, orchards and sometimes roadside tethering places. Most of us have spent many hours with a horse on the other end of a rope, standing with him to let him have a bite of grass.

Much 'snatched' grazing land like this is badly fenced, if at all, full of dangerous litter and pollutants (for example, **roadside verges**), and in areas where vandals or thieves can reach the animals.

Orchards are not usually available unless they have fallen into disuse, but even then a surfeit of windfalls in the autumn can result in digestive disturbance of serious proportions. Low branches are most dangerous for horses, and chemical pollutants may remain on the trees and grass from fertilisers and pesticides.

Ordinary **woods** and **spinneys** are valuable for cover but often harbour snares, traps and poisonous plants, not to mention protruding tree roots which can trip and injure animals playing about.

Although we cannot wrap horses in cotton wool all the time, these are dangers which must be considered and eliminated as far as possible before turning out horses.

Tethering

Tethering horses and ponies, donkeys and mules is subject to legal requirements which prevent these animals being tethered in such a way as to cause unnecessary suffering. If this method of grazing is used, the animal should wear a strong, well fitting headcollar or neckstrap and be on a swivel stake so that the rope does not wrap round and round the stake, imprisoning it in one tiny area – animals seem quite unable to unwrap themselves, but generally stand stoically until someone puts matters right.

The area chosen should be safe from vandals; it should provide access to ample food, and most important, to shelter and water. Although horses prefer to have company, they should not be tethered where enemies can reach them. If two or more are tethered together, they should not be able to touch each other, and should be far enough apart to prevent kicking matches.

Your own Back Yard (or Garden)

How many times have you looked in despair at the long, lush grass in your garden and thought about bringing your horse in to deal with it? But quite apart from his hooves damaging the turf, there are dangers here, too, even if the fencing is sufficient: most garden plants are poisonous, washing lines are dangerous, and garden tools too, and neighbours can be troublesome even if you offer them free manure for their roses.

Your own back patch *can* be made acceptable, and many do it, though you may just have to sacrifice having conventional garden plants and shrubs, and confine yourself to non-poisonous things which your horse may, or may not, eat in safety. Nevertheless, remove *all* possible hazards – if they're there, the horse will find them – and you may well have created a handy play-pen for your horse if you keep him a convenient distance away.

Land Improvement

First, the drainage will probably need attention, because wet land is cold and oxygen-starved and will never produce valuable grass. If you have the land on a longish tenancy, or if it is your own, having a good drainage system installed will be a real boon. If land you are inspecting for potential grazing supports tufts of spiky marsh grasses or even rushes, or seems very rough and rutted even in summer, this is a sign that it is naturally wet land which will be waterlogged for much of the year and therefore useless except for mainly exercise in summer.

Having a system installed involves laying drainage pipes underground which empty into a convenient ditch or other outlet; this will have to be maintained to be kept clear.

Soil Analysis

This comes next in sequence and is a subject that has already been discussed.

To Plough or Not to Plough?

Horses do tend to gallop about their fields and their hooves can do a good deal of damage. Horse pastures are better with a covering of old turf – the springy mattress of turf and roots cushions the impact with the ground and protects both the land and the horses' feet and legs. Such old turf should *not* be ploughed up and started from scratch except in extreme cases.

Having a field ploughed and reseeded means it will be out of use for at least a year and the 'mattress' will be destroyed for several years to come. It is normally better to remove unwanted vegetation and fertilise according to your analysis, and provide a seed-bed by giving the field a tough harrowing with a pitchpole harrow to thoroughly tear out old, dead grasses and roots and aerate the soil. This will not unduly damage live, healthy roots. The chain harrow can then be run over the field, the seed mix sown over the existing sward and the land possibly rolled to level and consolidate it.

When can we use it?

A field so treated in spring may be ready for light grazing in the autumn and normal use the following spring. If the work is carried out in the autumn, light grazing could start in the spring and increase throughout the summer, in line with a grazing/resting rota detailed below.

Making hay

If nitrogen has been applied – and high levels of nitrogen are certainly *not* what horse paddocks need – a hay crop must be taken off the land before horses are grazed on it, as the resultant growth of grass will be too nutritious for horses, and especially cobs and ponies, and you could end up with digestive disorders and laminitis.

If you do not wish to use the hay yourself you could always sell it and put the income towards other hay and feed, or into your land management kitty.

Rotating your Grazing

Once the land has been improved, it should be incorporated into a proper rota as all land needs resting for at least three continuous months out of every year if it is to remain in good heart. Fertilisers will also be needed periodically, according to the advice your consultant has given.

Ideally, land should be divided up into at least three paddocks so that each can be used, treated and rested in turn. If you want your land to provide a significant amount of your horse's nutritional requirements, you will need up to 4 acres (1.6 hectares) per horse (about half this for a pony) with about half as much again per extra horse if the land is to be kept in good heart, more if the land or grazing, or the management, is of poor

Grassland Management: the Key to Success

Well cared-for grass saves so much money in horse feeding that looking after it really *is* worthwhile. Even if you do not own your own land, or if you can only rent it on a seasonal basis, this chapter and section will, I hope, at least give you some idea of the quality of the land you are considering, and how to give it basic care with short-term benefits while you are using it.

Finding rented land is extremely difficult in some areas, mainly because the 'wasteful' grazing habits of horses and the damage their hooves can do are anathema to many farmers. The only land normally available is that usually grazed by horses anyway, and that, except for a few privately owned establishments (leaving aside well run studs), is normally patchy in the extreme with long, rank, rejected grass in the loo areas and bald grazing 'lawns', worm-ridden, weed-infested and virtually useless from a food production point of view. However, even a little basic care can improve such land and make it safer and more pleasant for your horse.

quality. The two driest paddocks should be alternated for winter use, or you can simply set aside the driest, not using it during the autumn so that it builds up a good grass cover for winter.

Put the horses to graze in spring in paddock 1 for two or three weeks, and when it starts to look patchy, with some areas noticeably shorter than others, move them to paddock 2. Paddock 1 should now have cattle put on it for a couple of weeks; this should not be too difficult to arrange, as most farmers are glad of a bit of free grazing for youngsters or dry cows. The cattle will eat off the long grass the horses will not touch (either because it is in their loo areas or is of a type they do not like), they will not be offended by horse droppings, and will use the horses' grazing areas for *their* lavatory, so adding much needed natural fertiliser to those constantly depleted areas. Also, as mentioned, they will take in the larvae of equine parasites from the loo areas, thereby killing them off.

If you cannot obtain cattle, sheep would be better than nothing; and if you cannot arrange anything at all, you should at least top (mow) the long areas. Either way, you should then chain harrow the whole paddock. Harrow the loo areas carefully so as to break up the droppings and help the sun and air desiccate both them and the worm eggs, but do *not* spread the horse droppings to the horses' eating areas. These should be harrowed within themselves to avoid contaminating them with worm eggs and with the horse droppings themselves. The horses will not object to cow-pats.

Perhaps the farmer whose cattle are enjoying a change of scene on your free grazing would do this work for you. If you are having difficulty in arranging it and cannot do it yourself, in the UK your ADAS representative should be able to put you in touch with a contractor who would do it – for a fee. In the USA you would need to approach your local County Extension Agent.

The paddock should now be closed off to rest and grow again. When paddock 2 starts to look patchy, move the horses to paddock 3, and give paddock 2 the same treatment, carrying on rotating like this throughout the growing season. There is usually a flush of grass during about September, so this would be a good time to stop using the winter paddock.

Fertilisers

Some fertilisers are used only every few years, some every few months depending on requirements. The time to apply the latter is at the end of a paddock's 'shift' so that it has time to be assimilated and used by the regrowing grass before the horses return.

When treatments such as spraying and fertilising are being done, horses usually need to be kept off the land to prevent possible poisoning or other adverse effects; this may be from a day to a few weeks depending on the product and whether there is significant rainfall, so your rota will have to be carefully arranged so that the land gets its treatments and rests and your horses their freedom and grazing.

More about cattle

Grazing cattle in the same field at the same time as horses is policy on many good studs, and can be a sound practice provided the cattle are free from brucellosis and ringworm and are dehorned. It does depend on what the cattle are being additionally fed, however, as

some substances such as hormones and nutrients which are toxic to horses could be passed out with their droppings on to the land which the horses will be grazing.

Discuss this with your adviser, and check with the owner of the cattle as to their diet. For the same reason, spreading your land with cattle manure – a good fertiliser which disguises the contaminating smell of horse droppings, therefore encouraging the grazing by horses of their previous lavatory areas – could produce problems if the manure is so contaminated. Straw-based farmyard (cattle) manure is very scarce now, modern practice being that many unfortunate cattle are not given bedding, and the resultant slurry (droppings plus urine) can be too concentrated for horse paddocks; so again, check on this with your adviser.

Other farm manure, particularly from pigs and poultry, can result in too rich a growth of grass for horses and should be rejected for horse paddocks. At the very least a hay crop must be taken first, or the land grazed by other animals in the spring when the grass is at its richest, putting the horses on later in the year – hardly an attractive proposition for horse owners with only a small amount of land.

To summarise

With such a rota your land will remain healthy and productive, and so should your horses. Mentally, too, they will be much happier and more content. If you can only divide the land up into two paddocks, you can still look after it; and if you can only manage one, give it the best care you can and search around your premises for corners from which to make play-pens. Also, try to rent other grazing in the area, both for the sake of your horses and what land you do have.

Left: In wild and feral conditions different species of animal graze together, their different feeding habits complementing each other. Sheep and cattle make good grazing partners for horses provided the cattle are polled (as most are these days) and are free of disease which could affect the horses

Inset: An outdoor surfaced manege is ideal for turning out horses for exercise when pasture is not available. Haynets can be hung around the fencing, if high enough, and two horses can be turned out and will keep each other on the move. They will be quite happy out together provided the weather is not extreme

Ponies do best on the sort of grazing used for sheep, which are just as good doers! Low nutrient-content grass helps prevent them becoming dangerously overweight, particularly ponies and cobs. Horses evolved to live and thrive on large areas of sparse to moderate keep, and they do best on this sort of pasture in domesticated conditions

Farmland Grazing

Mention has already been made of the dangers inherent in rich dairy-type grazing for horses, and particularly ponies and cobs. It is unlikely that most horse owners will have access to such pasture, and in fact this is a good thing because its high sugar and protein content readily causes animals to become grossly overweight with the concomitant problems of possible laminitis.

The best type of agricultural grazing to use is the less rich, short sward normally used for sheep. This is far safer for horses, which are better kept on poorer quality grazing and their diet supplemented as needed; they can then be left out for much longer periods with no danger of their over-eating. This is better than giving them shorter periods on richer grazing, although this may be necessary if the latter is all you can get. Dividing such grazing into small areas, or strip-grazing it as for cattle, are other means of keeping intake down.

Agricultural Applications

The pesticides and fertilisers used in non-organic, modern agriculture can also cause health problems, so it is important to get details of just what has been used on the land from the farmer renting it to you, and checking on possible problems with your vet or other adviser before you turn your horses on to it.

Wire

Another real hazard regarding farmland grazing is the ubiquitous presence of the barbed wire used for fencing it. Many horse owners do graze their animals inside barbed wire, and some advisers who should know better actually pass it as being safe, or even advise it!

My own experience is that it can be lethal stuff, and in my opinion it has no place near horses. You may graze your horses within it for years with no problems, but it is like the sword of Damocles – a potentially serious accident waiting to happen. Avoid it, if you possibly can. Squared, plain wire sheep fencing is also dangerous for horses and ponies: they can very easily get a hoof through it, injuring and terrifying themselves as they struggle and pull to get free.

What to Choose

The safest fencing for horses is wooden posts and rails; otherwise posts and taut plain wire. Best of all is thick, high, prickly hedging, although on land which is not your own you may find that poisonous plants growing in the hedgerow are a hazard.

This trough is very dangerous for horses. It has sharp corners and the concrete buttresses on the ground can also trip and injure horses' lower legs. The fencing is excellent apart from the fact the fence posts protrude above the top rails which, again, is not the safest structure for horses which can catch headcollars on them. Such posts can also cause severe injuries to horses who may jump paddock fences

This post and rail fencing is excellent in that it is sturdy and the top rail is flush with the tops of the posts. However, the rails are fixed to the wrong side of the posts. They should be on the inside so that horses playing and galloping along the fence line, as they do, are unlikely to injure the points of their shoulders on the square posts

This type of square, wire sheep-netting is dangerous fencing for horses, who can easily get a foot or leg caught through the lower squares. This can result in bad injuries if the horse panics and tries to pull its leg free or in severe stress, exposure, lack of water, bullying or vandalism if the horse is left trapped there

An obscured dyke, like this, is a danger to horses who can easily fall in and become trapped

High, thick natural hedgerow can make excellent fencing for horses, providing a windbreak as well as herbs not found in the pasture. Unfortunately, it may contain poisonous plants so a sharp watch should be kept for these. The shallow, dry ditch in this picture may be an added deterrent to the height to discourage horses from jumping out but it is not uncommon for horses to roll or fall into ditches and become stuck until someone spots this. It is probably safer to fence off ditches if at all possible

Key Facts

- Keeping a horse out at grass or turning him out can be fraught with just as much risk, even though this may seem a 'natural' way to feed him. Too much grass at once, particularly rich spring or autumn grass, or poisonous plants for which he may acquire a taste, can certainly kill him. Grass sickness, too, is now found in most areas of Britain. Treat grass as a proper food, and do not overdo it.

- Horses, and in particular cobs and ponies, do best on a large range of fairly sparse keep: such grass is of low feeding value, besides which the animals have to take a great deal more exercise when wandering to graze.

- Rich, lush pasture high in nitrogen is bad for any horse or pony. If renting grazing, remember that sheep pasture rather than cattle pasture is safest.

- Horses are very efficient grazers, but they are also choosy, and 'wasteful'; paddocks soon become 'horse-sick' from selective grazing and defaecating habits, and should be rotated and treated to remain productive and palatable to horses.

- Horses and ponies should be turned out as a regular routine – probably daily, not as an occasional treat – and grass regarded as a major ingredient in their diet when it is growing. There are suitable seed mixes for all categories of horse and pony today, and the creation of suitable grazing is not too difficult.

- Inter-grazing horses with sheep and/or cattle helps to keep the land sweet and the grass evenly used.

- It is cheaper to spend money on making grass a suitable food than to buy in other types of feed.

- Horses normally dislike grazing near their own droppings; also, the droppings contaminate the land, and even when picked up they leave an off-putting smell on the ground (unless they are removed within thirty minutes). Picking up droppings as often as possible is an important management technique, but disguising the smell is also important. This can be done by spreading cattle manure on the land, although modern-day cattle-feeding methods sometimes involve the use of in-feed hormones, and these can be dangerous to horses; advice should be sought on this topic, depending on the source of the cattle manure.

- Making hay from your own paddocks is advisable as a safety measure before grazing again if a high-nitrogen fertiliser has been used. Be sure, too, that you have made best quality hay before using it for your own animals! Otherwise sell it, and use the money to buy better hay.

Eating soil

This is something which puzzles many owners, and although when done in moderation it is no cause for concern, if horses do it significantly and regularly it can mean that their diet is deficient in minerals and possibly roughage. The same can be said of chewing wood.

If this is a problem with your horses, therefore, simply get their diet checked, and supplement or change it as necessary.

6

THE BALANCED DIET

What is a balanced diet? It is a diet which contains all the correct proportions of all the nutrients required by a horse. It has nothing to do with amount. A horse can be on a correct, balanced diet but be receiving too little or too much of it, in which case he is still not being correctly fed.

The expression has come into horse management over the past decade or so as the discovery of specific nutrients and their importance is being more and more appreciated thanks to research. Feeding is an extremely complex subject and it is obvious that there is still much to learn. It is truly a case of 'the more you learn, the more you realise there is to learn'.

Balancing a diet, it has to be admitted, is still informed guesswork. We still do not know enough about the bacteria populating the horse's gut or their precise requirements and life-cycles. Vitamins, minerals and other nutrients often interact in very complicated, precise ways which we need to understand better, and it is not yet possible to stipulate exactly how much of what nutrients a horse needs for certain. The best we can do is formulate diets according to our present state of knowledge.

How Precise Need We Be?

How long is a piece of string? It obviously makes sense to be as precise as modern knowledge allows, and correct nutrition is more critical the harder a horse works and the more competent he is expected to be. However, horses have survived for millions of years without our balanced diets. In more recent times they have helped us win wars, have won medals, bred, earned our living, been happy and given us a lot of pleasure, long before we had any real knowledge of scientific nutrition. The horse's body is good at picking out the nutrients it needs from the food which gets into the digestive tract, and it is able to make some nutrients itself from raw materials. Basically, therefore, a horse will reject, use and store what it needs from its food, and provided it seems content and healthy we are probably not going far wrong.

Nevertheless, it is still obviously sensible to feed a horse as correctly as we know how, and time and trouble taken over formulating a suitable ration for him is well spent.

Achieving a Balanced Diet

The knowledge available to the 'ordinary', non-scientifically minded or not particularly knowledgeable horse owner is increasing and improving all the time. It *is* well worthwhile trying your best to give your horse a balanced diet: correct nutrition improves a horse's feeling of wellbeing, the entire way his body and mind function, the speed and efficiency with which he recovers after an accident or illness, and the standard at which he is able to work and for how long; also how he tolerates and recovers from stressful events such as travelling, competing, learning a difficult lesson, weaning or being involved in a frightening or very exciting or upsetting experience.

By giving a horse the best balanced diet we can, we are helping him to stay strong and healthy, to work well for us, and to cost us less in management and health care.

How to Achieve a Balanced Diet

Bearing in mind the above, it is not too difficult! The easy way is to use branded feeds of known analysis, to feed them according to the recommendations and instructions of the maker, and to seek the maker's advice on combining roughage or forage and concentrate feeds so that you get the overall balance right. If you are mixing different firms' feeds you will need the advice of a specialist to make sure they are correctly balanced in themselves and compatible with each other. Again, this should not ruffle any feathers, as firms which make roughage sources often do not make concentrates and vice versa, and it is quite understandable that you wish to feed compatible types of feed to obtain an overall balance.

Even the hard way has been made easier. What is the hard way? The hard way to balance a diet is to work out the nutritional content of different straights, roughages and supplements, and to work out, with the help of tables and a calculator, the overall nutritional content and balance of the diet you are proposing. This may well be too complicated or onerous for many owners, but those who want to try can make the job very much easier by referring to my book *Horse Care and Riding* (published by David & Charles); here, guest contributor Gillian McCarthy, a freelance nutritionist and management consultant, has given a very detailed but easy to follow (if you concentrate) method of working out a ration using a calculator and table giving known analyses of commonly used feedstuffs. It takes a little while, but is very satisfying once you get to the end of it.

The Role and Importance of Analysis

This has been mentioned several times. Without the precise knowledge provided by a laboratory analysis of the nutritional content of every batch of feed you intend giving your horse, you cannot be exact, even using the method advised above, and most owners would find this inconvenient and expensive. Tables giving probable nutrient contents of feedstuffs can be a good guide, however.

The advantage of using reputable branded products is that the analysing has already been done for you by the company.

Choosing a Ration

The nutritional content is only part of the story, however: the diet must also **physically satisfy the horse**. We *could* give him all his nutrients in highly concentrated form, say cubes (pellets), but he would not be physically satisfied without bulk and texture; hence the failure (mentioned earlier) of so-called 'complete' cubes which are fed with little or no roughage source.

Then there is **the taste**. Horses being particular feeders, mostly fussy about what they eat (although there are gannets in every species!), no amount of correctly formulated feed is of any use if the horse will not eat it – and horses are notorious for refusing food they don't fancy, even though they are very hungry. Smell, taste and texture are probably more important to the horse than anything.

And finally there is **cost**. Most of us have to be cost-conscious these days, but it is still possible to produce balanced, suitable feeds without using the most expensive ingredients. Obscure feeds which are available to feed manufacturers will be analysed and their suitability assessed, and if they are cheaper than some other ingredient they may be included in a recipe for cost reasons while still producing a perfectly acceptable product.

It may be cheaper for owners to feed straights and try balancing their own rations. And if you don't wish to work through the balancing method described above, you can always use the only method available until scientific analysis became possible: feed your horse as you think best, and observe carefully the effect of your diet on his appearance and behaviour. This wait-and-see method is certainly cheaper than using branded products, and it may still be fine to use it and maybe give the recommended dose of a broad-spectrum supplement, particularly for horses not working hard.

For hard-working, breeding, growing, old or debilitated animals, however, a diet of known content and suitability is worth the extra expense.

If you wish to feed by the scoop, this is fine, but it is better to know how much of each ingredient your scoop holds. You can keep closer track of what your horse is eating, how long your supplies will last, and how soon you'll have to pay out for more!

It is also important to weigh your hay, as even if you feed it *ad lib* it is useful to know how much of his total feed ration a horse eats in hay or a hay alternative. If you do not use haynets, put your hay on an opened-out polythene feed sack and hang the four corners on the hook of the spring-weigher

What Affects a Horse's Dietary Needs?

All horses, as any other creature, need the basic nutrients to maintain life and health, but there are several other factors which govern how much of what a horse will need:

- The horse's own type and individual constitution determine whether or not he is a good doer or a poor one.
- His breed and type affect his reaction to his environment, his management and the weather.
- His temperament plays a part, too. Nervous worriers usually need more food than placid, carefree types.
- His workload obviously determines how much of what type of food you should give him – the harder he works the more food he will need, particularly energy-giving.
- His bodily condition should be your starting-point in deciding quantities (see Chapter 7). If he is overweight, feed less than the recommended amount, and vice versa.

Chapter 1 covered the probable protein needs of different categories of horse and pony. In addition to getting the protein level right the main area of dietary manipulation is the energy content.

Native ponies and cobs are notoriously good doers and often difficult to keep slim and fit. They are not naturally lean types, so the best guideline is to feed them so that you can feel their ribs fairly easily but not actually see them. This New Forest pony is in good working condition for his type

Constitution

For reasons we don't precisely understand, horses, like people, vary in their efficiency at using their food. There seems to be no criterion to guide us in this. It is something that sensitive, observant owners will absorb as they get to know their horse, and is at least one reason why a horse/human partnership is so much easier to build up when one person is mainly responsible for care as well as work.

Breed and Type

In general it may be said that 'blood' horses – those with a good deal of Thoroughbred blood in them – will probably need more food than other types of animal. Arabians are hot-blooded horses, too, with thin skins and desert-type features aimed at releasing heat from the body rather than conserving it, as with British native ponies, for example; however, in practice they are good doers needing much less food for their height than Thoroughbreds. But individuals can certainly vary within breeds, and some Thoroughbreds are very good doers.

The more pony-like, or cold-blooded an animal is in type, the less food in general, and concentrates in particular, it will need for maintenance. However, when these 'stuffier' types of animal are put into athletic work, it is often found that energy-giving food – usually oats with their ability to hype horses up – is needed to give the animals more 'zip' for work.

NOTE: It must be borne in mind that no amount of dietary manipulation can alter a horse's basic character, or increase his optimal performance abilities.

Temperament

Excitable, nervous horses, and particularly those which stew things up inside them and worry a lot, usually need more food than others and may always look lean and hungry, even tucked up (looking tense and thin behind the ribcage and in front of the hips with perhaps sunken hollows here, and little belly).

Horses of a calmer nature which don't ever work themselves up unduly, and which never seem to worry or anticipate exciting events, and are generally laid-back sorts, need less food and are often easier to keep in good condition.

The well known stallion Romany Rye in good to lean condition ideal for stud work. Overfat stallions are not in the best condition for achieving high fertility rates

Workload

There can be a big difference between the amount and type of food a horse needs when he is in hard work, and his diet when resting. Fast work such as racing, or work involving spurts of energy such as polo or show-jumping, will demand quick-release energy from concentrates to a greater extent than endurance-type work such as eventing, hunting, carriage-driving and so on for which the best type of energy is that derived mainly from fibre – nutritious roughage sources – or feeds with a higher fat/oil content.

McRaffles, ridden by Sophie Newman at Tetbury, shows correct condition for the fast endurance-type work, with often formidable obstacles to be negotiated, involved in eventing

Bodyweight and Condition

The most accurate way to decide how much to feed your horse in total is to calculate his total daily feed requirements as a fraction of his bodyweight, as explained in Chapter 7. If the horse is in work and you are using concentrates in addition to a roughage source, you also need to decide how to split the proportions so that he receives appropriate amounts of both types of feed.

In general, children's ponies are better without any concentrates, and certainly without oats. Larger family cobs and ponies may be difficult to assess, because if it is decided to give them more feed for extra energy to carry the larger, more competent members of the family, say for a particular event, they may become too 'hot' for less competent or younger family members. However, a middle course can often be found as you get to know your animal.

Feeding Different Categories of Horse

The types of horse most needing quick-release energy-boost feeds are those doing hard or fast work of short duration; these will include flat racehorses, polo ponies, gymkhana ponies (with care) and show-jumpers. Research work seems to indicate that, as this starchy/sugary energy is digested and absorbed more quickly than the carbohydrate derived from cellulose, its availability to the muscles coincides with the time we usually allow after a feed before we work a horse, namely about two hours.

Horses doing more sustained work of a slightly or considerably slower nature will do best if their energy is the slow-release sort generated from eating hay, hayage, forage feeds and feeding straws, with the addition of extra oil to their diet as a concentrated, and again slow-release form of energy. Such horses include steeplechasers and point-to-pointers, event horses, hunters, driving horses, endurance horses, show horses and dressage horses.

All-rounder types, such as the family or riding club horse, will have different energy-category requirements according to the nature of the work being asked of them at any particular time; but provided the ingredients remain constant, you can 'tinker' with the amounts of each energy source as appropriate. However, it is unlikely that such horses will be asked to work to the limits of their ability, as do high performance horses, so the proportions of the different sorts of energy source will not be critical.

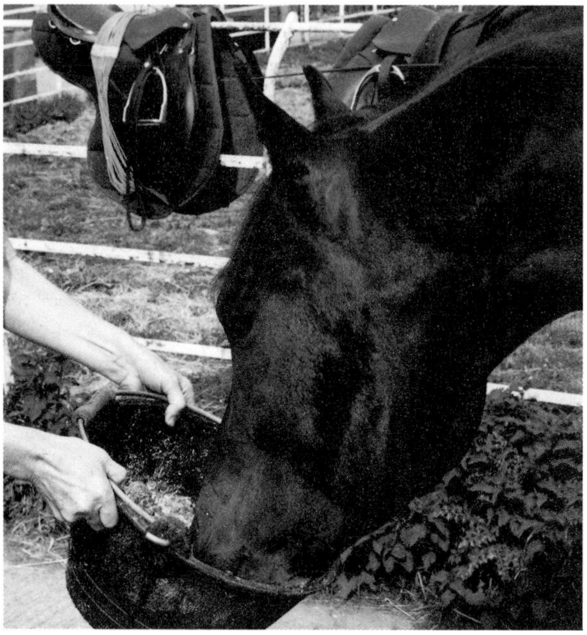

A correctly fed horse should look forward to his feeds and ideally eat up each one. Some horses on high-concentrate rations, however, often take a while to eat up and although this may simply indicate a naturally 'picky' attitude, it can mean that the diet is not well balanced and that the horse needs something else, or simply wants a change

Feeding for Fitness

It is well known that feed increases according to work during a fitness programme. In fact, the total daily weight of feed may remain constant, though the proportion of concentrates increases and that of roughage lessens as more work is done and energy expended.

There is a belief in some quarters that a horse will get fit simply by increasing his concentrates, without giving him the progressively taxing work needed to build up stamina, tone and muscular strength. At the very beginning of a fitness programme – that critical two to six weeks of walking – concentrates may well not be needed at all if the roughage source is of good enough quality and nutrient content; however, as faster, more demanding work is introduced, so should the concentrates, reaching the correct level for each stage of fitness the horse reaches at successive points in his programme.

Introducing concentrates

If the horse has been having no concentrates, these can be introduced by adding just a handful per feed, a seemingly insignificant amount, towards the end of the

Feeding good quality, high-energy hay or hayage is the best way to keep outdoor horses warm and well fed in winter. An *ad lib* supply of this type of roughage/forage/bulk food is far more effective than concentrates which provide a quick boost of warmth and energy which is soon used up

walking phase of his programme. This will very gradually get his digestive system used to the idea that a new food is on the way and needs to be processed. Once significantly faster work is introduced, weigh the concentrates properly and start off with possibly only $^{1}/_{2}$lb (0.25kg) a day at first, gradually building up according to how the horse seems.

Blood tests and hair analysis

For horses in serious competition, blood tests and profiles are often carried out to give an overall picture of the horse's progressive fitness and health. These can be organised, and sometimes carried out by your veterinary surgeon, who will anyway have to explain the significance of the results to you. They are well worthwhile, and often spot some dietary overdose or deficiency, or some metabolic disorder not apparent during daily management. Disease conditions can also be highlighted before they become apparent, or some sub-clinical, chronic condition which may have been adversely affecting a horse's performance for some while.

Hair and horn analyses can also be carried out, but these are not too popular, nor easy to arrange, in Britain.

Feeding in Winter Weather

Exposure to cold, wet and windy weather can greatly increase the amount of food and energy a horse needs because it is more difficult for him to maintain his body temperature. Outwintered horses *must* be given a constant supply of high-energy roughage, concentrates as needed on a regular basis (once, twice or more times *daily*, not less often) with possibly a feed block of vitamins and minerals in the field to help them metabolise their feed properly, maintain condition and keep warm.

The digestion of food takes energy, which creates warmth. Roughage feeds such as hay, hayage, forage feeds and straw are digested and fermented in the large intestine low down the gut and take longer to digest, providing the horse with internal 'central heating' on a 'timed energy-release' basis. The warmth/energy is made available gradually and constantly over several hours, whereas the quick boost received from a concentrate feed is soon over and the horse is cold again.

A hungry horse is a cold horse, and probably vice versa. A well fed animal with some roughage always being digested feels much warmer and more content.

Turning out fit horses in winter and early spring

Being turned out daily for several hours freedom is a great way to relax a horse and give him enjoyment, and it should be a vital part of every horse's régime. However, turning out fit horses in winter, or roughing them off too early in spring after a winter's work, can cause considerable suffering.

One of the objects of getting a horse fit is to adjust his body condition so that he carries as little surplus fat as possible. However, fat is, of course, a great insulator, and the fat layer under a horse's skin goes a long way towards helping him ward off cold winter weather, one of the reasons why it is permissible to have a horse a little tubbier in winter than in summer (when he may need actually to lose body heat). Thus not only will a fit horse in winter have little subcutaneous fat (under his skin), he will probably also have been clipped quite significantly; and so he has already lost two important methods of heat retention. A fit horse is therefore not necessarily hardy when it comes to weather resistance.

It is important to give fit horses that are turned out in winter a constant supply of hay if they are going to be out for more than an hour or so, and to dress them in a well fitting, wind- and rain-proof turn-out rug, possibly also with a neck hood and tail flap, particularly if their tails are pulled. Both these items will go a long way towards helping a horse keep warm and comfortable. When roughing off horses in spring, provide them with proper shelter and turn-out rugs, and do *not* be in a hurry to cut down their feed, particularly their hay.

Key Facts

- **The emphasis placed on feeding a correctly balanced diet today is not just a marketing ploy by feed and supplement companies. A properly balanced diet is more effective and safer than an unbalanced one.**

- **Once you have decided on which feeds to use as being suitable for your animal, feed the diet as recommended by the manufacturer in its correct amounts, and if you have any doubts or queries do not hesitate to check with the firm's nutritionist; his or her advice should be free.**

- **There are no significant differences between the digestive functioning and abilities of ponies and those of horses. Most people overfeed ponies and cobs, however, which is probably the main reason why they are so often obese and the victims of laminitis. They are normally better off without concentrate feeds, provided their roughage source and grazing are suitable.**

- **Feeding a suitable, balanced diet alone will not make a horse or pony physically fit for work. Both feed *and* exercise need to be progressively increased to obtain fitness.**

- **The digestion of food takes energy, which creates warmth. Roughage feeds take longer to digest than concentrates, and provide the animal with internal 'central heating' on a 'timed energy-release' basis over several hours; this is the most effective way of feeding for warmth in winter.**

- **Good brands of forage feeds and hayage will have their energy, protein, fibre and vitamin/ mineral analysis on the bag. From this, maybe with expert help, you will be able to determine whether or not your animal needs a supplement to adjust his diet.**

7

HOW MUCH TO FEED

The previous chapter explained the importance of the different factors affecting a horse's dietary requirements. This chapter aims to explain how to decide how much to feed animals of different types (horses, cobs and ponies) and also how to split the diet between roughage and concentrates (if used) in appropriate proportions.

Left to themselves and with adequate supplies, horses will obviously eat as much as they feel they need and with the so-called greedy types, this can easily result in overfeeding. It is always safer to slightly underfeed an animal (particularly cobs and ponies) than to slightly overfeed. This is especially important where concentrates are concerned.

However, with good hay or with forage feeds or hayage of a high energy grade, feeding *ad lib* may mean, with the greedy types, that they are overfed. It is not uncommon for owners to be surprised when such animals go down with laminitis or azoturia as it is simply often not realised just how high the energy content of such feeds can be.

How to Recognise Good or Bad Condition

It is not too difficult to learn to recognise good or bad condition, and to tell the difference between fit condition, where many horses appear to be on the thin side, particularly those trained for endurance pursuits such as endurance riding, steeplechasing (and similar) and eventing; and condition which indicates that a horse is actually thin, or 'poor' as it is euphemistically called in the horse world.

What to Aim at

Most privately owned 'pleasure' horses are in what can be described as light to medium work – and many of them are too fat. High-level performance horses might include those competing actively, and those working fairly to very hard in non-competitive spheres such as hunting or range work; these are usually kept in good to fit-lean condition. I feel most horses and ponies whose owners are reading this book will belong to the former category.

For them, the correct condition to aim at is so that you can feel the animal's ribs fairly easily but not actually see them. In winter, particularly with animals out a good deal, you can allow a little more rib-coverage. Horses whose work approaches hard – one-day eventing, regular hunting/hunter trials, lower-level endurance riding, and driving competitions with an endurance phase as opposed to simply presentation or showing – can be harder in condition and, depending on individual type, leaner, so that you can just see the last two pairs of ribs but with the spine and hips not too obvious. The muscles should be well developed, too.

This native-type pony is in fair condition for average work. He is not overweight, but is not lean and hard either

Individual Type

As mentioned, some horses and ponies are naturally leaner than others. Animals which do not seem to need much food to keep weight on are called 'good doers'; those which seem able to eat their heads off and still look 'lean and hungry' are called 'poor doers'. There is no term for the ones in-between!

It is important that you absorb by experience your animal's individual type and characteristics, and treat him accordingly. Even if you do not 'do' him entirely yourself, you should be familiar with his condition under all circumstances – in work, resting, healthy, sick or injured, winter and summer. Even if he is the naturally lean type, his spine all the way along should be well covered with flesh without being podgy. But if he is a good doer, watch out that you do not allow a channel to develop along his spine so deep that water could run down it! At one time this was regarded as a plus point in show animals, and it still is in some old-fashioned quarters.

Measurement/weight tables

Table 1. Ponies and cobs

Girth in inches	40	42.5	45	47.5	50	52.5	55	57.5
Girth in cm	101	108	114	120	127	133	140	146
Bodyweight in lb	100	172	235	296	368	430	502	562
Bodyweight in kg	45	77	104	132	164	192	234	252

Table 2. Horses

Girth in inches	55	57.5	60	62.5	65	67.5
Girth in cm	140	146	152	159	165	171
Bodyweight in lb	538	613	688	776	851	926
Bodyweight in kg	240	274	307	346	380	414
Girth in inches	70	72.5	75	77.5	80	82.5
Girth in cm	178	184	190	197	203	210
Bodyweight in lb	1014	1090	1165	1278	1328	1369
Bodyweight in kg	453	486	520	570	593	611

(Tables based on work of Glushanok, Rochlitz & Skay, 1981)

Cobs are generally very good doers, needing less food and often a different, lower energy food than blood animals like Arabs and, particularly, Thoroughbreds

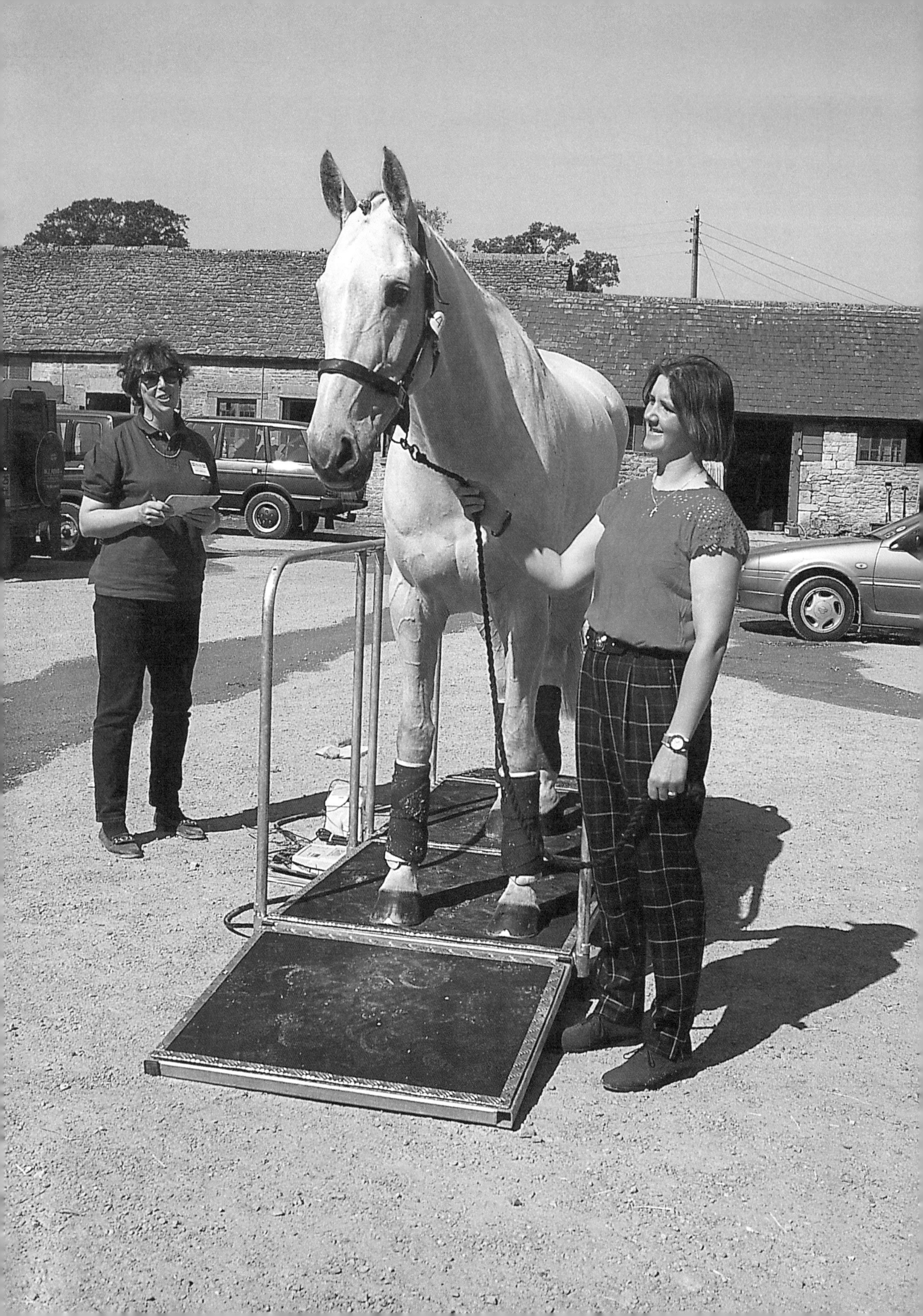

Keep an Eye on his Weight

By far the most accurate way of deciding how much of what to feed your horse is to feed according to (a) bodyweight and (b) the type of food that suits him and which he finds palatable. A **weighbridge** is ideal for accurately discovering his weight; even if you only visit it occasionally, knowing a horse's weight in any given condition – when he is too fat, too thin or just right – will give you a correct starting-off point.

Weigh-tapes are the next most accurate way to get a fair idea of what the horse weighs. These are calibrated, and tell you what the horse weighs and usually the total amount of feed he should be given each day, depending on the make of tape used. You can obtain them from most good saddlers, tack stores and some feed merchants.

Ideally, weigh your horse on a weighbridge and then use a weigh-tape, and see how far your tape reading is from the weighbridge figure. Then you can deduct or add on accordingly for an accurate figure each time you use the tape at home.

If you have no tape, use a piece of string or some pieces of binder twine knotted together to measure him, and then use the tables given here to work out his weight according to his girth measurement.

To use a tape or string correctly:

Measure the horse just behind his withers round his ribcage, keeping the tape straight (vertical to the ground) and not twisted; the tape should be just tight enough to press in his flesh a little when you hold it in place. Also, measure him and hold the tape firm at the appropriate place as he is breathing *out* . This may not be easy! The most reliable way to find out when he is breathing out is to have a helper hold a mirror up to his nostrils and tell you when it has misted up, then quickly hold the tape firm and read off your figures; or if you are using string, hold the string firmly at the right place and measure it.

It is important to be as accurate as you can, as even a half-inch (12mm) out can give quite a variance in your consequent feed amounts.

Measure with the tape held snug but not too tightly round the ribcage just behind the girth, keeping the tape smooth and vertical with the ground. Measure as the horse breathes out

Left: Checking your horse's weight on a weighbridge is the most accurate way of discovering his bodyweight so that you can calculate correctly his likely feed requirements

Cobs and Ponies

Cobs and ponies and animals with a good deal of that type of blood can be very difficult to assess and feed. They are almost always good doers – indeed, excessively good doers – perhaps a bit (or very) greedy and prone to laminitis or azoturia, if worked, at the slightest overdose of starches or sugars in their feed Nowadays there are several proprietary feeds designed just for them, and these are certainly well worth investigating.

Basically it is usually best to avoid high energy concentrates, and to make the main, or even the entire diet consist of clean meadow-type hay, or poor – but again, clean and well cared for – pasture, the best pasture for them being the short, poorer sort used for sheep rather than the rich type used for cattle. They should especially be kept off dairy cattle pasture except for very short periods (perhaps for an hour or two in the evening, when the sugar content of the grass is low).

How Much to Feed – the Crucial Question

Once you have your animal's weight you have to decide whether he is in fat, good or poor condition; since the total daily amounts of feed required are worked out as percentages of bodyweight, you would obviously be overfeeding a fat horse and underfeeding a thin one if you did not make allowances for his condition. Thus for a fat horse you reduce the total you arrive at, and vice versa for a thin horse. Very obese or emaciated horses may be special cases requiring the help and advice of a vet or nutritionist as regards their feeding.

Feeding for Lifestyle

Feeding can be purely for maintenance, to keep a resting horse or one in very light work ticking over; it can be for light work, for moderate work, or for hard work; for breeding; or in youngstock up to three, for growth. And when feeding sick horses, expert guidance may be needed.

The exact amount you feed will depend on the factors already discussed, and any information given in a book or feed manufacturer's brochure can only be regarded as a guide, if a fairly accurate one. The final decision will be a knowledgeable guesstimate on your part, aided, perhaps, by expert help. Also, if a horse's circumstances change even from day to day, such as an enforced or intended rest or, conversely, more work than intended, the diet should change accordingly.

■ **A daily maintenance ration for a pony, cob or good doer** should be about 2 per cent of his bodyweight, maybe even less, particularly if he is already fat. It should be 2.5 per cent for other horses.

■ **For youngstock and lactating or late-pregnancy broodmares**, none of which will be working, maintenance would be 3 per cent of bodyweight daily.

■ **For light work** such as gentle exercise, activity when turned out, relaxed hacking for an hour three or four times a week comprising some trotting and maybe a little cantering, 2.5 per cent daily of bodyweight is adequate.

■ **For moderate work** involving average Pony Club or riding club activities, half a day's hunting at weekends, schooling or a lesson a couple of times a week and longer hacks a few days a week, cantering and some jumping, feed at 2.5 per cent of bodyweight daily but probably use higher-energy feeds.

■ **For hard work** such as competitive eventing, hunting three or four full days a fortnight, competition driving, endurance riding or similar activities, feed at 3 per cent of bodyweight daily and possibly give extra oil in the feeds.

■ **For example:**
If your horse weighs 1,000lb (453.5kg), feeding him **for maintenance** at 2 per cent would mean giving him 20lb (9kg) of food daily, or 25lb (11.3kg) at 2.5 per cent. **For resting or light work,** this would be fed entirely as good quality roughage depending on the individual. If some concentrates are required, up to one third of the total weight could comprise concentrates, but probably more likely up to one quarter for this category of work. The dietary energy level could be about 8.5 MJ of DE per kg.

Medium work could be performed on the latter ration, but the proportion of concentrates to roughage could be perhaps narrowed, feeding up to half the amount as roughage and half as concentrates as a maximum.

Table of suggested energy requirements in diet related to work

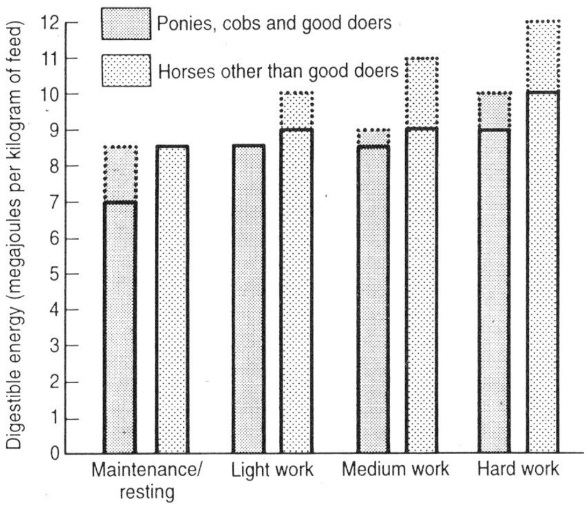

Maintenance/resting: not working, box rest, exercise in field or surfaced yard at liberty.
Light work: walking and a little trotting three or four days a week, possibly some gentle cantering and a little light schooling.
Medium work: working on most days, comprising schooling, active hacking for up to about two hours, half day's hunting, show at weekends.
Hard work: full day's hunting (three or four days a fortnight), eventing, competitive carriage driving, cross-country work, racing.

Many horses will manage **hard work**, too, very well on that sort of ratio, but for those needing more concentrates, I feel it is better to add oil to the diet rather than to reduce the roughage further. If the latter course of action were felt desirable, give two thirds as concentrates and one third as best quality roughage. However, nutritionists are now recommending that even hard-working, athletically fit horses should not have their roughage ration reduced below 50 per cent of their diet as this can significantly impair digestive efficiency and make the horse feel uncomfortable in himself. This is certainly my experience. Some horses on large amounts of concentrates often eat less hay of their own accord and some eat straw instead, given the chance, to 'dilute' their rich diet. The energy level could be 10MJ of DE per kg for medium work, or about 12MJ for hard work.

For horses which need a good deal of food to exist and work satisfactorily, those in **very hard work** or **out in winter**, up to 3 per cent of bodyweight could be fed, although it may be better to keep to 2.5 per cent and add a cupful of corn oil, soya oil or animal-grade linseed oil or cod-liver oil, to make the feed more energy dense, rather than overface the possibly reluctant horse with too many concentrates. Vitamin E with selenium should also be supplemented in such cases. The energy level should not be less than 12 MJ of DE per kg.

Back to balance

Remember that once you have worked out seemingly correct amounts for your horse or pony, you still have to ensure that the correct balance of energy, protein, vitamins and minerals is obtained, as explained in Chapter 6. Feeding the right type of branded feed for your horse or pony is a good way to do this, if not the cheapest. It is easy to feed solely by amount but still be maintaining your horse in an unbalanced nutritional status.

Playing Safe

Always increase the work before the feed, and decrease the feed before the work. It is far safer to slightly underfeed your horse, and particularly your cob or pony, than to slightly overfeed 'just to be sure'. This is particularly important for animals who have had even one

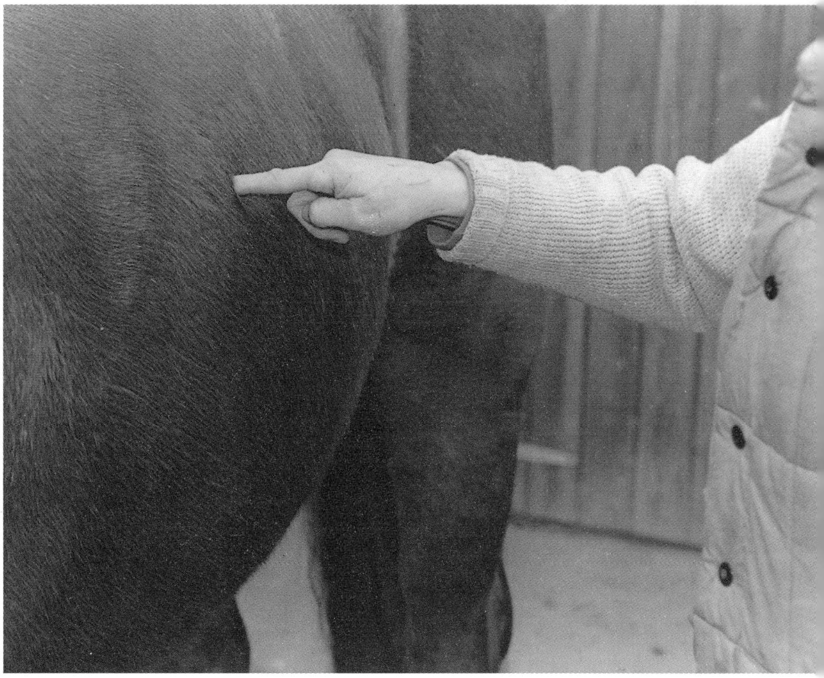

Feel through your horse's coat regularly with your fingertips to check how well covered are his ribs. You should be able to feel them easily but not actually see them, for a healthy, working weight

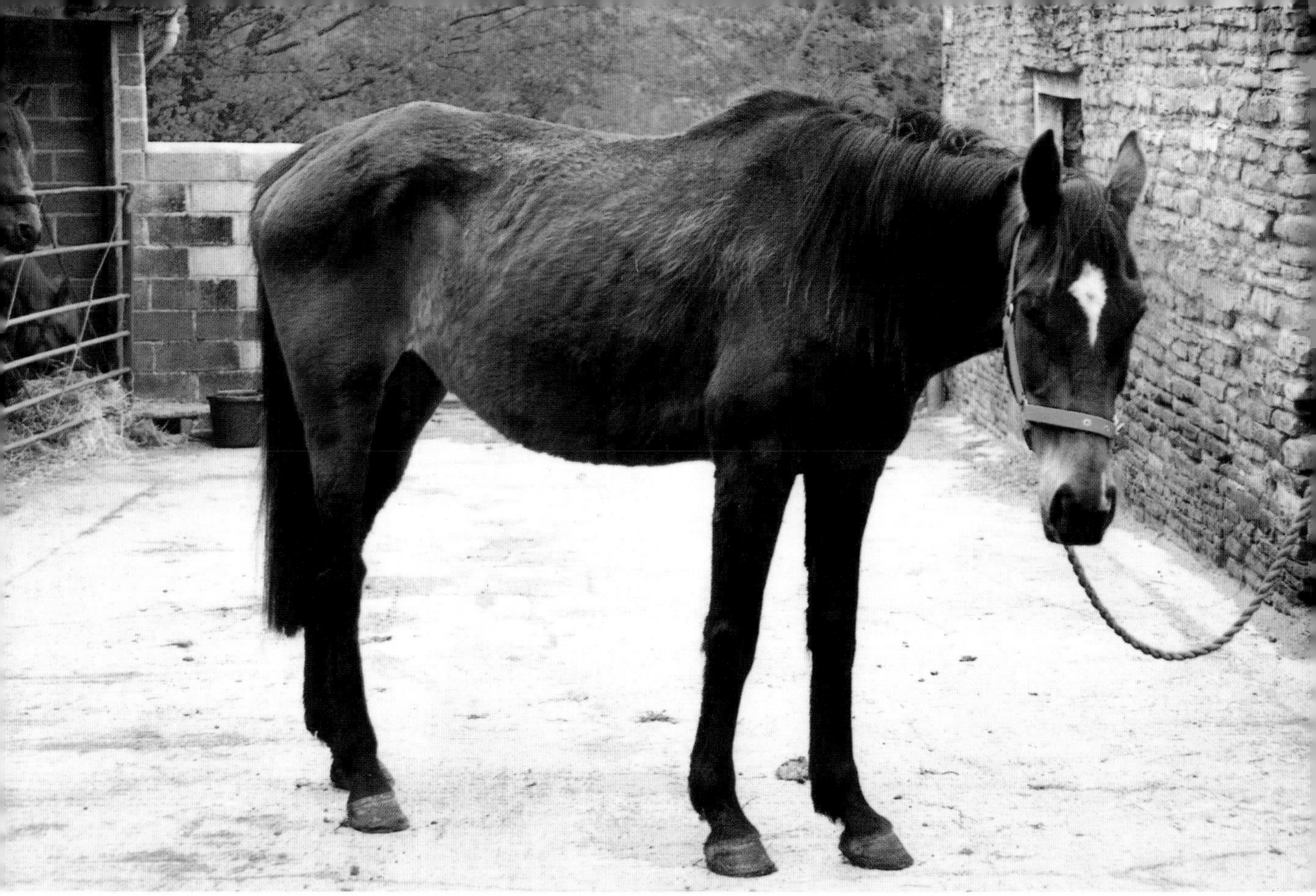

This appalling condition is the result of completely inadequate nutrition; however, look at the difference in the same animal after some months on a suitable diet

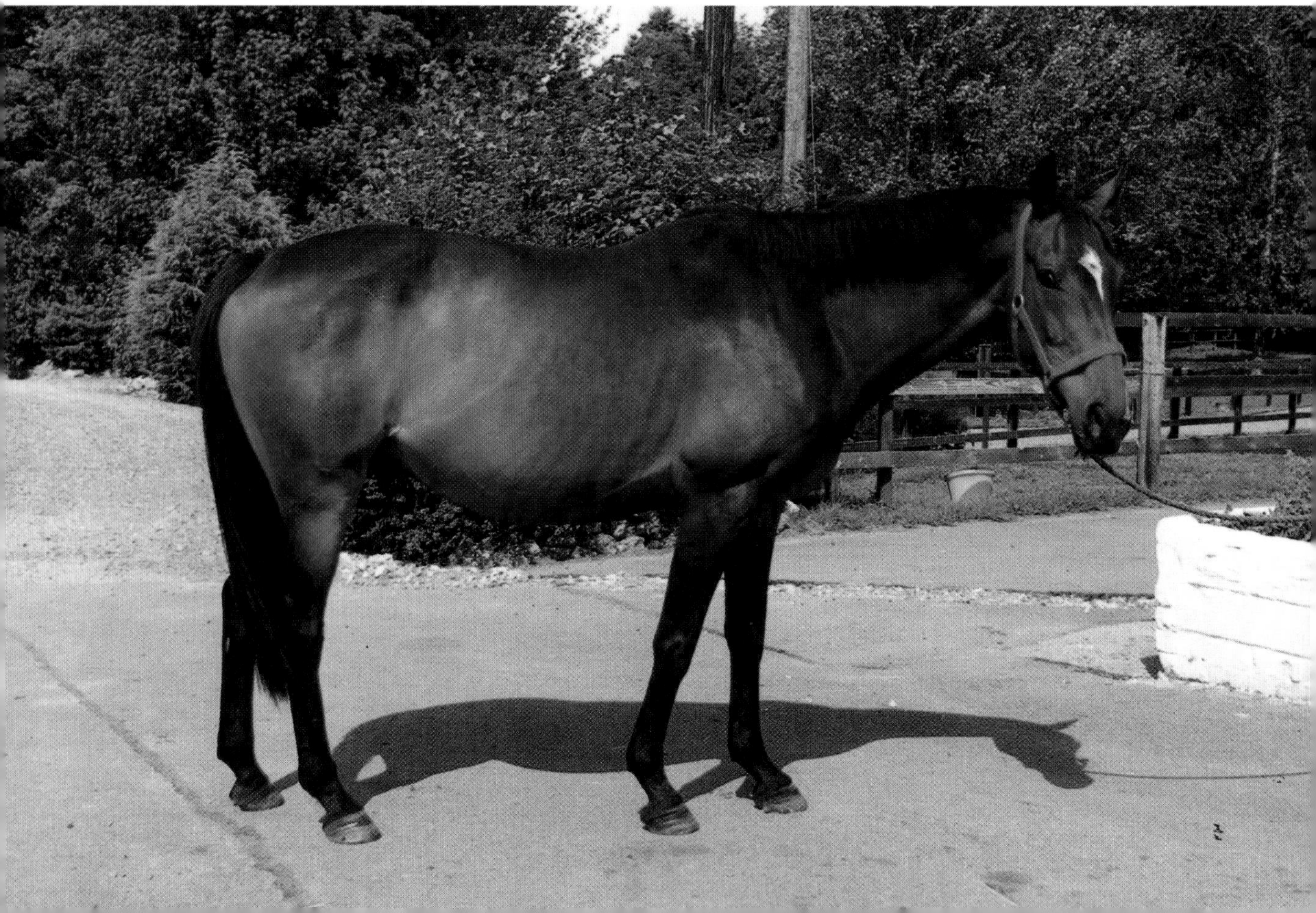

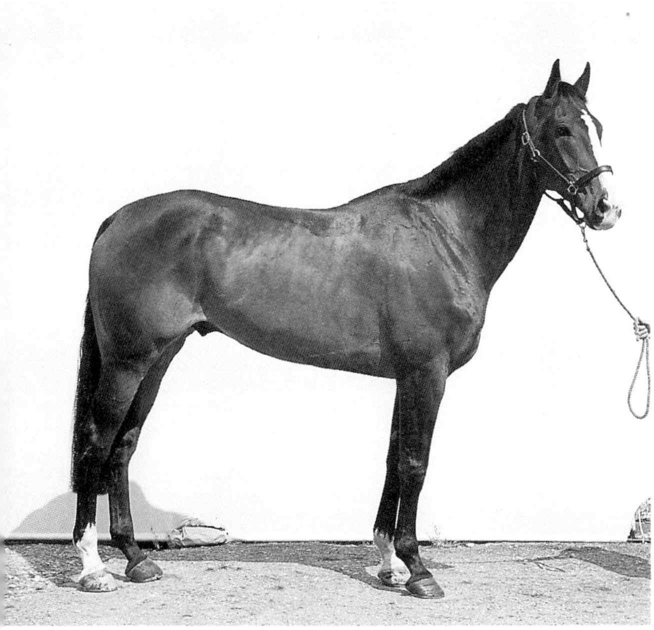

Mary Thomson's three-day event horse, King William, photographed at Badminton in 1991. He is lean, not carrying any surplus fat, hard and ideally fit for his gruelling job

The Arab's body type is much lighter than the cob's, for example. Although Arabs are often good doers, they cannot usually compare with cobs of similar height; but they are often better doers than their 'offshoot', the Thoroughbred

Resting horse at grass – well covered but not fat

Condition Scoring

The condition of a horse can be measured by using a scoring system from 0–10. This measures displacement over the neck, back, ribs and quarters.

The two extremes of condition.
Inner outline = level 1; outer outline = level 10

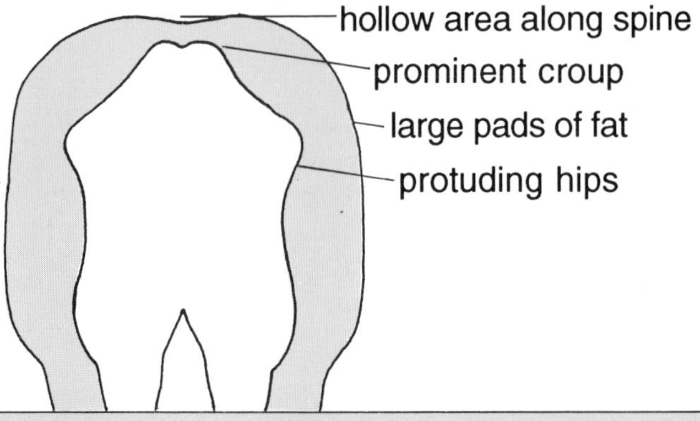

1–4 All levels of poor condition
1 Starvation level
Back view: croup and hip bones prominent and very sharp. The horse is 'cut up' behind and there is no tissue fat or muscle definition. *Side view:* vertebrae in the neck are palpable with a hollow in front of the wither. Sunken temporal fossa and eye. Spinous processes of the thoracic and lumbar vertebrae sharp, well-defined and easily palpable. Rib cage prominent with all ribs showing.
2 Similar to **1** but less obvious.
3 The checkpoints (withers, croup etc) are still defined but less sharp. A little more muscle definition but still hollow in front of the wither.
4 Bones beginning to lose their sharpness. Front half of rib cage covered, the back half still defined. Neck beginning to fill up in front of the wither.

Checkpoints for condition scoring

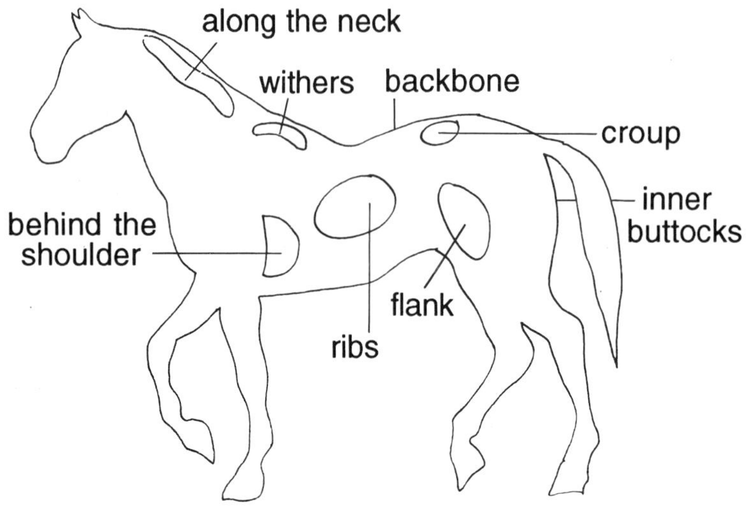

5 Approaching normal
Withers, croup and hip bones still well-defined but less easy to palpate. Inadequate muscle definition.

6 Normal
Hip bones and spinous processes defined but not prominent, well-covered in muscle and tissue. Rib cage covered, with last three pairs of ribs still palpable. Muscles well-defined.

7 Beginning to carry too much weight
As the horse gets fatter and more round, the bones become more difficult to palpate.

8 Fat
Definition of bones is lost between levels 7 and 9. Rib cage fills up – the last three pairs cannot be seen. Neck becomes hard and cresty.

9 Obese
Horse carries masses of weight on neck, quarters and back. Rib cage can be felt but only just. Deep palpation is needed to feel croup and hip bones.

10 Very obese
Excessively round backside. The horse so fat that the spine makes a hollow. Huge pads of fat on quarters and on back. Impossible to feel hip bones, croup, rib cage. No definition on shoulders.

Condition scoring (giving your horse or pony marks) for fatness or thinness is an excellent way of keeping tabs on his weight and teaching yourself to have an eye for condition. The places where horses noticeably put on or lose condition (fat) are along the crest of the neck, on either side of the withers, behind the shoulder muscle just above the elbow, on the sides, flanks and in the loin area.

If you can see the horse's ribs easily, if his withers and hipbones and even his spine protrude significantly, and if he appears 'cut up' between the thighs so you can easily get your fingers between his thigh muscles under his tail, then he is surely very underweight! Even horses which are naturally lean characters should not look like this.

If, on the other hand, you can't even feel your horse's ribs let alone count them, if you can't begin to guess where his backbone or his hipbones are because of the rolling fat covering them, and if he waddles like a pregnant duck (or resembles a broodmare heavy in foal when he is really a gelding), he is obviously too fat.

Common sense and educated judgement are needed. The diet can always be adjusted as you go along, but remember not to make sudden changes. Don't chop and change, but try to keep the horse on as settled a diet as possible.

The diagrams should help you to understand the difference between obese and emaciated (condition scoring), and will also show you where the main fat depots should be visible when considering the outside of the horse.

attack of laminitis or are even at risk of it, as is any overweight animal.

When in Doubt

If you haven't a clue what to feed your horse, cob or pony under a particular set of circumstances, particularly if he is new to you and you have no guidelines from a previous owner or no one experienced handy to ask, remember you can rarely go wrong if you give him a constant supply of clean water and nice meadow-type hay. Even Thoroughbred-type, poor doers can manage very well on a maintenance diet when fed as much of such hay as they want to eat.

In the unlikely event of your only being able to get top class, rich 'racehorse' hay or similar, which is not suitable for good doers resting or in light work, you can still use it if you feed it 50/50 with clean oat or barley straw. The old argument about barley straw not being suitable and causing colic due to the awns on it no longer applies, as present-day harvesting methods remove them. Wheat straw commonly used for bedding can be offered if you are desperate, although there is a lot of indigestible woody fibre (lignin) in it. Rye straw is rarely available.

An Alternative Rough Guide to Feed Quantity

If you want a lightning calculation of how much feed a particular horse might need and have no measuring facilities available, let alone a weighbridge, you can use the following method: take the horse's height in hands and then double it. The answer, taken in imperial weight (pounds and ounces), is a slightly over-generous estimate of what a horse or pony in moderate work might need.

For instance, if the horse is 15hh, twice that is 30 – so 30lb (13.6kg). Reduce that slightly to about 25lb (11kg) and you have a reasonable daily total feed weight for a Thoroughbred-type horse in moderate work. It does at least give you an off-the-cuff starting-point, and can be amended for different types of animal.

Assessing height

Not very good at guessing a horse's height? Use your own height (which you surely will know) as a 'measuring stick'. Remember that there are 4in (10cm) to the hand: a 16hh horse would, therefore, measure 64in (1.6m), which is exactly the height of a 5ft 4in human.

The difference between so-called hot-blooded physical features, as in the Arab shown below, and cold-blooded features, as in this native pony, is quite distinct, particularly when they are seen together

'Hot' and 'Cold' Physical Features

A horse or pony's physical type and features are an excellent guide as to where his ancestors evolved, in hot regions or cold, and therefore to how he is likely to react to wintery weather conditions. Exposure to cold, wind and wet, particularly together, always depletes horses' energy resources as the body uses up more energy to keep the body temperature up to a workable level; but animals with 'cold-climate' features will have a much more efficient natural resistance, using less energy to withstand such conditions than those with ancestors from hot regions.

Animals can adapt or acclimatise somewhat to changes in habitat and climate, but not sufficiently to enable them to withstand climates which are very different from those their physical features were evolved to cope with.

Features Typical of 'Hot'-Blooded Horses

The main breeds which can be regarded as 'hot'-blooded (which means they evolved in hot regions, not that their blood or body temperature is higher than others) are the Arabian, the Barb, the Thoroughbred (largely descended from the first two) and the Caspian. Other breeds or crosses with a good deal of such blood may also, for practical purposes, be regarded in the same way.

Probably the first thing we notice about such animals is their thin skin with small blood vessels close to the skin surface, and their fine, short coat; they also have more sweat glands, and sweat more readily than other horses. Their nostrils can flare widely during excitement or exercise. They have a head which is fairly short or small in relation to their body; their mane and tail hair is fine, their ears often comparatively large and open, and their tail carriage is high, particularly in the Arabian. Their neck may seem fairly long and their jaw or jowl area curved, open and airy. They have longer legs and a more oval-shaped barrel.

Their thin skin, and the readily visible blood vessels which carry heat-containing blood from within the hot core of the body, mean that excess heat can be easily radiated out through the skin to the outside air. The short, fine coat and fine mane and tail hair help in this. The flaring nostrils allow a greater volume of hot air to be expired easily, and their heads are fairly short because in their countries of origin the air is already warm so doesn't need warming as it is inhaled before it reaches the lungs. The largish, open ears, well supplied with blood, also help heat removal to the outside air.

The high tail carriage allows body heat to be wafted away by the air from a very thin-skinned area of the body, as does the open jowl structure. The generous supply of active sweat glands assists better heat removal by another means, evaporation of heat-containing moisture; their longer legs again make for free air movement around the body, and their oval barrel permits easier heat loss to the outside than a rounder structure. Even in winter, their coats are never very thick – and certainly rarely up to combatting the high wind-chill factor created by the cold, wet, windy conditions of a normal temperate-zone winter, let alone that of sub-Arctic or Arctic areas.

Features Typical of 'Cold'-Blooded Horses

Compare, now, animals from cold regions of the earth. Their skin is measurably thicker, with blood vessels less obvious and a longer, denser coat which traps warmed air near the body and so helps to insulate it; some even grow a double coat in winter, with a soft, furry underlayer and a coarser, longer top coat with long hairs under the jaw, down the sides and on the legs which help to drain the rainwater off the body. Even their summer coat is not so short and fine as that of their hot-blooded cousins.

Their nostrils are smaller and more slit-like to conserve heat, and their longer head contains correspondingly longer air passages to warm the cold air being breathed in. The mane and tail hair is often thick and dense, sometimes wavy or even curly to trap more warm air near the body and protect it from cold, wet weather. They have a low tail carriage for the same reason.

Their smaller, woolly ears help to reduce heat loss, as does their more closed, angular jaw. It is always easier for heat to pass from a thin object than a rounder one – just think of a radiator – so the neck of cold-climate horses and ponies is shorter than others, again to minimise heat loss. They have short legs compared to their height; a rounder, heat-retaining body; and fewer sweat glands, as these are simply not needed so much.

Dressage and showing are two examples of equestrian sports in which horses and ponies are still often presented too fat for good health. Dressage in particular is hard, gymnastic work for the horse and surplus fat causes unnecessary distress and difficulty for the horse. This horse is just right

Dietary Needs

We have already seen how an *ad lib* supply of high quality roughage greatly helps to keep animals warm in winter. For those whose bodies are not designed to withstand so-called temperate or colder-region winters, it is an absolute necessity if they are to spend much time out in winter. Those of pure, or mostly, Thoroughbred and Arab blood which will have to be out a lot in winter should *not* be clipped excessively, if at all; they should have a good field shelter and turn-out rugs, and their manes and – especially important – their tails should be left untrimmed, and/or a rug with a tail flap used.

Without this sort of help, such horses are unlikely to winter at all well, and could suffer greatly, if they survive.

An interesting study in the United States of America a few years ago using two control groups of similar horses showed that those with full, unpulled tails maintained bodyweight and needed less food than those with pulled tails. This is because a horse's natural reaction is to stand with its tail to bad weather, the natural tail being intended to shield the body from cold. With a pulled tail, a horse has lost most of that protection, so it will lose a lot of body heat from this area, heat which the body then

Recognising a pot belly

Horses suffering from malnutrition may have distended, pot bellies particularly if the food they have been receiving has been very high in indigestible, woody fibre (lignin) such as in a straw-only diet, or very poor hay. This rounded belly may lead some people to think the animal is actually fat – but check his top line.

If the horse or pony has a normal, curved top line with a well fleshed upper neck, back, loins and quarters as well as a big belly, he may well be overweight; but if his neck is poor and slab-like, maybe dipping in front of the withers, if his withers and shoulders are very bony, his back sunken at the sides, his spine protruding, along with his hips and croup, and with hardly any cushioning flesh or fat on the back, loins and quarters – then that plump-looking belly is, indeed, a pot belly and a sign of a severely undernourished animal.

tries to make up from its energy resources (supplied only by food); as a result, the horse will be extremely uncomfortable – another factor which increases energy and, therefore, food usage.

Animals with cold-climate features do withstand the winter weather better, but they, too, should be given reasonable conditions in domesticity to mimic as far as is practicable the facilities they would be free to find in the wild: shelter, food, and the full protection of their natural coats, manes and tails. Again, a proper field shelter is best, with somewhere dry to get out of the mud where they can lie and rest; hay or its equivalent to make up for the winter grass which on a small paddock will have no feed value at all (compared to the wide range they would enjoy in the wild – unless they have many acres available to them); and they should be left unclipped and untrimmed, or at the very least given turn-out rugs to wear.

In a mild winter, supplementary feeding (ie concentrates) for such animals may not even be necessary *as long as* their other requirements are taken care of.

Key Facts

- **As a safe guide to a correct 'working' condition for most animals in moderate work, feed so that you can feel the ribs fairly easily but cannot actually see them.**
- **The most important factor in deciding how much to feed your horse or pony is to use his bodyweight as a guide to quantity, fine-tuning it according to the other determining factors such as workload, weather, temperament and constitution.**
- **For cobs and ponies, it is normally best to avoid concentrates, particularly in moderate to large amounts, and to rely on good fibre sources for their energy and nutrient requirements, such as good meadow-type hay, hayage and forage feeds. Sparse pasture grass is also a good feed for them.**
- **Do not be too quick to cut down the roughage portion of a horse's ration: current thinking advises more roughage than was formerly believed adequate. Even horses in hard work and on high concentrate rations should not have their hay/hayage reduced below one third (by weight) of their daily ration.**
- **Learn to condition-score your horse or pony, and check him or her weekly until you get used to his natural condition under different circumstances. Even allowing for individual tendencies – such as those animals who are naturally tubby and those naturally lean – there should be no marked variation either side of their working average.**
- **Always increase work before feed, and decrease feed before work.**
- **An *ad lib* supply of meadow hay and water is a safe starting-point for virtually any horse or pony.**
- **If you have no means of assessing a horse's bodyweight to calculate his probably daily feed total, a rough guide is to take his height in hands and double it; this will give you a slightly generous daily food allowance in pounds.**
- **If you cannot guess his height, use your own height to assess his.**

8

WATER AND WATERING

The horse's body is roughly three-quarters water, young bodies containing more than old ones. Water is needed in most body processes, and the whole body is full of fluid – inside the cells, between them, in the blood, milk, digestive juices and lymph. Sweat and urine are mostly water, and are the means of carrying waste and toxic substances away from the body; and particularly in the case of sweat, they also carry heat away from the body. The eyes are filled with fluid, as are the canals inside the horse's ear which help with hearing and balance. Thus water is needed for the entire body metabolism.

Left: An ample supply of clean, palatable water is essential to good digestion and health

How Much Does He Need?

In a comfortable temperature, a non-working horse might drink about 5 gal (23 litres) of water per 24 hours and a pony obviously less, so you can see that actual requirements vary considerably. Those needing most – say, 12 to 15 gal (54 to 68 litres) per day – are horses working hard in hot weather which sweat a lot, and lactating broodmares which obviously need the extra fluid to make milk.

Most stable buckets hold only about 5 gal (23 litres) so it is obvious that one bucket twice a day, which is all many horses receive, is not enough.

These days, most yards keep water constantly with their horses, either in ordinary containers such as buckets or small plastic dustbins, or by means of automatic waterers which do save a great deal of work in large yards. If these are used, though, it is best to use the kind with a meter so you know how much your horse is – or is not – drinking.

Water intake is a good guide to general health and condition, and if your horse or pony suddenly starts drinking a lot more or less than usual you will know there could well be a problem.

A Horse's Water Requirements

Depending on his work and the weather, a horse can drink up to about 12 gal (54 litres) per day and occasionally more in hot weather and during hard work. However, much depends on the water content of his feed. As an example, grass will normally be about three-quarters water, although its water content does vary according to weather conditions and the time of year; fresh grass in a wet spring will be high in water, whereas shrivelled grass in a dry summer, or old winter grass will contain much less. This can have unhappy consequences: during a very dry summer a few years ago, grass was shrivelled up and parched brown; horses were pulling it up and swallowing it without much chewing, and several died of intestinal blockages. This was in spite of their having ample water available, and appearing to be drinking freely.

Hay may contain up to only 15 per cent water, and hayages a little more. Coarse mixes (sweet feed) will contain about the same, but cubes and undamped cereal concentrate feeds will contain only a small amount of water.

Availability of Water

Even those who always keep water constantly available to their horses may feel it wise to remove the bucket when a horse is given his feed, and not to replace it until about an hour afterwards, bearing in mind the old rule 'water before feeding' and the dictum that if he drinks water *after* feeding it can result in undigested food being washed through to the intestines which may cause colic.

However, current scientific thinking on this is that drinking water just before, during and even after feeding actually stimulates the digestive juices and aids digestion, *provided* the horse does not take a big drink. Besides, horses which have water always with them very rarely take in several gallons at once; the small amount they do drink does no harm and can, as mentioned above, do good. It is certainly a fact that many horses, on being brought home and expecting a feed, will refuse to drink at all until they have eaten.

If you really feel you want your horse to have a drink before his feed, offer him the (fresh) water in which sugar-beet pulp has been soaked. Most horses enjoy this and will drink it readily. It also contains a limited amount of non-cereal energy and important electrolytes.

Many horses will take short drinks between mouthfuls of short (manger/bucket) feeds, about two or three swallows at a time, in the same way that we might sip a glass of water or wine. It is also not uncommon for horses purposely to dunk their hay in their drinking water before eating it; some will even refuse to eat their hay if they cannot do this, usually because the owner has removed the water to stop the practice! As horses' natural food has a high moisture content, it is not surprising that some do not like eating comparatively dry hay.

As for dry concentrates, it used to be advised by some experts that feeds should not be damped because it was believed this significantly diluted the saliva and digestive juices and so impaired digestion, and also discouraged the horse from chewing his food properly. This does not seem to be a common opinion now, however, and the benefits obtained by damping the feed – that it 'binds' the ingredients together, lays any dust/flour, and makes it more comfortable and pleasant for the horse to eat – far outweigh any very minor dilution of saliva and digestive juices. This would surely be infinitesimal – and in any case, the current thinking is that water during feeding, and damping feeds, is a good thing.

Methods of Watering

In the wild or in feral environments, *equidae* (horses, ponies, asses and zebras) do not always have water nearby, but probably have to trek to the nearest watering sources; this they do mainly mornings and evenings. They drink long draughts then, but only twice a day. In between times, they return to their grazing grounds. Zebras have been noted as going as long as four days between trips to their only distant water source, staying for about a day and really drinking their fill, then trekking back to their grazing; this length of time is unusual, however, and one noted mainly in camels rather than the horse family.

In natural conditions where water is readily available, *equidae* drink more often and in smaller amounts.

The Traditional Way

In the past, horses were either taken to water or it was brought to them, and this still applies in many traditionalist establishments such as some military and police stables, breweries and others. Then, as now, the rule was always to water before feeding to be on the safe side, for the reasons already given, and most people feel that this is still excellent advice in such circumstances.

Taking the horse to water

Horses led to drink at a communal trough may be at slightly higher risk of catching diseases from each other, but if they are kept in close quarters they will probably all succumb, anyway. In large yards it is certainly less laborious to take the horses to water than to take water to them in buckets in their boxes or stalls, although this is done in some yards.

With any such system, it is important that horses are given plenty of time to drink their fill, and that circumstances permit and encourage them to do so. Choose drinking partners carefully so that a more timid horse is not afraid to drink because of dominance or actual bullying by another. The presence near the yard or the actual trough of something a horse is afraid of – a vehicle, a dog, flapping polythene, someone waiting at a bus stop on the roadside with an opened umbrella – should be considered too, as many horses will not drink if at all worried by anything. This is an instinctive wariness, developed in the wild, when herds of horses were/are at particular risk at a water-hole: predators always gather at a water source knowing there is food readily available, and tension is high, with frequent skirmishes breaking out, in such circumstances. Horses will not usually drink until they feel it is quite safe to do so.

When horses are watered in this twice- or three-times-a-day method, it is important to realise that they take some time to satisfy themselves: they will take an apparently long, satisfying drink and will then raise their heads and perhaps look around. But wait with them, and you will find this is just a rest – they will often put their heads down again to drink, and a very thirsty horse may even repeat this process a third time. If we drag him away during one of his 'rest' periods, he will not have slaked his thirst and we shall be depriving him of water. If we do this repeatedly at both of the day's waterings, we could inadvertently be dehydrating the horse ourselves. Usually, horses will leave the trough themselves when satisfied, and we should certainly wait for them to do this.

Taking water to the horse

When taking water to horses in their stables, we should be prepared to take as many buckets as a horse seems to need to satisfy himself, remembering that the entire process may take up to about twenty minutes. Another important point to remember is that even a very thirsty horse may not drink for several seconds (up to half a minute) when first offered water, and may then spend a good ten minutes or more drinking and resting.

A horse will take in about two-thirds of a pint (one-third of a litre) at one swallow; you can see the swallows by watching the underside of his neck as he drinks, so you can check approximately how much he has taken in – this is useful to know, because at times, such as if he is hot after competition, his water intake must be small and gradual.

The Modern Way

Even watering horses *ad lib* is not free of potential problems, the main one being that of simply not leaving enough water. Likely consumption has already been discussed: simply make it a priority never to leave your horse without a full container of clean, fresh water, and to leave two buckets or small plastic dustbins if it is going to be several hours before anyone can give him any more.

Another occurrence with stabled horses is that sometimes they do a dropping in their water bucket. This cannot be prevented unless the bucket is sited at an uncomfortable and unnatural height, higher than the horse's tail. However, you can partly alleviate the problem by leaving two buckets in different corners, and use the same corners so the horse knows where to find them in the dark; if you do this, the chances are that the horse will always have some clean water to drink.

Horses watered in this way may also find it entertaining to play with their bucket or container when looking for something to do. Thus all containers should be firmly fixed to the wall by a safe, strong fitment to prevent the horse tipping the bucket over, depriving himself of water and possibly injuring himself on the loose container.

Automatic waterers

These are plumbed in, and it is best to use the type with a meter so you can check consumption, and which have a recessed plug in the bottom; this makes it easier to empty and clean them – daily.

Automatic drinkers certainly save a lot of work, but try to use the type with a meter so you can check consumption, and with a drain-hole and recessed plug in the bottom for easy cleaning

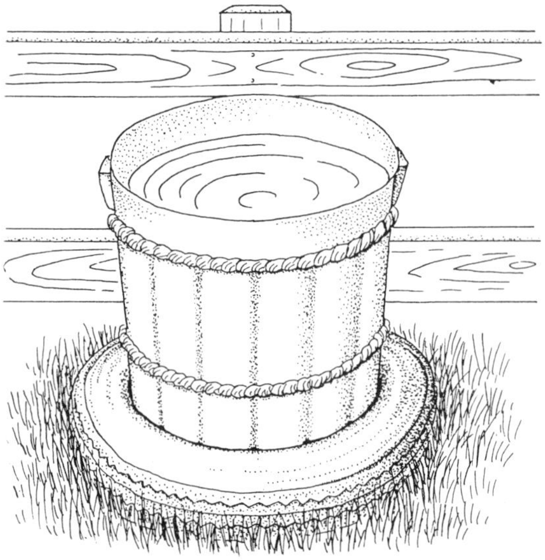

Plastic dustbin seated in an old tractor tyre and tied firmly to the fence-post behind; easy to empty and scrub clean. In wet weather these can be moved along the fence to prevent the land immediately around them being unduly poached

Watering Yarded and Outdoor Horses

Yarded horses and those at pasture can be watered in similar ways. The most convenient is to have water laid on to the paddocks, or at least readily available by hosepipe so the containers can be filled up regularly. Self-fill containers of whatever sort are normally the safest because they ensure that the supply is constantly topped up, provided they are in correct working order.

Conventional **troughs** are fine, provided they have no sharp edges or corners on which the horses can injure themselves, and that the filling mechanism is covered to prevent them interfering with it, as they undoubtedly will if they can, being so inquisitive, and sometimes mischievous by nature.

Plastic dustbins tied to the fence-posts are good: they are filled by hosepipe and can be easily emptied and cleaned, and also moved on down the fence a little way each day to prevent poaching of the land around them.

Siting a trough

If you use a long, rectangular trough, do not site it crossways to serve two fields because it will project into each of them and is then dangerous not only to horses milling around there, but to those galloping along the fence-line; these, believe it or not, may not see the

Carefully sited, troughs can be made to serve two fields at once. They should be set along a fence-line so as to avoid a right-angled projection into the field, which can be dangerous as horses tend to gallop along fence-lines and do not always look where they are going

The existence of a pond in a field is no guarantee of a suitable water source. Apart from the water possibly being stagnant or polluted, the approach, as here, can be an accident waiting to happen

projection, or may simply forget it is there, and gallop into it with disastrous consequences.

Instead, site it along the fence-line so that horses from both sides can reach it. The problem here can be that it may be necessary to remove the top rail of the fence, otherwise some horses may be put off drinking and there is also the risk of them banging their heads on it. Once removed, however, the trough on its own provides an invitingly low jump from one field into the other, which may not be quite what you want!

If you use the crossways method, fix rails from the corners of the trough diagonally back to the fence to steer horses round it, and paint them white for easier visibility. This reduces the drinking area but makes the arrangement safer.

Of course, yarded and outdoor horses can be led to water two or three times daily, as described above, if strictly necessary.

Natural supplies

It is advisable to have any natural water sources regularly analysed, a procedure which you can arrange through your local water authority or veterinary surgeon. It is tempting to feel that if you have a stream, pond or river on your land you need make no further arrangements for watering your horses. In reality, such supplies often have unsafe or off-putting approaches, and sometimes even form dangerous traps for horses – for example, in freezing weather animals may wander on to the frozen surface and fall through the ice; they may contain stagnant or polluted water.

In general, sad though it may seem, it is often safer to fence off natural ponds and ditches and use artificial supplies.

Watering Horses in Hard Work

For generations it has been the accepted practice to deprive horses of water for several hours before hard or fast work, the reasoning being that it is bad for the horse to have a lot of water swilling around inside him during galloping or jumping, and that it would unavoidably adversely affect his performance. Nowadays however, research on competition horses and particularly in the endurance riding field, has led to the conclusion that this is counterproductive and that such horses are highly likely to become dehydrated even if the weather is not very hot.

Water Quality

Horses may be very fussy over the taste of their water. A common cause of animals not drinking enough in their home surroundings is dirty or tainted containers. Buckets and other stable containers should be scrubbed out daily with a clean brush kept for the purpose to avoid slime and algae developing on them. Soap is not necessary but hot water is a help. Rinse very thoroughly.

If the horse does a dropping in his container, you can clean and disinfect it by using a baby-type steriliser fluid, or one of the special equine disinfectants safe for feed and water containers. These leave no smell which will put off a fastidious horse further. Never use ordinary household or agricultural disinfectants, or bleach, many of which products can be toxic, and in any case leave a lingering smell to offend the horse.

If your horse suddenly refuses to drink water which is apparently all it should be, and you are sure the container is not at fault, get the water analysed as he may have detected some change in it, or pollution. Refusal to drink is also a sign of sickness of course, which your vet should check.

Water temperature

Temperature does not seem to matter to the horse, although it is generally felt that hot horses should not be offered very cold water. In practice it will be found that horses drink more, and more freely, if the water is of a comfortable temperature, rather like ourselves, and it is not a bad idea to pour a little boiling water into the bucket if the water is near freezing, for a horse returning from work who may want a good drink.

Drinking muddy water

If your horse or pony consistently prefers drinking muddy water to clean water, he is probably short of minerals in his diet and you should consult a vet or nutritionist to have the diet corrected.

When to Water

It is currently recommended that horses should have water freely available to them for up to one hour before work, or even only thirty minutes. You can check the most up-to-date advice with a nutritionist or vet interested in performance horses.

During endurance-type work – endurance riding itself, hunting, long hacks, and at appropriate points during the endurance phase of horse trials and carriage-driving trials – it is advised that horses be encouraged to drink at appropriate times and places to allay the onset of dehydration. Indeed, in competitive endurance-riding competitions, horses not allowed to drink frequently become seriously dehydrated.

During such events and when hunting, horses should be allowed to drink their fill whenever a convenient place is reached and at a convenient time. Between phases at horse trials or at certain carriage-driving trials, horses can be allowed up to about 4 pints (2 litres). It is also important to remember to allow the horse to stale whenever he wants to, or to encourage him to do so at convenient points.

Even if the horse is hot and sweating, he can be allowed about 4 pints (2 litres) provided you keep moving on afterwards, ideally at a walk for a little while; water passes down the gut quite quickly.

After Work

If the horse is hot and tired after he has worked, offer him the above amounts every fifteen minutes during his

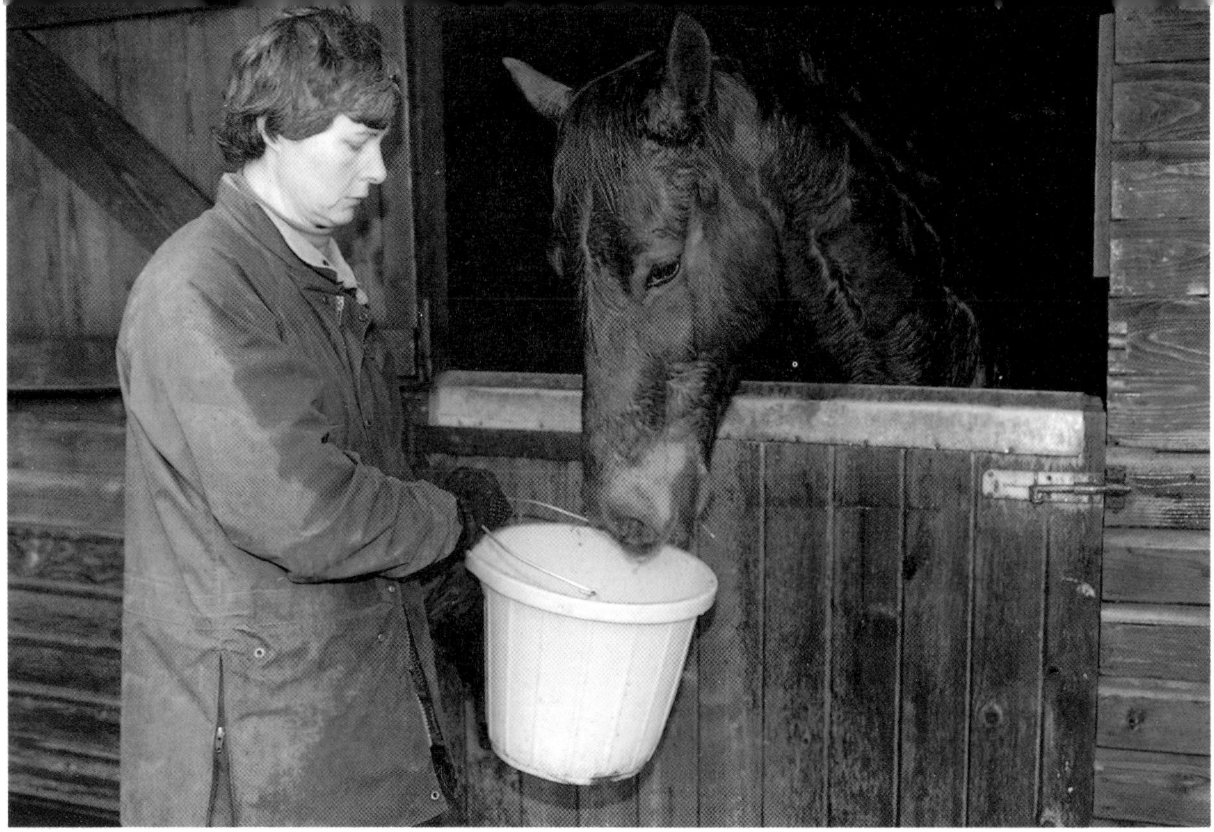

It is wrong to deprive a hot horse of water. A few swallows every 15 minutes or so puts back lost body water, helps alleviate thirst and makes the horse feel better. Once he is cool he should be allowed water *ad lib*

Body heat, protein and electrolytes are all lost in sweat, and a great deal of energy is used up in hard work. Correct watering and the replacement of electrolytes are needed quickly after stressful work to start the recovery process immediately, followed by balanced, appropriate feeds (not bran mashes) to restore energy walking/cooling out period. Once he is significantly cooler and has stopped sweating, and his temperature, pulse and respiration are more or less back to normal resting rates, he can be allowed *ad lib* water as usual.

If you finish your work with the horse already cool (following the old adage that you should never bring your horse home hot and blowing) you can safely allow him to drink his fill unless he has been sweating freely and has been without water for several hours; in this case, offer half a bucket every quarter of an hour until he seems to want no more, then leave him an *ad lib* supply.

Dehydration

Horses needing water soon begin to show signs of discomfort and illness: they lose their appetite, look dull, anxious and lethargic, and in cases approaching the severe, actually appear to shrink in body mass. This is not surprising, because if a horse is dehydrated the tissues are short of water, and it is water which plumps them out.

Further Symptoms of Lacking Water

The skin loses its body and elasticity, and other tissues also become drier and 'thinner'. The blood volume is reduced so the blood's solid elements (cells and so on) are left to circulate in less fluid. As the blood becomes 'thicker', this puts a strain on the heart which is forced to pump the thicker material round the body; the blood vessels, too, are under greater strain and the blood's functions of delivering and taking away nutrients, gases and waste products are impaired, so the horse's general health suffers.

The constant chemical messages travelling round the body in the form of hormones cannot be delivered so effectively, and the fighting of disease – the joint task of the circulatory and lymphatic systems – is impaired.

In practice, the horse's whole body suffers if it is short of water, whether this shortage is large and sudden, or of a lesser and more chronic nature. The competition horse deprived of water for several hours before competing, or the family pony largely in the care of children or the unknowledgeable who simply do not give enough water or give it regularly, are both at real risk of serious health problems.

It has to be said that water is of more immediate importance to the horse than food.

Watering when Travelling

People often do not realise how stressful travelling is to a horse and that he is using his muscles, often in an unnatural and tiring way, all the time simply to stay on his feet in a moving, swaying vehicle which gives him no prior warning of its movements. Travelling is both mentally and physically draining to horses, and those subjected to journeys of several hours may arrive at their destination far from fresh and ready to work, but in fact stressed, fatigued and on the way to dehydration.

The horse may appear cool and dry on arrival, but depending on clothing and ventilation in the box, this does not mean he has not been sweating: the moisture could have evaporated or been absorbed by the clothing, besides which horses don't have to be hot to sweat; some will often break out in a cold sweat due to anticipation.

Horses may not be happy to drink while their vehicle is in motion, so it is advisable to stop and offer water every two hours on long trips; they should also be unloaded, and led out in hand and allowed to graze if at all convenient. This goes a long way to warding off dehydration, resting them and relieving their muscles, and relaxing them mentally.

On arrival, once the horses are unloaded, and have relaxed and perhaps been settled into temporary stabling, they should be allowed to drink their fill. Some will not drink strange water, so you may well have to take a large container filled with 'home' water for them. They should be allowed at least one hour's recovery time for every hour on the road, and more in hot climates.

Some experts recommend adding a very small amount of molasses to strange water to encourage a horse to drink when he is away, but this may only work if he is used to having it occasionally at home.

Testing for Dehydration

To test if your horse is dehydrated you can test his capillary refill time, or use the skin-pinch test.

Capillary refill time

This is the time it takes for the tiny blood vessels (capillaries) in his gums to refill with blood after you have pressed the gums firmly with your thumb, leaving a white mark. The mark should disappear in no more than two seconds; any longer and the horse is mildly dehydrated.

The skin-pinch test

This is done by simply pinching up a fold of skin on the horse's neck just in front of his shoulder; it should fall back flat more or less immediately, and if it does not, the horse is dehydrated. If it stays up for a few seconds you and he have a serious problem which certainly needs veterinary assistance.

The Treatment of Dehydration

Treatment falls within the sphere of the vet. On a practical level, while waiting for the vet to come, you can certainly offer the horse water which he will, surprisingly perhaps, possibly not drink. Offer an electrolyte drink as well. If he won't take either, sponge fluid into his mouth; do not, however, try to drench him (pour fluid down his throat) unless you are sure you know how to do this or have the help of a suitably experienced person; it is very easy to choke or drown a horse using this formerly common treatment.

When the vet arrives, he or she may well have to administer fluids by tubing the horse – that is, siphoning fluids into him by means of a tube passed up a nostril and down into his oesophagus – as well as by means of drips administered intravenously (into the veins) and/or subcutaneously (under the skin).

Preventing Dehydration

Dehydration can be prevented mainly by the methods already mentioned: allowing horses to drink during work as advised above, and by making sure that not only do they have a clean, fresh supply at all times whenever possible, but also that they are allowed plenty of time to drink their fill, particularly if a constant supply is not available.

Check that horses are not afraid to drink, for reasons already discussed: a bullying companion, an off-putting approach to the water source, a container which rattles or of which they are afraid, or which smells or tastes unpleasant.

Key Facts

- Water is the horse's most important nutrient. He will very quickly die without an ample supply of clean water.
- Water intake is a good guide to general health: if your horse or pony starts drinking a lot more or less than usual, look for other signs of illness and consult your veterinary surgeon.
- Provided the horse does not take a long drink, it is quite safe for him to drink before, during and even after feeding. Current scientific thinking is that drinking actually aids digestion rather than hampers it, in moderate or small amounts.
- A horse's natural food is moist. Some horses need to 'dunk' their hay in their water before they will eat it. Do not discourage or prevent this practice.
- It is dangerous to deprive hard-working horses of water for several hours before work. It is currently advised that they should have water freely available up to an hour or even half an hour before hard work.
- Even if a horse is hot and sweating he can be allowed up to about 4 pints (2 litres) – roughly six swallows – provided he is kept walking on afterwards.
- Use the horse's capillary refill time to check whether or not he is becoming dehydrated, rather than the skin-pinch test, which only gives a result once a horse is significantly dehydrated.
- Watch your horse drinking, both in the field in company and alone in his stable. If for any reason he is being prevented from drinking, he may become dehydrated.
- Horses can become dehydrated in winter as well as summer if the water sources are frozen so they are unable to drink. Many horses will not break even thin ice themselves.
- Check both piped and natural supplies regularly for safety and/or pollution. Your veterinary surgeon or nutritionist can advise how to get this done.
- If your horse or pony consistently prefers drinking muddy to clean water, he could be short of minerals in his diet.
- When cleaning drinking containers, use the products which are marketed specially for cleansing and disinfecting equine feed utensils, and rinse very thoroughly. Strong soaps and disinfectants can leave traces of unpleasant smells and tastes even after thorough rinsing.
- Horses often drink more, and more freely, if the water is of a comfortable temperature. A little boiling water added to your horse's bucket when he is likely to drink (for example after returning from a ride) is a good idea on a very cold day.

Left: Hot and humid weather adversely affects horses, particularly working horses, much more than many people realise as it makes it very difficult for the body to cool itself down during and after exertion. To help prevent dehydration, horses in such conditions should be allowed to take short drinks at convenient moments – say a quarter of a bucket (ideally containing electrolytes if the horse will take them). Current research on heat stress in horses seems to show that the application of cold water to muscle-mass areas (including the quarters), which are rich in heat-carrying blood, is probably the most useful way of cooling down a horse

9

THE NEW 'GOLDEN RULES' OF FEEDING

There are no so-called 'Golden Rules' for any other aspect of horse management, only for feeding; this alone should impress on us why feeding is so important and how complex a topic it is, which in turn may be why initially someone decided we needed clear summaries and guidelines to set us on the right road. However, times change and so do feedstuffs and our knowledge of nutrition. The Golden Rules of yesteryear were fine so far as they went, but even so, many people failed to interpret them correctly – as they do still and so nutrition-related problems still occur.

The following survey of the Golden Rules confirms some established practices, encourages a different look at others, and adds a few new thoughts in the hope of improving the way we feed our horses and ponies and, therefore, their health and wellbeing as well.

1. Feed Little and Often

This is usually the first rule and probably the most famous. It is meant to encourage us to feed the horse as closely to nature as possible, although in practice most people still do not do so.

The horse's natural feeding habits have been fully discussed, as has the functioning of his digestive system, and it is probably obvious that the usual interpretation of 'little and often' – two or three short feeds a day with hay only night and morning – is *not* little and often when compared to nature's way and the way his digestive system evolved to work.

A Constant Diet

Remember that the horse has a small stomach, and if you are feeding concentrates you should give no more than about 4lb (1.8kg) in one feed; when swollen and soaked with saliva, this is quite enough for the stomach to cope with. Give as many small short feeds (if you feed short feeds) per day as you can possibly manage to ensure optimal health of the digestive bacteria and quality of digestive enzymes and so optimal digestive efficiency, and try to give an *ad lib*, more or less continuous supply of roughage, whether this is hay or an equivalent.

A good, old-fashioned way of giving a consistent, constant diet is to put the horse's roughage in a large, open manger-type holder and mix the concentrates in with it so he gets some of each in each mouthful. An excellent, modern way to feed consistently is to give a good forage feed which is scientifically balanced to contain a higher feed value than most hays, so he gets all he needs from one type of feed – as Nature intended. Because forage feeds used as hay replacers are fed more or less *ad lib*, the horse always has food around him, never gets hungry, bored or impatient due to lack of food, and his digestive bugs stay in good health.

Working owners will bless this system as they don't have to give many tiny feeds a day, but can still feed their horses as well as if they were.

Hayage and other branded preserved forages can also be fed on this system, and if the right grade is fed for your horse's lifestyle, again you should need few, if any, concentrates.

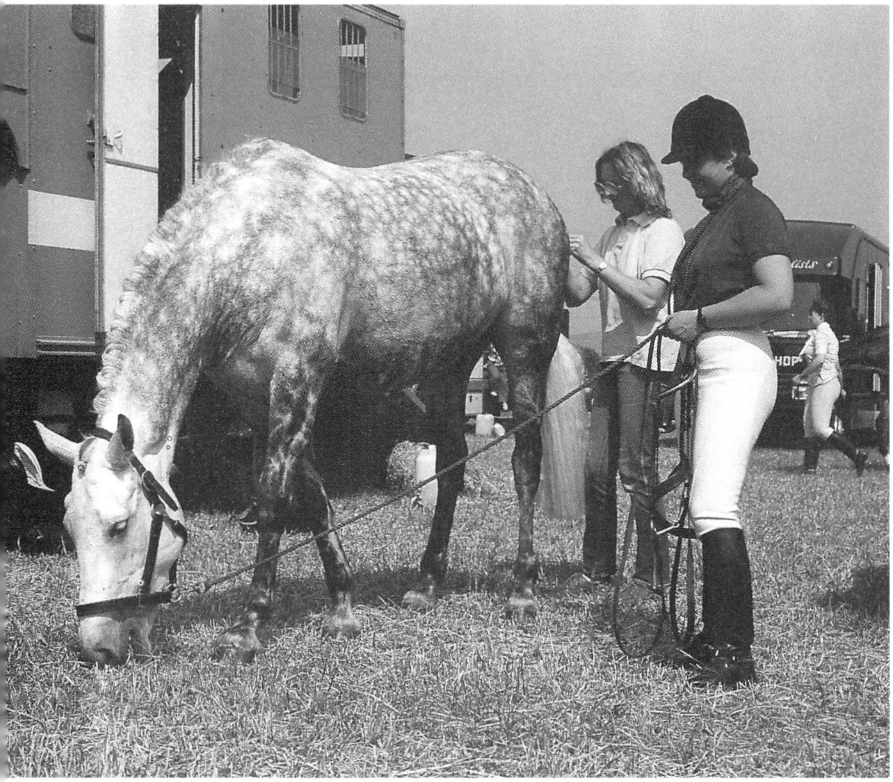

If at a show and you have no feed with you, let your horse nibble grass when convenient to keep his digestion ticking over and to make him feel more comfortable and relaxed

Feeding Short Feeds

Here you have more of a problem. If you cannot feed all forage as described above, you should understand that giving short feeds only every twelve hours (just twice a day) does not make for optimal digestive efficiency: you may therefore wish to feed in smaller amounts more often. If you cannot get to your horse at lunchtime, you may have to inveigle friends, family or co-owners to feed him when you cannot, or resign yourself to paying someone to feed him at midday if you really want to keep feeding separate short feeds. You could also investigate the possibilities of using automatic feeders, which make erratic appearances on the market.

One way of improving the digestion of short feeds is to make their volume bigger by adding plenty of chop and succulents.

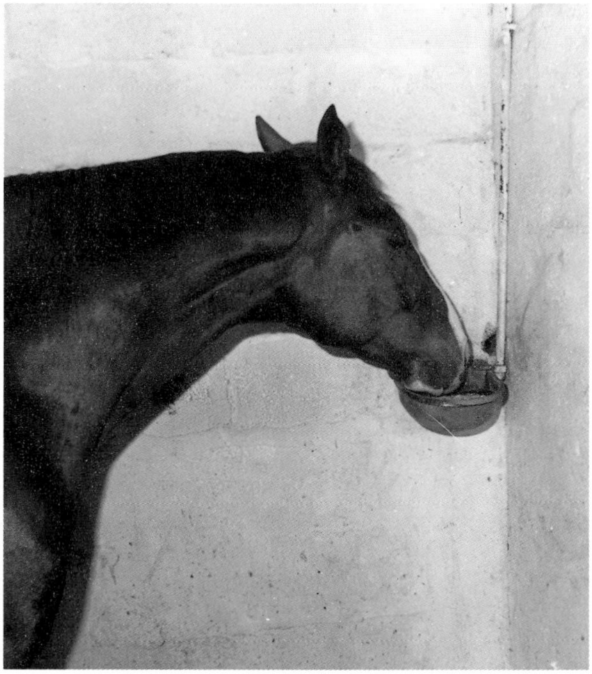

An automatic waterer is a labour-saving way to ensure your horse always has a constant supply of water, but it must be checked daily to ensure it is working and that the water is clean

2. Water Before Feeding?

This rule is less vital than it used to be in circumstances where horses have water with them all the time. Where you have to take horses to water, or vice versa, two or three times a day, it still holds good, for the reasons given earlier.

A Constant Supply

The important point is to make sure that your horse never goes short of fresh, clean water. Ignore the traditional advice to deprive horses of water for several hours before hard or fast work: this is just asking for dehydration and all its effects. Let your horse have water available until half an hour, or certainly no longer than an hour before work, and during endurance-type work let him drink at every convenient opportunity. On other occasions, such as between phases at horse trials, five or six swallows – about 4 pints (2 litres), will refresh him and make him feel better, plus allaying dehydration.

Drinking a little before, during and after feeding is *not* harmful and probably actually aids digestion: it will certainly make the horse feel happier, if this is what he wants to do.

3. Make any Changes in Diet Gradually

This is also an extremely important rule not often followed properly. Sudden changes in diet are in fact still carried out as traditional practice, and include giving a weekly bran mash, and giving different ingredients in each feed; for example, nuts for breakfast, barley for lunch and something else for tea and/or supper, according to the whim of the person doing the feeding. We may feel that, like us, the horse wants a change and doesn't want the same old thing all the time. Actually, the opposite is true: supplying the same ingredients in each feed provides the consistent diet that the horse and his digestive system need to stay healthy.

The Way to Success

Varying the *amounts* of specific ingredients is another matter. The way to success is to keep the ingredients themselves constant, but to reduce or increase their quantity according to the horse's workload, exposure to the weather and so on. For instance, if the horse is off work for any reason, cut the cereal-concentrate portion (if any) of his diet drastically to avoid the potentially serious effects of over-feeding this type of energy, but do not cut it altogether unless you cannot envisage the horse needing this type of feed in the forseeable future. Giving a few grams or ounces of cereal concentrates in each feed keeps a 'skeleton staff' of gut micro-organisms for that type of feed, ready to increase when that feed is increased. You can make up the volume of the feed with other things such as chop, low-energy coarse mix (sweet feed), succulents and so on, as long as these are already part of the regular diet.

Mashes

Feeding a mash once a week is a *really* sudden change in diet, even if bran is used in the ordinary feeds. It is simply too much at once, fed in a form the horse does not get every day, and as you will be able to see from his droppings the following morning, it really upsets his digestion; this is surely *not* what you intended. This has been discussed fully in Chapter 3.

Alternatively feed a mash made up of chop, dried grass and soaked sugar-beet pulp, for example; or if you

Bran mashes may have a place in the stable yard if a veterinary surgeon, for example, advises their administration to clear out a horse's gut for any reason, but their use as a regular part of feeding régime is not recommended as they are nutritionally imbalanced, not easy to digest and constitute a sudden change in feeding, going against one of the rules of feeding

want a feed of mainly roughage, but palatable enough for the horse to enjoy, simply soak chop with black treacle melted in hot water, adding roots if you wish. Just make sure the mash (or 'false feed' as such a feed is called) contains small amounts of ingredients the horse gets in his normal feeds.

Introducing New Feed

When introducing a genuinely new feed, start off by feeding just a few ounces or grams of it in with his ordinary feed at first and gradually, over at least three weeks and preferably four or more, increase the amount of it, probably at the expense of some other ingredient which it may be replacing.

It should also be remembered that even different batches of the same type of feed can differ significantly. Make sure your new feeds arrive before your old ones run out, so you can feed them both together for a while, gradually making the new batch take over. This goes for any feed, including hay.

4. Do Not Work Immediately after Feeding

The horse does have an 'escape mechanism' which is essential to him in the wild, when he may have to take to his heels whilst still chewing a mouthful of grass. In practice, you *can* work a horse soon after he has been eating provided you only walk for about half an hour. However, it is better to arrange your timetable so that you exercise him first and feed him later.

Bad Effects

If you do work a horse fast or hard very soon after feeding, you can certainly cause colic and respiratory difficulties because exercise calls for the blood supply to be largely diverted to the muscles, heart and lungs and away from the digestive system. This means the food will not be digested properly. Also, a full stomach may well press on the lungs which lie adjacent, separated only by the sheet of muscle called the diaphragm (which separates the chest from the abdomen) and the pressure will interfere with the working of both the lungs and the stomach.

Thus the old advice to leave a good two hours after feeding before working the horse fast or hard does still hold good.

5. Daily Succulents

Really this rule should read 'feed something succulent in every feed'; or better still, 'turn the horse out to graze for several hours every day'. Succulents might include sugar-beet pulp, a good old favourite which also counteracts the calcium deficiency in many concentrate diets and provides other minerals plus non-cereal energy. Coarsely grated carrots and apples are justifiably popular, and you can try leaving whole turnips, mangolds or fodder beets in the horse's manger for him to crunch on. Hydroponic grass is another excellent way to give this sort of natural feed. However, all succulents should, like any feed, be regular ingredients in each feed.

The Grand National winner Seagram, an excellent example of a hard, fit steeplechaser

6. Feed the Individual

Feed according to work, weather, constitution and temperament: in fact, these requirements are easier to follow today than ever before; although many horses are still fed too many concentrates, particularly cereal concentrates, or they are given too high an energy grade of feed.

Low Energy Feeds

When looking for a feed of low energy – a 'non-heating' (non-exciting) feed, or something for resting or sick horses – do not go only by the name of the feed, for example 'Calm Cubes': go by the energy content on the bag, which should not be more than 8 MJ of DE per kg. Also try to ensure that the energy is not cereal-based, but of a non-cereal source.

Clay additives claim to 'soak up' the toxins created by a high cereal-concentrate diet and which are the cause of erratic, fizzy behaviour, but feeding these is only a short-term solution. It is far better to change over gradually from cereal concentrates to non-cereal ones for horses so affected. Alternatively, of course, feed your horse on all-forage feed or branded roughage of the most suitable energy grade.

7. Feed at the Same Times Each Day

This procedure is not so crucial with an *ad lib* roughage type of diet, or if you mix your horse's concentrates with his roughage. And if you provide separate concentrate feeds with his roughage, it is not disastrous if you are half an hour late with the concentrates.

The Dangers of Hunger

The real problems occur when horses are allowed to become hungry (which they should not do on an *ad lib* roughage diet). Particularly with horses in the field, they congregate round gates expecting their people to turn up with feeds, and when they do not the horses become fractious, and skirmishes and injuries are very likely to occur.

Hunger is not natural to horses in normal circumstances. When any horse becomes hungry his digestive system becomes badly affected, for reasons discussed several times, and so it is something to be avoided in your management régime.

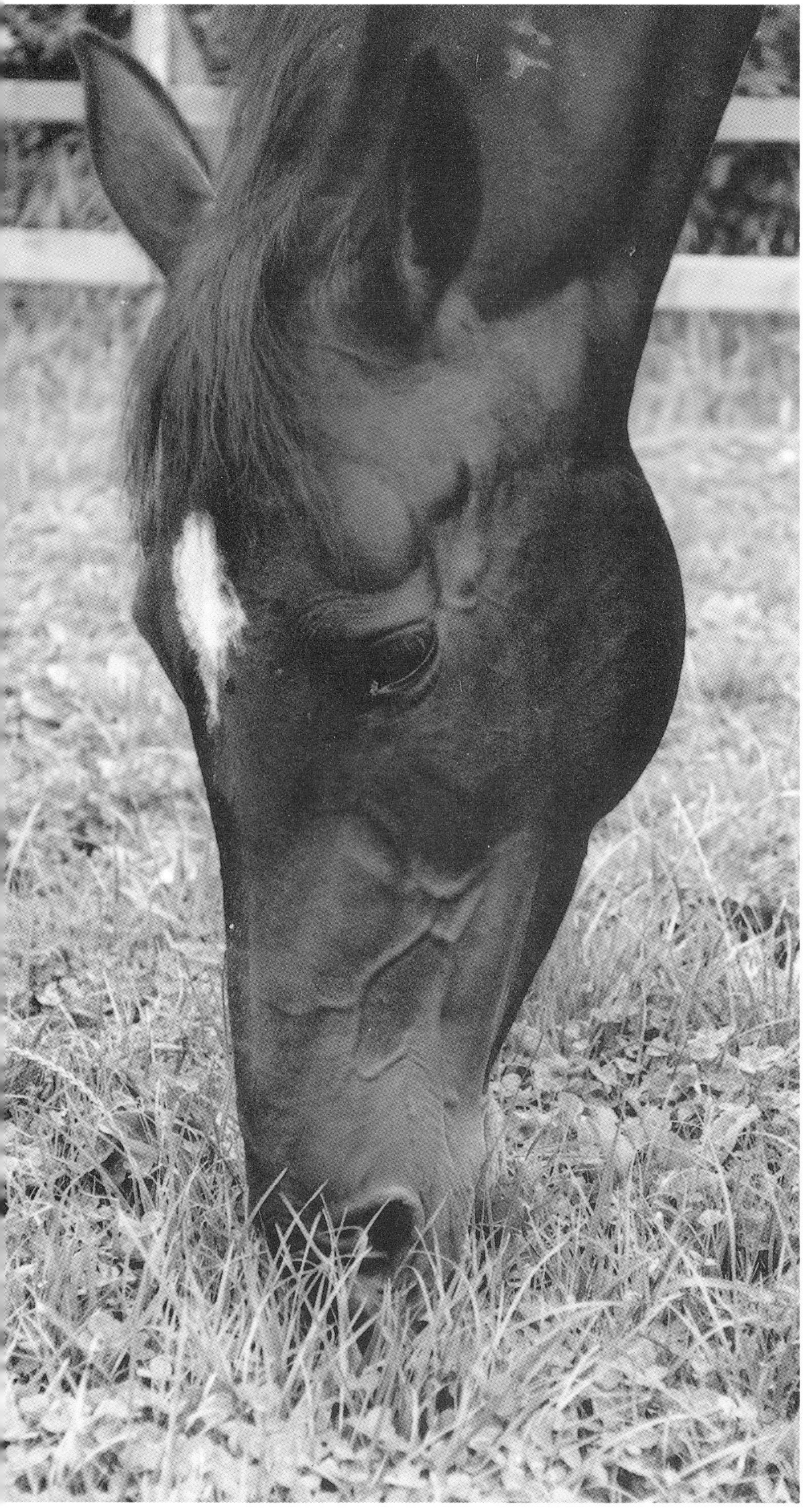

8. Use Good Quality Feed

This is common sense for an animal with as sensitive a digestive system as the horse.

Modern Feeds

These should be in excellent condition when you buy them, and you can bank on freshness by using one sack at a time of one product (bearing in mind the remarks on introducing a new batch above), rather than having several sacks open at once which can mean, particularly with coarse mixes (sweet feeds), that they go 'off' before you have finished them.

Low Quality Feedstuffs

Do not be palmed off with low quality feeds, whether it is hay, roots, concentrates or anything at all. If they are delivered in your absence, get them taken away and do not pay for anything unless you are happy with the quality. If you pay for sealed, bagged feeds and find it unacceptable when you get it home or open it, ask for it to be exchanged, or demand that your money is refunded if the supplier refuses. It is consumer law, now, that goods must be of merchantable quality, and you can actually kill a horse or pony by giving it unfit feeds – if it will eat them.

Grass and other herbage are important parts of a horse's diet and régime and every effort should be made to ensure that horses get a regular chance to graze, even if only in hand

9. Feed Plenty of Roughage

What is plenty? Basically, as much as the horse wants. If he is getting fat, feed a lower energy grade of roughage, but never poor quality. If your hay is top class and your horse is putting on too much weight, halve it and make up the volume with oat, barley or fodder straw or a low-energy grade of forage or hayage, or mix it with meadow hay if it is seed hay. Keep up the quantity and the quality, but reduce the energy.

Horses in Fast Work

These should not have their roughage reduced below one third of their total daily feed intake, and probably not even this far. The better the feed content and quality of the roughage, the fewer concentrates you need to feed, even for hard or fast work. Roughage is the foundation of the diet, not concentrates, and especially not cereal concentrates.

There is ample alternative in the form of readily-available hayage products or cleaned forage products to feed any horse plenty of roughage today, even if he is troubled by COPD (Chronic Obstructive Pulmonary Disease or broken wind).

Horses at Grass

These can have access to unlimited grazing provided it is not rich or high-nitrogen/protein grass. Sheep-type grazing is ideal, or have your land seeded with the special seed mixes now available for paddocks for athletic performance horses. Even laminitic ponies can be catered for, given poor grazing and other suitable roughage sources which provide their specific nutritional requirements (for example, alfalfa-based roughages).

Remember, spring grass is the richest in nutrients, and grass contains more sugar in the morning than later in the day, so you can arrange you horse's turnout times appropriately.

10. Weigh All Feeds

Do not measure out feeds just by the scoopful, as this can result in highly inaccurate feeding, an inappropriate diet, and bad effects on your horse and your bank account! Using the same scoop, weigh out into a proper weighing scale one scoopful of every ingredient you use so you know how much of what your scoop holds. Once you have done this you don't need to weigh every single feed. Weigh roughage in the net, or in an opened-out sack, on a spring-weigher with a hook. Even if you feed *ad lib* roughage, you should know how much your horse seems to need. Also weigh any leavings so you know the extent of any variance in appetite.

Key Facts

- **Feeding little and often copies nature's way, where the horse is eating almost constantly. A virtually *ad lib* supply of hay or its equivalent and water is the best way to achieve this in the domesticated, stabled horse.**
- ***Ad lib* water, similarly, is normally the best way to ensure your horse has an ample supply of this most essential nutrient.**
- **Making no sudden changes in feeding procedure means using the same ingredients in each feed and ignoring the old practice of feeding a weekly mash; it is also important to mix old and new batches of feed, even when these are of the same type, and to make changes from one feed to another over three or four weeks (not days) to ensure that the horse's digestive system has a proper chance to adapt.**
- **Do not underestimate the value of succulents, which should be included in each feed.**
- **As a general rule, be generous with hay, and mean with cereal-based concentrates.**
- **It is safer to feed an energy grade feed which is slightly too low than one which is too high.**

VITALITY & PERFORMANCE

10

EQUIPMENT AND PREPARATION

Knowing how much to feed your horse or pony, what to feed and when is obviously vitally important. Also important is how you store your feedstuffs and how you prepare them to give to the horse. Practical considerations such as these make a big difference to the success, or otherwise, of your feeding régime.

Storage which is too hot or damp can ruin most feeds. Feeds which contain syrups, honey or treacle (molasses) are particularly susceptible to warm storage conditions. Rain on forages stored outdoors can ruin them and bagged feeds (such as cubes kept in their paper sacks) stood on damp or wet floors can also go 'bad' very quickly.

Contamination can occur from other animals or birds urinating or defaecating on feeds, and this is an effective way to spread disease to the horse. Contamination can also occur by allowing such substances as insecticides, disinfectants and liniments to come into contact with feeds. At best, the smell will discourage animals from eating the feed: at worst they can cause illness if an animal does eat it. Dirty containers and mixing utensils can have the same effects.

Left: These galvanised bins make ideal storage for feedstuffs such as cereal grains, chop and cubes. The lids should be properly closed after use and fastened to prevent accidental access by loose animals and vermin. Use scoops of known quantity for accurate feeding and wash scoops and containers daily

Storage

Feeds of all kinds do deteriorate in feed value and general quality if improperly stored – feed supplements are particularly sensitive. Do not buy supplements, or any bagged feedstuffs, which have passed their 'use by' or even their 'sell by' date, which have been stored in sunlight or damp, or in hot or humid conditions (and don't keep them in such conditions yourself), or where the packaging has been damaged or opened. Also, don't buy more than you can use within the recommended viable period (check with the manufacturer if in doubt), and reseal the pack properly after each use to reduce the presence of air.

Shorts and Succulents

Roots

These keep best in cool, dark, airy conditions with the soil on. Rinse them just before feeding to remove soil and any other chemical residues. A plastic mesh laundry bin is suitable as storage for small yards.

Concentrates

These are best stored in galvanised bins with the lids kept down and preferably locked to prevent accidental access by horses – and others if you keep your horse away from home. If storing concentrates in sacks, keep them off the ground and *dry*. Plastic dustbins are good, although rats can chew through some types. Keep the lids firmly on, perhaps by means of a long pole poked through the lid handles and wedged into holders at each end of the line of bins, like a sliprail.

Coarse mixes (sweet feeds)

These, and any product containing molasses (including sugar beet) or syrup of any kind, keep best in cool conditions. In summer, unless you have a natural stone-built feed room, you could buy an old, tall fridge, remove the shelves and keep a sack or two in that. You should buy no more at a time than you can use within a few days, and again, it is best to open one sack at a time.

Hay

Hay can present practical storage difficulties. It should also be kept in well ventilated, dry conditions: old-fashioned hay lofts kept hay truly dry (provided the roof was in good condition!), but too often today we see hay stored in open barns with simply a roof and no sides, which does nothing to protect the side bales from driving rain and can result in considerable wastage.

Use your imagination in creating dry storage conditions, and if buying new hay, pay particular attention to ventilation to prevent it becoming mow-burnt. Even older hay (and don't be persuaded to buy 'good' two-year-old hay because its feeding value will have dropped greatly by that age) needs reasonable ventilation, dryness and preferably off-ground storage. Pallets or planks on bricks (provided a cat or terrier can get underneath to sort out vermin) are helpful here.

One often sees hay and straw stored round the sides of indoor schools or outdoor manèges. This is very poor management because the rising dust from the flooring will penetrate the exposed bales and contaminate them to the detriment of the health of any horse eating such forage. Hay and straw should be stored downwind of stables, particularly where there are any horses susceptible to respiratory problems, otherwise the spores from it can be blown into the stables, affecting the horses.

Hayage

This should be delivered in undamaged sacks – if they are damaged at all, do not accept them. Open one sack or bale at a time to prevent waste and deterioration; they can often be stored outdoors where they won't be damaged by rodents.

In the Stable

Here, you can actually manage without any fixtures at all, although you may find **haynets**, **hayracks** (the corner type are safest) and **automatic waterers** (again in a corner) handy. Many top studs do feed hay on the ground, as they claim – and it is undeniably true – that in the first place it is more natural for horses to feed this way, and second, there is nothing for foals to get caught up or injured on. However, it can be a rather wasteful method unless your horse is a tidy, quiet feeder.

Mangers should be the corner type, fixed so that the top is at the height of the horse's elbow; alternatively they can be fitted into holders on the ground if you wish to feed *au naturel*. Not all horses actually find it comfortable to eat this way, however, so watch yours carefully to see how he feels about it.

Haynets need very strongly fixed rings or brackets so the nets can be tied at horse's head height; then when they are empty they will not sag so low that the horse is likely to risk getting a hoof caught in them. **Hayracks** should be fixed at the same height; if they are too high, bits fall down into horses' eyes and ears.

Large **corner units** are available, with a roughage holder at the top and a manger below; this also catches any bits of roughage which fall down and which the horses then eat. These units are a good idea as long as they are smooth and firmly fixed.

Water buckets or **bins** are most practicably held in special holders fixed to the wall in a corner. Many horses like knocking their buckets over so they should be fixed somehow. Standing the bucket in an old car tyre is also a good idea, and one quite commonly used.

If you wish to feed out of a **free container** rather than a manger, whether your horse is stabled, yarded or out, you can use a large washing-up bowl; a wide, shallow cattle-feed bucket (more convenient for and attractive to the horse than the taller, narrower conventional plastic stable bucket which is only really suitable for water); or a travelling manger which will hook over the stable door or the top rail of a wooden fence.

Equipment

Storage buildings and bins are obvious necessities; you will also need a scoop of known capacity, a kitchen-type weighing scale for concentrates and similar, and a spring-weigher for roughage. Ideally you would have hot and cold running water in your feed room too, or maybe a wall-mounted instant water heater if you have no hot running water, and of course a sink. The following list of items makes for a well equipped feed room: a wooden spoon which is excellent for mixing; washing-up gear for washing portable buckets and mangers; and a scourer, a dishcloth and a kitchen towel for cleaning and drying fixed ones. If you really do want to mix cooked or hot feeds, a kettle and maybe a camping ring will be needed, unless you are going to do these at home; in any case, kettles are useful for coffee breaks! Finally, a very important item is a decent broom so you can quickly sweep up any spills which could attract vermin.

Feed rooms should be kept clean and tidy, partly to avoid waste and partly for reasons of hygiene. Spilled feed soon attracts vermin which contaminate feed with urine and droppings, carry disease and eat feeds. Metal feed containers are best as rodents can chew through even tough plastic. Containers, feed bowls, buckets and scoops should all be kept clean to avoid the build-up of old feed, particularly if moist or syrupy, which soon harbours disease

Field or travelling mangers, which can be hooked over a rail, are a convenient way to feed outdoor horses. Behavioural studies indicate that they should be spaced at least 16ft (about 4.8m) apart to help prevent horses from harrassing others and stealing their food. This post and rail fencing should have its top rail flush with the tops of the posts for safety, and the type of square mesh fencing used to fill in the lower half is dangerous as horses and ponies can easily get a hoof caught in it. Ideally, the gate, too, should have its bottom half filled in with a strong mesh grille. It is always safer not to leave headcollars on outdoor horses if at all possible

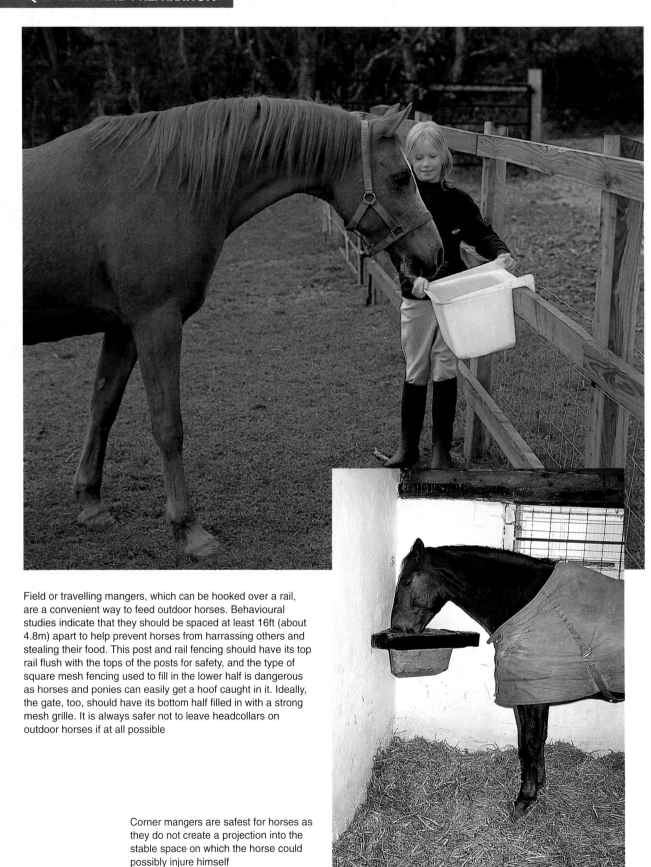

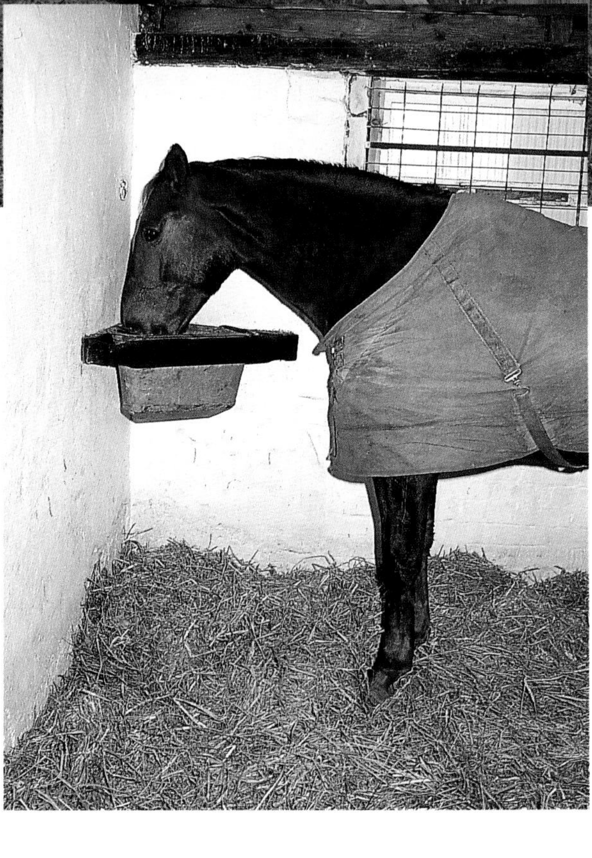

Corner mangers are safest for horses as they do not create a projection into the stable space on which the horse could possibly injure himself

This is a commonly-used type of large hay holder for groups of horses. However, the round sort is safer and there should be no places where the horses could catch their feet, as there are here

Haynets are a tidy, economical way of feeding hay but this one is too low: it should be tied up at the height of the horse's head and so that, when empty, it does not hang lower than his elbow, to make less likely the chance that he may get a hoof caught, particularly when rolling

This picture shows a good type of corner hay rack

This is a combined hay holder and short-feed manger. Bits of hay falling down are caught in the manger and likely to be eaten by the horse rather than trampled in the bedding and wasted

There are also on the market various proprietary feed containers which are usually of a semi-rigid material such as polypropylene; they have built-in carrying handles at the sides, and are wide and shallow enough to suit the horse, yet big enough to make it less likely that he will tip the container over or scoop his feed out.

Yarded or Outdoor Horses

Horses managed in this way can have their concentrates in the type of containers mentioned above, and their hay or other roughage tied in haynets and put either in their field shelter, or attached to fence posts in the field (provided these are high enough) or to convenient tree branches (provided the net can rest against the trunk for the horse to get some purchase on it so as to get the hay out easily).

Long, head-height hayracks running along the walls inside a field shelter are a good method of communally feeding roughage to outdoor horses, and there are also available large portable hay holders-cum-mangers, with a hay area above and a manger part running round the middle which will catch any hay that falls out, and into which concentrates can also be put. These can be moved around a field to prevent excessive poaching, and are excellent provided there are no sharp corners or places in which a horse could get a hoof stuck, or on which he could bang his head easily.

Foal Creeps

A foal creep is simply a fenced-off feeding area which foals can enter but mares cannot. Creeps ensure that foals get enough of their special rations once they start eating 'hard' feed (concentrates), and prevent their dams stealing it or keeping them away from it. The simplest are just a series of posts with a single rail which the foal can walk under. Obviously, the creep has to be big enough to allow the feed container to be sited far enough away from the rail so the mare cannot crane her neck over and reach the food.

This is a selection of feed containers. There are many types on the market: the safest is the type made of semi-rigid material without the usual metal handles. Feed containers must be cleaned out daily – ideally after each feed – and should not be left in the box or field after the horses have finished

Cleaning Equipment and Utensils

Really it goes without saying that containers and mixing utensils with old, caked-on feed stuck to them harbour disease and taint new food, which can easily put horses off eating. Thus feed equipment should be thoroughly cleaned each day. If soap is used to remove oils, rinse very thoroughly. Water containers should be scrubbed out at the same time as mangers to prevent the accumulation of slime, and it is much better to empty and refill them when needed, rather than to keep topping up the water which may be thoroughly stale and flat and already have old saliva, bits of dirt and other debris in it. Auto-waterers with drain plugs are easier to clean than the ordinary sort. Field troughs should be checked daily for debris falling into them, such as leaves and dead birds; they also need emptying periodically – say, once a quarter – and scrubbing out before swilling out and refilling. It is not necessarily true that fish in a trough mean that the water is clean enough to drink, and in any case their presence will put some horses off drinking! Nor should long mangers in field shelters be overlooked, either, but regularly cleaned.

Disinfection

There are several brands of suitable disinfectants these days specially made for cleaning horses' equipment and that will not leave a lingering offensive smell, putting the horse off eating. Otherwise, baby-equipment sterilising fluids are suitable; they should be used in cases of disease, or if a horse has done droppings in a container. A monthly session with suitable disinfectant for all feeding equipment would not go amiss.

Cooking Food

Some practices can be detrimental to the nutrient content of the feed, and one of these is cooking food, which can destroy many heat-sensitive nutrients and, therefore, significantly reduce the value of the feed. The practice of cooking feed was originally to make it more digestible, but with today's pre-cooked and processed feeds, this is not necessary. If you do provide cooked feeds, remember that the vitamin content will probably be damaged by the high temperature so you may wish to add a supplement to restore it: if so, wait until the feed is cool enough to eat before adding it, otherwise the vitamins in the supplement itself will also be damaged.

Feeding Supplements

When feeding a supplement in any feed, half fill the container, then add the supplement and finally the rest of the feed, and mix thoroughly; this ensures that it is evenly mixed, and that a powdered supplement does not blow away.

Adding Medicines

Sometimes it is necessary to give horses 'doctored' feeds containing medicines of various sorts, even if only worming pellets, and you may quickly discover how sensitive are a horse's senses of smell and taste. Many will curl up their top lip and simply refuse to eat at all. The usual remedy to this is to add plenty of molasses or something else the horse likes; this generally does the trick.

Another tip is to mix the medicine, if practicable, with toothpaste of a strong minty flavour, and to spread the mixture on a piece of bread, which the horse will very likely accept. You might also try putting the mixture into an old, cleaned-out wormer syringe, and squirting it on the back of his tongue in the usual way.

Avoid Contaminating Feedstuffs

Wash your hands before handling the feedstuff itself as any unpleasant smells on your hands such as droppings, liniment, or your own cheese and onion sandwiches will be transferred to the feed, and some horses would then refuse to eat.

Preparing Feeds

For many owners, preparing their horses' feed is one of the most enjoyable tasks of horse management, and they take great pleasure in watching the horse tuck into a carefully prepared feed after the anticipation of what's coming. Besides, thoughtful preparation *is* important for good digestion.

A commercial hay soaker/drainer from Gregory Enterprises. This photograph shows two full bales of hay soaking. The tank is tipped to remove the water and let the hay drain, and it is finally tipped out ready for feeding

Hay can be effectively soaked in a clean plastic dustbin, half an hour maximum being the currently recommended soaking time (although five minutes is probably enough). It is vital to change the water regularly, preferably after each soaking, as nutrients leach out of the hay and will ferment if left. The nutrient-rich water can be used for watering plants! Let the hay drip for a good half hour before feeding, but do not let it dry out as any spores will then shrink back to a size enabling them to be inhaled into the small airways, making the soaking a waste of time and reducing the feeding value of the hay

Take the time to watch your horse eat and drink so you can spot any abnormalities: is he happy with his feed container, or is it rattling and putting him off? Is it too deep, or in an unfavoured corner, or too high for him or too low? Feeding from the ground in a stable can cause problems as horses can catch their feet in the containers, and dirt can easily get into them.

Food prepared in advance can be mixed, but should not be damped or cooked as this could well turn it sour and cause those ever-looming digestive problems. If premixed feeds are left overnight, cover them with a heavy object such as a plank the width of the container, so that rats and mice cannot help themselves and contaminate the feed with their droppings and urine.

Soaking Hay

Current thinking is that hay should not be soaked for more than four hours, as this results in too many nutrients being leached out. Some experts recommend that one hour is sufficient to swell fungal spores to such a size that they cannot be breathed down into the tiny air spaces where they cause trouble. Do not let the hay dry out, however, as the spores will shrink again.

Change the water used for soaking hay *very* frequently – ideally after each soaking – to avoid contamination of subsequent loads. Because of its nutrient content, it is good for watering the garden, if fresh.

Feeding Horses in Company and Alone

Many horses can be put off feeding by a higher-ranking animal in the same group. Stabled horses, even when they cannot see each other, can suffer in this way if stabled next to an enemy or a dominant individual, and horses living out can be chivvied away from their rations.

Sensible and Sensitive Management

Give stabled horses amenable neighbours; and when giving outdoor or yarded horses their concentrates, stay to ensure fair play. Horses seem to prefer a personal space of about 16ft (4.8m) around them when eating man-provided food, and this is important when putting out hay. Have at least one more pile than there are horses, but spacing is perhaps even more important.

Horses fed in field shelters should be watched to see each is eating peacefully. If not, the underdogs should be fed separately; you may even have to bring them in for the purpose. Quite often, simply leading the bully away and feeding him at some distance while you hold him on a halter or a headcollar and lead-rope does the trick. Don't let him go, however, until the others have finished their concentrates in peace. If he also chases others off their hay, simply put various supplies in different places around the field, ideally where horses choose to rest or shelter.

Remove the bully

Although there is a natural herd hierarchy, in domestic situations where a real bully (often not the actual herd leader) is causing continuous problems, it is best if he or she is removed from the herd entirely and accommodated elsewhere. Stress, fear and harassment can certainly cause digestive problems, as in humans and other species, and it is good management to prevent them by keeping only compatible animals together.

The Effects of Stress

Any disruption or stress of this nature will upset the digestive micro-organisms and the general functioning of the digestive system. What food is taken in may be poorly digested, which can result in gases and excess toxins being formed, micro-organisms dying and rotting, energy-giving and other nutrients not being properly absorbed, and toxins and other products of metabolism not being efficiently excreted. All this can result in significant illness.

Feeding during Journeys and 'Away Days'

Days out are often times when a horse's normal feeding routine is seriously disrupted. Apart from the excitement of the trip, which is enough on its own to put some nervous animals off eating, the timing is disrupted, the travelling is physically and mentally stressful, and the horse's schedule on arrival may prevent normal feeds. Unfortunately, however, the attitude of some owners to this is simply: 'This is what I keep the horse for – he'll have to put up with it!' Then they wonder why their horse breaks out or goes down with colic some time after they have arrived home, or even at the venue if they are staying overnight.

Avoiding Trouble

The way to avoid all this is to try to arrange your schedule as nearly as possible according to the horse's normal one, and to feed the same kinds of feeds at, as nearly as possible, the usual times. Even doing something as simple as taking a couple of polythene bags full of feed in your jacket pockets to give the horse a nibble out hunting or on a long hack can keep the bugs – and therefore the horse – feeling fed and comfortable.

On journeys in transport, take your home supplies of roughage, concentrates and maybe water, too. Out hacking or hunting, do let the horse graze when convenient: this is, I know, a contentious point with some people, but the fact is that it is a serious disadvantage to your horse to go without food for many hours, as you will by now appreciate if you have read this far. It is also bad management and unkind to the horse. You can use your common sense as to when a convenient time arises, but whatever the situation, take every suitable opportunity to keep a little food going through your horse and you will go a long way towards avoiding problems later.

During transit in a horsebox or trailer, horses can have a haynet to nibble at, and can be fed at intervals from travelling mangers, or unloaded and allowed to graze, stretch their legs and stale. If you are going to work the horse actively at, say, 11am, take his haynet away at 9am to be on the safe side, but allow him to eat normally once he has cooled down after work.

I feel it is not a good arrangement to carry hay in open cages on the outside of a horsebox where it is exposed to pollution from vehicle fumes, but it may well be better to do this than to not take enough due to lack of space inside.

Feeding After Work

During work, the circulatory system is mainly concerned with providing adequate blood to the muscles and other parts being asked to perform. Waste products also need removing in the blood. One of the reasons for not feeding too soon *before* work is to make sure adequate blood is available to carry the digested nutrients round the body or to storage depots, as appropriate. Once work starts, blood is diverted to help fuel it, so incomplete digestion may result, as explained earlier.

Time to Recover

Once the work or exercise finishes, it still takes a while for the circulatory system to help the body recover. It continues for a few hours to work as a priority to help restore energy, protein and other nutrients to the body, to refill energy stores and replace tissues used up during work and, of course, to carry away waste products which continue to form.

If the horse is given a large feed very soon after work, the job of recovery and that of digesting the food may both suffer, the latter probably most of the two. It is wise to give the horse small rations of easily digested food for several hours after hard work. (For watering after hard work, see Chapter 8.) Furthermore, for many years the accepted practice and advice, unfortunately still followed by some, was to give the horse a supposedly easily digested mash (which we now know is *not* , in fact, easily digested) before giving him a more or less normal feed later that evening.

The Best Course of Action

A mash is not the kind of food that will help the horse recover, however, or get his digestion going again. The best course of action is to give him some hay or his normal roughage as soon as he is cool and dry, and his temperature, pulse and respiration are more or less back to normal. After another hour or so, give him half a normal feed or even a little less, which will help restore his energy without overtaxing his digestion. At the next feed time he should be able to tackle a normal feed without problem provided he has not been over-tired, which he should not be if he is fit enough for the work you are asking.

If he is resting next day, go easy on the cereal concentrates. It may be better to use mainly non-cereal concentrates and high quality fibre as sources of energy.

Right: Ponies as well as horses need correct feeding for fitness work to ensure that they are fed for energy without getting too fat. This pony is a good example and is doing hill work as part of his fitness programme

Key Facts

- Most feeds keep best in cool, dry, well aired but fairly dark conditions. Sometimes air must be excluded, such as in vacuum-packed forages or feed supplements. Hay and straw, however, need good ventilation. Never buy dated products which have passed their sell-by date, and always reseal supplement packaging as best you can after each use.

- Consider getting a large, old refrigerator for the feed room in which to keep heat-sensitive feeds such as coarse mixes, supplements, molasses and so on.

- Buying in large quantities is *not* necessarily economical: certain types of feed deteriorate easily if you cannot use them within a short time.

- All stable fittings should be smooth and safe. Corner mangers, racks and waterers are best. Haynets should be avoided for youngstock, and all fittings should be securely fixed to avoid accidents.

- Weigh your feeds to make sure you are feeding the correct amount.

- Keep things clean without using strong soaps or disinfectants. A hot water supply is a real boon: wall-fixed heaters for instant hot water are not expensive.

- If using cooked feeds, add any vitamin supplements *after* they have cooled to eating temperature, as excessive heat will kill many vitamins.

- Wash your hands before mixing feeds so as not to transfer unpleasant smells to the feed. This can easily put off fastidious feeders.

- Take time occasionally to watch your horse eating and drinking, alone and in company, to make sure he is at ease and getting his full rations.

- Do not soak hay for more than an hour: this is probably sufficient, provided it is properly immersed, to ensure that any fungal spores swell to a large enough size to prevent their being inhaled down into the tiny air passages where they cause trouble. Do not let soaked hay dry out too much before feeding as the spores will shrink again. Change the soaking water after each use.

- Give horses congenial neighbours in stable and field to ensure contentment and good digestion.

- Stay to ensure fair play when feeding horses loose in paddocks. Remove bully horses or hold them on a lead-rope to feed well away from others.

- Do not make your horse go without food on days away from home as this seriously upsets the digestion. Try to keep a little food going through him most of the time: let him graze, or carry a few nuts in your pockets, and of course take proper feeds in your transport vehicle.

- Do not give mashes on return from hard work as these do not encourage either good digestion or restoration of energy. Once the horse has cooled down, give hay or its equivalent, later followed by a half-sized feed of the ingredients he normally receives.

PART II

FEEDING PROBLEMS

Azoturia

Hard-working horses may show symptoms of azoturia if given strenuous work after a time of rest on full, high-energy diets. However, there are other causes of the disease, which is under active investigation by scientific research establishments

Q *I have recently bought a horse at a bargain price because he is prone to azoturia and cannot seem to take the sort of diet his previous owner felt he needed in order to do hard work. His diet seems very high in concentrates, even though the horse is admittedly a poor doer. I have gradually reduced the concentrate level to half whilst allowing him as much hay as he wants, turning him out every day and riding about four days a week on enjoyable but not very taxing hacks. So far the horse is fine but as the weather improves I want to get him fitter for harder work in the summer and am worried about his diet as I obviously do not want the azoturia to recur. How should I manage and feed him?*

A As you may know, azoturia – also called equine rhabdomyolysis, paralytic myoglobinuria, tying-up and set-fast, which are all varying forms of the same basic condition – usually occurs within fifteen minutes or so of exercise when horses have been kept in on a full ration of concentrates, usually cereal-based carbohydrates such as oats, barley, maize/corn or high-energy nuts or coarse mixes/sweet feeds. Spring grass can also cause problems because of its sugar content.

The reasons for azoturia

Energy is stored in muscle tissue as glycogen, which is present in excess amounts in such a diet, because the horse is being provided with more energy than he is using. When he is suddenly put to work, particularly without slow, thorough warming up, excess lactic acid (a waste product of metabolism) and other substances are also produced which damage the muscle tissue. A poisonous pigment called myoglobin is released into the bloodstream and is carried to the kidneys which filter it out and excrete it (along with other toxins) in the urine; this accounts for the characteristic amber to chocolate-coloured urine seen in azoturia.

Other causes

It is felt that other causes of the condition include imbalance of body fluids and electrolytes; possible deficiency or absorption of calcium; stress which upsets the body biochemistry; transportation which, particularly with an inconsiderate driver, involves almost constant use of the muscles simply for the horse to stay upright and balanced (not to mention mental stress); possible deficiency or inadequate absorption of vitamin E and selenium; changes in diet, weather or routine; hormonal disturbance; cold weather; inadequate blood supply to the muscles; and hereditary factors. Quite a lot to think about!

The effects of azoturia

A horse with azoturia will usually go uncertainly, and then start to stagger as his hindquarters appear to seize up. He may even fall down. The muscles of the back, loins and quarters (large muscle-mass areas) will feel hard, swollen and painful, and he may show signs of colic, pain and anxiety. He will probably have increased pulse and respiration rates and be sweating, and his urine, if he can pass any due to possible blockage of the kidneys with pigment and dead muscle tissue, will probably be discoloured.

How to deal with azoturia

Briefly, to deal with this situation you should not force the horse to continue walking, as this will cause even more muscle damage. Throw a rug or your jacket over his quarters and get the vet immediately. It may be necessary to get a low-loading trailer to get him home. Put him in a well bedded loosebox with water and an electrolyte drink available, but no food. Keep him warm and stay with him to reassure him till the vet arrives.

How to prevent azoturia

The vet will be able to give you advice on future management should the need arise. It is true that once a horse has had an attack of azoturia he may be prone to further attacks unless his management is corrected. Basically, make sure you follow the old adage always to **reduce the feed before the work** and **increase the work**

before the feed. Also, **do not let your horse stand in the stable for very long periods**. Even on days when you ride him, try to turn him out as well on poorish grazing: obviously, never leave him standing in on his day off. In cold weather put on a turn-out rug, and exercise in an exercise-sheet or rain-sheet.

Always warm your horse up very gently and thoroughly before asking him for taxing or fast work. This gives the muscle glycogen levels time to fall a little so the injurious amounts of lactic acid and other substances will not be produced. At least thirty minutes of walking and gentle trotting are needed before you even think of doing anything faster. If your horse shows even the slightest sign of stiffness during work, do *not* 'work him through it' as is commonly advised, because this can certainly make matters worse. Dismount and proceed as advised earlier, particularly if the case seems at all pronounced.

Probably the most important aspect of management is to moderate his diet. You have cut his concentrates by half, but presumably are still feeding cereal-based carbohydrates which seem to have caused the problem previously. To improve matters a step further, gradually change from cereal-based concentrates to energy sources based on roughage (hay/hayage/forage feeds) and soaked sugar-beet pulp, chop (molassed or not), fodder beet if you can get it, roots and grass, maybe grown hydroponically. Low-energy cubes and coarse mixes (sweet feeds) can also be used.

For the work your horse is doing at present, feed him a total daily ration of 2.5 per cent of his bodyweight and containing 8.5 MJ of DE per kilogram. When in the harder work you intend, you can feed probably the same amount but you could add oil (corn, soya, fish or animal-grade linseed oil) for increased energy, or use higher-energy roughages, so that his diet contains 10 MJ of DE per kilogram, and see how he is on that. This diet should be quite adequate for him.

Laminitis

Q *My pony had a mild attack of laminitis last spring and the vet said we were very lucky it was not worse, as he and my sister's pony were turned out with the cows on my father's farm. Why did my pony, an Exmoor cross, get laminitis and not my sister's? Also, how can I prevent him getting it this spring?*

A The sort of grazing dairy cattle need is the worst possible sort for ponies and cobs, and horses who are good doers. It is far too 'rich' and high in sugars for ponies, especially native types. Perhaps your sister's pony has some Arab or Thoroughbred blood in him, but even so, he was lucky not to go down with laminitis too.

How to deal with laminitis

Ask your father if there is some poorer grazing you can use for your ponies, such as the sort used for sheep. Alternatively, only turn your ponies out on to land which has been well grazed by cattle, so there is not very much grass left on it, and restrict their time out on it. Try to organise yarded accommodation for them, or stable them for several hours a day to cut down their grass intake, and try to give them as much gentle exercise a day as you can with cantering and other work, too, when they are fit enough. Never feed them rich hay, oats, or any cereals (barley, maize) at all, and certainly never give them feeds meant for other species such as calf nuts, as these are not balanced for ponies and can cause laminitis and other problems.

Keep your ponies' weight down so that you cannot see their ribs but can easily feel them. This does not mean starving them, which was the advice given in the past, but feeding them low-energy feeds (lower than 8 MJ of DE per kg) with properly balanced vitamins and minerals. Forage feeds based on alfalfa (lucerne) are excellent for ponies, fed in the amounts recommended by the makers.

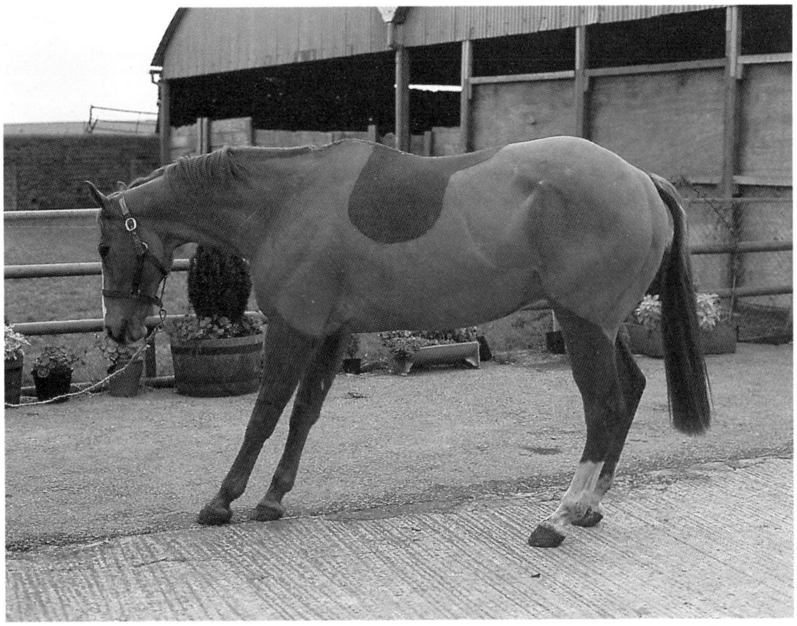

Laminitis is extremely painful and stressful for the animal affected. Immediate veterinary attention is essential if the animal is to be restored to health as the effects of this disease frequently mean the animal has to be destroyed

Allergic Reaction

Q *My horse is three quarters Thoroughbred, one quarter Welsh Cob. He is generally well behaved but is a bit sluggish so I give him oats to pep him up a bit. Unfortunately, even on a small ration of oats he becomes very silly and his skin becomes spotty and itchy and his coat dull. What can I feed him to avoid these problems, but to give him energy as well? He is not a good doer and is a bit on the lean side at present.*

A Many more animals than it is realised seem to have almost an allergic reaction to oats, showing the signs you mention. For these, bruised barley makes an excellent substitute for oats, providing energy without the troublesome side effects. You can feed a quarter less barley, by weight, than oats as it is a more energy-dense feed which 'weighs heavy'. You can also try feeding him a brand-name feed such as cubes (pellets) or coarse mix (sweet feed) with a stated energy level of 10 MJ of DE per kilogram.

The importance of diet

Make sure he is getting plenty of roughage and water: his digestion will not be fully effective if he is short of either. Also, get your vet or a nutritionist to check the entire balance of his diet for vitamins and minerals as these, too, affect how efficient his digestion is. For his hay, try giving him top class seed or mixture hay till he seems better, then gradually switch to good meadow-type hay to maintain his condition.

If you wish to try maize, do not use it as the main cereal in his diet but so that it forms only a quarter of the cereal ration as it is not well balanced as regards protein, vitamins and minerals. It is good for putting on weight, however, and providing energy.

Filled Legs

Q *My horse constantly gets filled legs when stabled, despite having a good two hours exercise a day. I have to bandage his legs all the time to keep them down. They go down after exercise, but in a few hours are up again. I cannot turn the horse out in winter, but I do so for the rest of the year, when the problem disappears.*

A You are describing a classic case of 'ordinary' filled legs, very common in stabled animals on restricted exercise and, often, too many concentrates. It has to be remembered that the hind legs, which are those which usually cause the problem, are the extremities at the furthest distance from the heart: this problem is quite simply caused by insufficient exercise. Although you give your horse two hours a day, this is not very much from his point of view. Horses and ponies are animals meant to be free to wander and exercise gently and constantly.

How to deal with filled legs

If you can give your horse two exercise periods a day – say, two separate hours or longer, rather than one stint of two hours – this would be preferable, but basically the horse would be better on the combined system at a yard offering year-round turn-out facilities.

You may also find some improvement if you change the concentrates in his diet to non-cereal ones, letting him get his energy from roughage/fibre and other sources rather than from cereal grains.

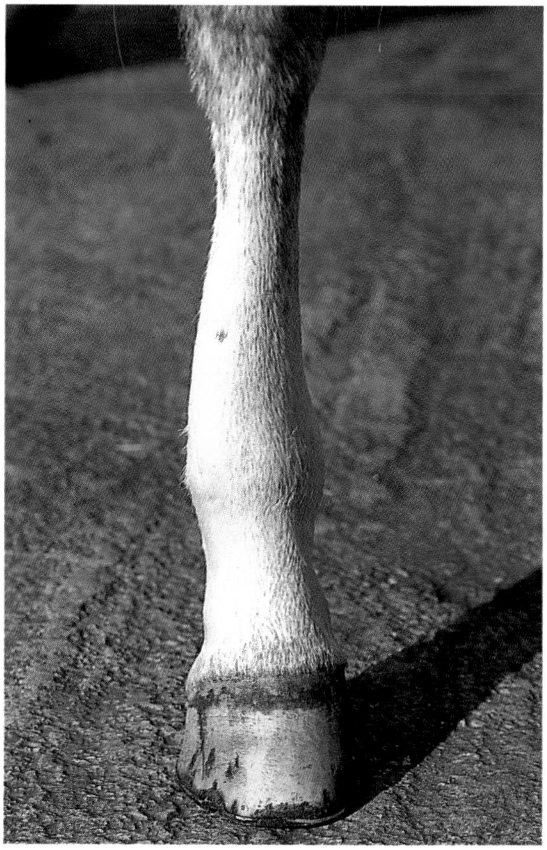

Some horses develop swollen, so-called 'filled' legs after standing in the stable for only a very few hours. This is caused primarily by insufficient exercise for the animal concerned. Such horses and ponies are better kept yarded, or out on poor keep if necessary, than stabled

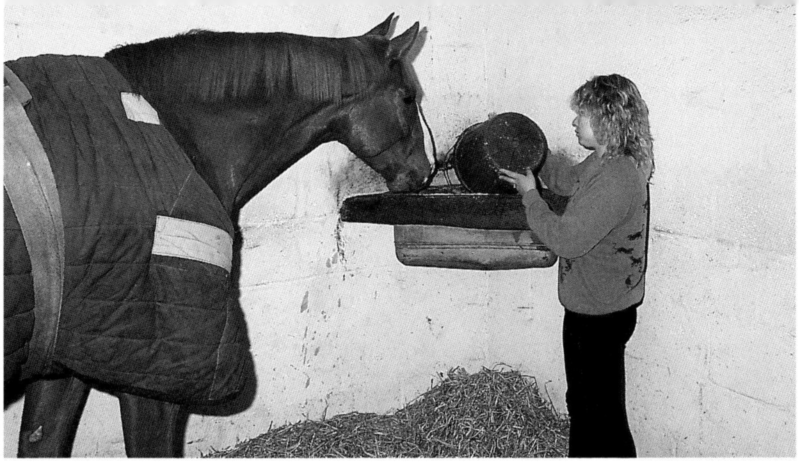

Suddenly changing a horse's diet can easily cause colic due to disruption of the digestive system. Even if the horse appears enthusiastic about the new feed, do introduce it very gradually, taking several weeks, if necessary, to change over

Introducing New Feed

Q *My horse has had colic twice in the six months I have owned him – his previous owner did tell me he was prone to it – and I am anxious to prevent it. The first time was a few days after he arrived, and the second when I brought him in after a summer out at grass, although I mashed him well for the first week like all the books recommended. Can you suggest anything to stop it happening again?*

A It sounds as if, on both occasions, your horse's colic was caused by a sudden change in his diet. There are different types of colic, of course, and 'colic' simply means tummy-ache and is not necessarily digestive in origin.

Causes of colic

In your horse's case, it seems he is particularly susceptible to changes in his diet. The equine digestive system works largely by means of enzymes and micro-organisms in his intestines and the latter, in particular, need plenty of time to build up populations of the right sort of 'bugs' to cope with new feeds coming along. Any sudden change can seriously upset them: they weaken and may die, which means any food which does arrive is not properly digested and colic can easily be the result.

How to prevent colic

Follow the old rule of making no sudden changes in feeding: it can take four weeks or even more for some horses to adjust their digestive systems to new feeds or management routines. Try giving your horse a course of probiotics now, and perhaps during any changes in his régime to help him adjust. Always mix old batches of feed with new ones – never finish all your supplies and then start straight on with the new. Remember that grass is a feed, too, and sudden changes from grass to 'stable' feeds can be just as disastrous.

Although many people do still recommend mashing horses when they come up from grass, ostensibly to help them adjust from grass to other feeds, mashes are not at all good for their digestive systems and can make matters worse. The best way is to start feeding your horse small amounts of hay and, if used, concentrates while he is still out at grass to accustom his system to them.

When you do bring him in (after a couple of weeks of this treatment), try to make the change gradual so his grazing time is reduced over two weeks or more, and graze him in hand as long as possible if you cannot turn him out at all.

Too Many Oats

Q *My horse is so badly behaved that I am becoming afraid of riding him. He is well schooled and I am not a bad rider, but my instructor seems unable to help us. He does not seem naughty but just over-fresh all the time. He is mainly stabled and is fed oats, chop and roots, plus hay. He is 16 hands high and currently receiving about 8lb (3.6kg) of oats a day. He is ridden for between one and two hours three days a week, with two or three hours a day at weekends. He works quite hard but I find I am beginning to look for excuses not to take him out! Please help!*

A Cut his oats down immediately to half his current ration, and gradually cut them out, over two or three weeks, altogether. Let him have as much hay as he wants, and aim to feed him only that plus chop, sugar beet and roots.

Turn him out as much as possible, and ride him as much as you can: try to get friends to ride him when you cannot.

The new diet alone will make a big change in his behaviour. He will not feel half so giddy or inclined to play you up, and the extra freedom and exercise will make things even better.

Cereal-based concentrates in general are vastly overrated, and most animals do not need anything like the amounts conventionally recommended. Once your horse's behaviour has stabilised, as it almost certainly will on the lower-energy diet, you can try, if you really wish to reintroduce cereal-based concentrates, feeding him on bruised barley (in smaller amounts than oats) or a low-energy cube (pellet) or coarse mix/sweet feed.

Proprietary Feeds

Q I recently changed my horse's diet to a proprietary feed advertised as being specially formulated for excitable horses, being 'non-heating', having had him previously on ordinary horse and pony cubes from a local feed mill. The new feed is not making any difference, and he has been having it for several weeks now. I feel he has to have some concentrates as I ride him quite regularly, but he is no fun to ride when he is spooking all over the place at nothing. If so-called 'cool' feeds don't work, what will?

A Have a look at the actual energy content of your new feed: this is what will affect his behaviour. Unfortunately, so-called 'cool mixes' or 'cool cubes' are sometimes called that because they have non-cereal concentrates in them but are still fairly high in energy. For horses in moderate work, such as active hacking with some cantering and schooling plus a little jumping, 9 or 10 megajoules (MJ) of digestible energy (DE) per kilogram of feed is quite enough; yet some of the types of feed you mention have as much as 12 MJ of DE per kilogram in them. Try a feed which states it has 8 MJ or 8.5 MJ of DE per kilogram, and you should find your horse much more amenable.

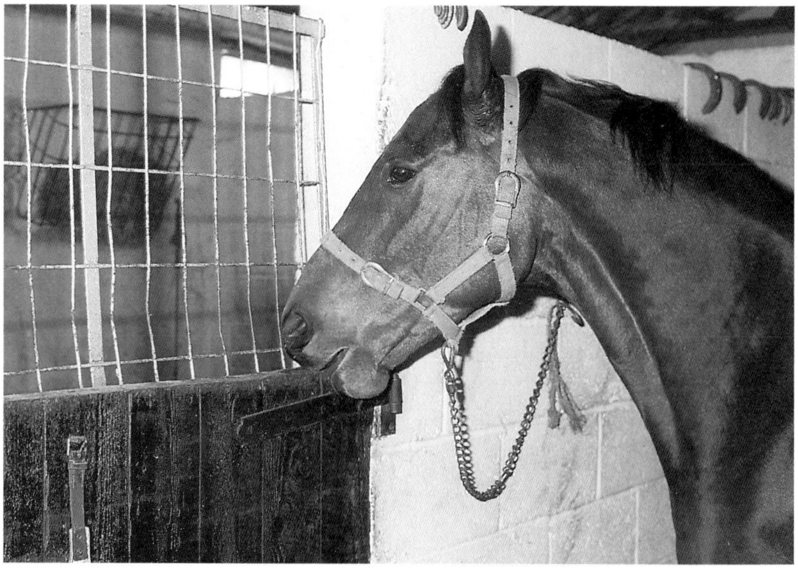

Stable vices such as crib-biting, shown here, are not now believed to result from horses copying each other. They are almost certainly caused by the frustration and discomfort caused by an unsuitable management régime. Some horses in a yard, therefore, may be affected, but others may not, depending on their individual temperaments and needs

Stable Vices

Q My horse is kept at livery in a yard where, I have noticed, several horses crib-bite and weave. I have been warned that horses copy these vices so I asked particularly for mine to be stabled out of sight of those horses, but to my horror he, too, has started wood-chewing and continually digging in his bed. He has always been very settled before wherever I have kept him and I have, unfortunately, had to move him around quite a bit because of my husband's job. What could be the problem here?

A It is very possible that both your horse, and the other horses in this yard are not being fed anything like enough roughage – hay, hayage or forage. It is no longer generally felt by behavioural experts that stable vices are copied, but if several horses in a yard are affected then it is likely to be the management which is stressing them, and vices are their way of relieving their discomfort and anxiety.

Horses *must* have a lot of roughage in their diets, partly because their digestive systems will not function properly without it, and partly because they seem to have an inner need to be chewing most of the time in order to feel occupied and satisfied. Check how much hay, or whatever, your horse is being fed daily, and how and when. It is highly likely that your yard follows an exaggerated version of the old-fashioned routine of feeding horses hay only night and morning, and of feeding too little hay and too many concentrates.

Instruct the yard that your horse is to be fed as much good hay as he wants to eat – or hayage, or a forage feed of the right energy grade for the work he is doing – with few, if any cereal-based concentrates. Once he no longer feels hungry and bored he will very likely stop looking for the release inherent in stable vices.

Coping with COPD

Q *My vet recently told me that my horse suffers from chronic obstructive pulmonary disease, in other words that his permanent cough and runny nose are due to broken wind, and has told me to keep him on a clean-air régime with dust-free hayage, feed and bedding. I am trying to do this, but it is not very successful as far as his diet is concerned.*

Although his cough and general health seem to have improved, he finishes his hayage very quickly and has started to eat his new coarse mix almost violently, seeming to be always hungry. I tried putting him back on hay whilst retaining the coarse mix and dust-free shavings, but he started to cough again.

A The answer is either to soak his hay, or feed him *ad lib* hayage of a lower energy grade.

Feeding soaked hay

If you want to soak his hay, remember it must still be good quality hay to start with – soaking is not a means of making dusty hay acceptable. Soak the hay for a minimum of five minutes and a maximum of one hour, and let it stop dripping before you give it to him; but don't let it dry out, as the spores will once again shrink to a small enough size to allow them to be inhaled and so cause trouble.

If you prefer to keep to hayage, use a lower-energy grade *ad lib* so that he is not being overdosed with energy but still has enough material inside him to be satisfied, occupied and not so hungry for his coarse mix.

There is nothing to stop you mixing soaked hay with hayage, or feeding straw such as oat, barley or fodder straw. Some owners find that their horses show no allergic reaction when dry straw is included in their diet as opposed to dry hay, so you could try mixing straw with soaked hay or hayage, till you find the right combination for your horse's needs.

Using forage feed

Another alternative is to feed the horse on a good brand of forage feed: these are safe for COPD horses and you can feed them *ad lib* which is the best for most horses and ponies. You should also find, as with hayage fed *ad lib* , that you need few, if any, concentrates.

A Balanced Diet

Q *Although I feed my horse plenty of hay and he is turned out to graze every day, he persists in eating soil, droppings and chewing wood. He cannot be hungry, surely, so what is the problem?*

A It could well be that your horse's diet is not properly balanced as regards mineral content, as eating all the above materials is a clear sign of mineral imbalance or an upset micro-organism population in the lower gut. Get the vitamin and mineral content of your horse's diet checked, and try giving your horse a course of probiotics, and you should notice a big improvement. Ask your adviser about yeast supplemements, too, as these can often help to stabilise the gut environment and improve digestion.

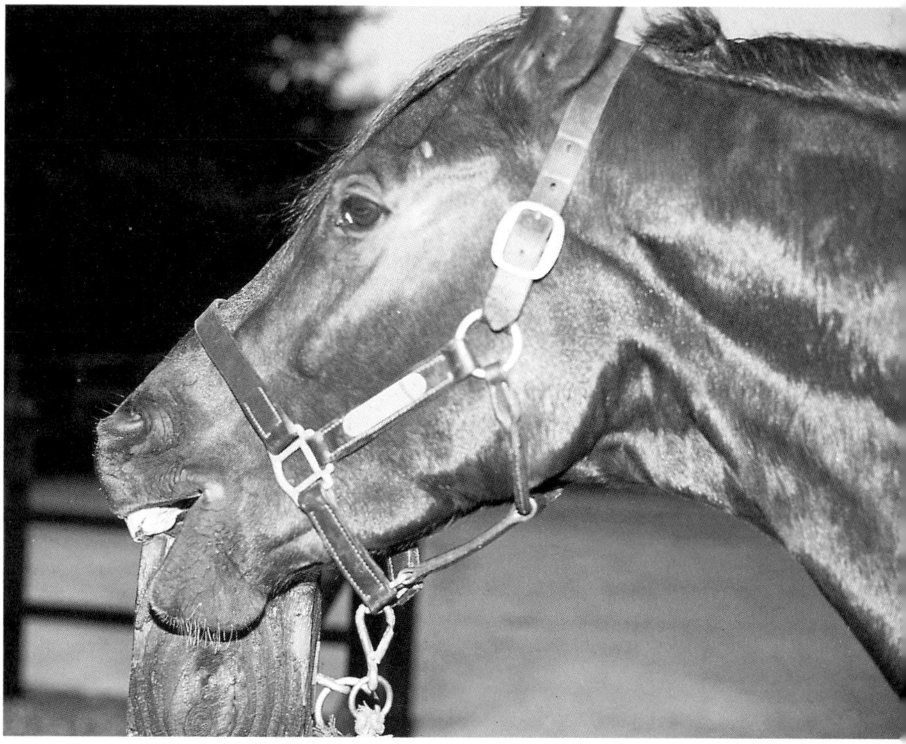

Chewing wood and dirt, and even clothing, manes and tails, may well be caused by lack of minerals in the horse's diet as well as by insufficient bulky roughage

A Bad Start

Q I have a small livery yard and it has recently been discovered that one of my residents is in foal. The mare was acquired by a client a few weeks ago in very poor condition and was not vetted before purchase. Last week the vet was called to check her over generally, to give vaccinations and so on, and he declared her to be about six months pregnant – something of a shock to all of us! Our main concern is that as she is so very poor – her topline and neck are extremely hollow and her ribs are showing – her foetus may have been damaged by malnutrition. Is it too late not only to get weight on the mare, but also to provide the foetus with what it needs for a fair start in life?

A From a nutrition and development point of view the most critical period of pregnancy is the last three months; you therefore have two months in hand, as it were, to start building up the mare and then you can continue the process during her last three months. The three months after foaling are also very demanding on her, as she has to produce maximum output of high quality milk for her young foal. Obviously, the ideal is for the mare to have good nutrition all through pregnancy, but the food she gets will go first to the developing foetus – so the chances are that the foetus will not have suffered unduly.

An appropriate worming programme

As she has obviously been neglected she will probably have a heavy worm burden, and you should ask your vet what you should worm her with: not all worming medicines (anthelmintics) are safe to give to pregnant mares.

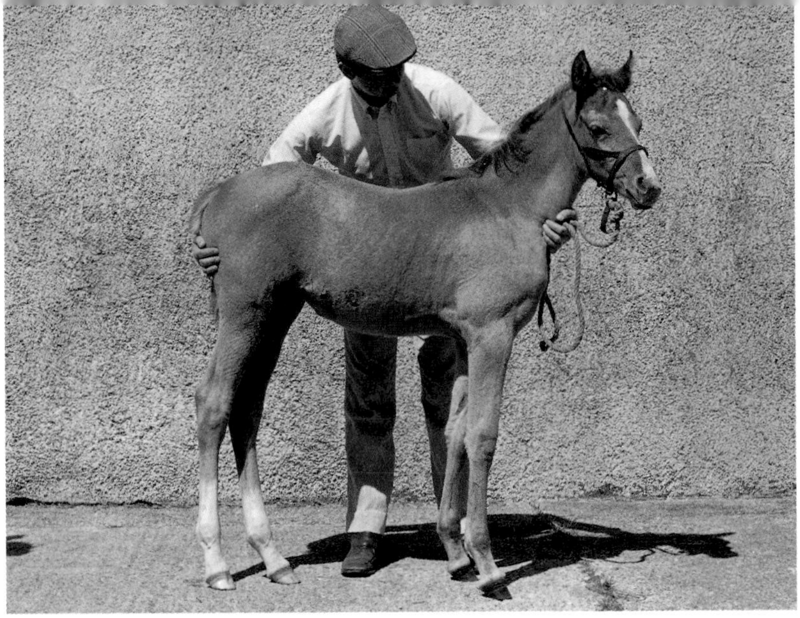

This picture shows a healthy, well-grown foal who is absolutely correctly covered – not too thin and not too fat – with strong, 'straight' legs. This is an ideal at which to aim and is perfectly possible with the right advice and diet

The foal when it arrives will also need worming regularly, again on your vet's advice, as foals have no immunity to worms. If the mare is well wormed now and you continue with whatever programme your vet advises you will minimise any damage she might suffer as much as possible.

Check her teeth

Presumably the vet checked her teeth and treated them as was necessary. Obviously, sound teeth and a worm burden which is as low as possible are most important in helping your mare make the most use of her food.

Introducing a better diet

You will be aware of the importance of introducing a higher plane of nutrition very gradually, particularly as the mare is obviously run down. The fairly failsafe way to feed her is to use products intended for breeding stock from one reputable manufacturer, as then you should be sure that the feeds will be of good quality, they will be individually balanced and will complement each other. The firm's nutritionist will also be on call for free advice on any feeding queries you may have if you are using their feeds.

The mare should be well covered over her ribs and topline without, of course, getting fat; you can condition score her, as any horse, to ensure that, allowing for her enlarging belly, she is in correct mid-way condition on a condition score scale. Being overweight can be as bad as being very thin, as it puts excessive strain on the mare's entire body and can make for a difficult foaling.

It is *not* advisable to pump her full of high protein feeds, even though she is poor. Allowing for her condition and stage of pregnancy, you could give her a diet of about 12 per cent protein at present. The normal recommendation for broodmares in the last three months of pregnancy is 11 per cent, which should be fine for her once she has improved in condition. After foaling she will need 14 per cent for three months, and 12 per cent thereafter until the foal is weaned. If a fairly natural weaning process is going to be allowed and the mare returned to work gradually, she can go on to a normal working horse's diet (initially for light to medium work) once the foal is about nine months old.

Feeding the foal

Once the foal starts to feed at about three months of age it will need a high protein diet of about 18 to 20 per cent. It will start gradually eating grass and trying to nibble the dam's rations, but at three months it would be best to ensure that the mare and foal get separate rations suitable for each of them, either by someone standing by whilst they feed to ensure that one does not steal the other's feed (this can happen either way!) or by feeding the foal in a creep in the field, a creep being a special construction of posts and a rail under which the foal can walk to reach feed in the middle but which the mare cannot negotiate.

With these diets and the advice of your vet and a good nutritionist, you should find that mare and foal come through a bad start very well.

Dealing with Tartar

Q *My old horse's teeth are covered in a brown film or layer which seems very hard and won't scrape off with my fingernail. I have not tried anything harder such as a file. He seems to eat all right and is not in poor condition. What could it be and is it important? He has mainly soft food as he is old.*

A The layer sounds like tartar which forms when horses have a good deal of soft food such as mashes or cooked feeds. Has your veterinary surgeon told you specifically to feed soft food, I wonder, perhaps because of worn teeth in an old horse? Natural feeds for the horse are grass and hay, and most concentrates which are traditionally fed have natural fibre, such as oats with their husks, and these would constantly scrape the teeth fairly clean; soft feeds, however, cannot do this.

Tartar can eventually cause inflamed and bleeding gums and predisposes these areas to disease. Contact your veterinary surgeon and ask him if the soft feeds are really necessary and whether or not he feels it would be worthwhile to file away the tartar.

Stress-induced Colic

Q *Twice now my gelding has gone down with colic a couple of days after a competition; they were just mild attacks but were upsetting for both of us. The vet was called out each time and the horse recovered, but I want to stop it occurring again. Why should it happen at such a specific time, and what can I do to prevent it?*

A As this occurs after a disruption in the horse's routine (a competition) it is probably because the digestive régime is interrupted; it could also be in response to the stress of the excitement and the change in his daily living/working pattern.

The causes of colic

Any stress, even 'pleasant' stress such as excitement, can change the body's blood chemistry and this can, in turn, affect the horse's whole body; it can certainly disrupt the digestion and upset the microbial population of the hind gut. Travelling is particularly stressful, of course, especially if the driver is not sufficiently considerate of the precious cargo behind him. During a long journey it really is advisable to stop somewhere suitable every two hours so as to unload the horses and let them stretch their legs, pick a bit of grass, and stale; many horses will not stale in the horsebox. You should also allow one hour's recovery time for each hour the horse spends on the road before he competes.

Many people still follow the old practice of not giving the horse a haynet during the outward journey. This 'fast', combined with the recovery time he is given on arrival, means that the horse will be without food passing through his gut for too long: the 'bugs' in his gut will therefore be considerably weakened, and some even killed off, all of which makes for disrupted digestion. The horse should be able to have hay safely for the outward journey. Also, try to ensure that he is fed other feeds as near to his normal 'at home' times as possible, depending on when he will be required to work. In other words, keep his routine as near to his home routine as you can.

Ensure that he has plenty of opportunity to drink both in transit and at the event, as depriving him of water can certainly contribute towards a disturbed digestion. Take a large container of 'home' water for short periods away, and mix it with the water at the venue if you are going to be away for some time. Professional show animals, showjumpers and so on have to get used to foreign water tastes all the time, and some owners and grooms like to add something to make the horse feel that the water is familiar, such as a drop of peppermint essence or a little diluted molasses.

Why it is delayed

The reason for the slight delay in the occurrence of the colic ('a couple of days') after the competition is that it may take this long for the diminished efficiency of the depleted gut micro-organism population working on the food coming through for digestion to take full effect.

If you try to maintain your routine, make journeys as stress-free as possible, and keep your horse well fed and watered, you should greatly reduce the chances of colic later; you might also discuss with your vet or a nutritionist whether or not a susceptible horse may be a suitable candidate for probiotics, which help maintain and stabilise the micro-organisms.

Controlling Middle-age Spread

Q *My part-Arab horse that I use for riding club activities has started to get middle-age spread! I feed him just as I always have and he has the same medium level of work, but I am having great difficulty now in keeping his weight down. He is turned out for several hours daily on poorish keep and has* ad lib *hayage with small concentrate feeds. He is admittedly a greedy horse, but gets very fractious if stabled with no food at all. What can I do?*

Middle-aged horses, like other animals – and humans – often develop 'middle-age spread' so owners must be prepared to adjust their animals' diets accordingly as their metabolisms change with age

A His feed will have to be rationed whether he likes it or not, but it would be wrong to put him on a severe diet as this can cause serious digestive upset in a trickle-feeding herbivore such as a horse. You could reduce his grazing time, but as you say the keep is fairly poor this may not help much, and it would be better to use a low energy grade of hayage.

Use lower energy feed

Most hayage products, either branded or farm-produced, are significantly higher in nutrient content than hay and owners often do not realise just how 'rich' they are if using hayage of unknown nutritional analysis. Put your horse onto a hayage product or forage feed of no more than 8 MJ of DE per kg. Use his bodyweight to calculate how much total weight of feed per day he should have and then reduce it slightly as he is overweight.

Until he loses weight he should not really have concentrates in significant amounts: to fulfil his expectations at feed time just give him unmolassed chop with grated carrots; this will make a low-energy feed for him. Molassed chop has sugar in the molasses and is therefore higher in energy than the plain type; and carrots are not going to increase the energy content of his diet as would soaked sugar beet, for example, and in particular, obviously, the molassed sort.

Use a small-mesh net

Give him his hayage or a long forage feed in a small-mesh hayage net so he can only get out a few strands at a time; it will therefore take him longer to eat what he has. Give him several small nets a day with the largest at night – it is bad for him to have many hours with no food available – and accept that there will be shortish periods when he has no food at all in front of him. Remember that in the wild, equidae eat for roughly sixteen hours a day – not twenty-four!

How to prevent boredom

If boredom becomes a problem, try, if you can, to turn him out onto a surfaced (non-grass) schooling area with another horse and limited amounts of roughage feed, such as feeding straw, oat straw or barley straw. The company, low-energy roughage-type feed and the fact that he is outdoors should mean he has other things to occupy his mind than 'pigging out' all the time.

Exercise is as important as diet

Of course, dieting is only half the story with any overweight creature, equine or whatever: exercise is the other half. Give your horse as much steady work as you can; if he is very overweight, fast work should only be used judiciously until he is slimmer, as working a fat horse at a fast pace damages legs, heart and lungs. Long walks with spells of steady trotting and, ideally, hill work, will all use up energy and, hopefully, tire him too so he feels like resting when stabled and not eating all the time.

This régime should produce a definite improvement in him over a few weeks or months; if the weather or his work suggest that he needs more food, assess his condition carefully and his bodyweight before you consider increasing the energy level of his diet and perhaps feeding concentrates again.

What if my Horse won't eat Hayage?

Q *I am trying to change my horse over to a clean-air régime as he has a slight but permanent cough which my vet says is due to a mild allergy to dust and moulds. The only drawback so far is that the horse will not eat hayage and does not like soaked hay. He is not really a picky feeder and used to wolf down his ordinary dry hay. What can I do?*

A You can look in the advertisements in the equestrian press for a firm which sells vacuum-cleaned hay. There are several firms now doing this, and they claim to remove around 90 per cent of dust and moulds from the hay (and straw) they sell. You could also ring your local and regional feed merchants and tell them what you are looking for. (If they do not have it, do not be fobbed off with a sales pitch for other good hay as susceptible horses can still be affected by the spores which will be present even in what we would consider to be excellent hay.) If you have a local or regional horse magazine, ask the staff if they know of a supplier in your area: it is their job to keep up to date with what is available in the districts they cover.

One of the new bagged dry forage feeds used as a hay replacer would probably be quite acceptable to him.

Friendly persuasion

You can also try thoroughly mixing hayage with ordinary hay so the horse has to take some and gets used to the taste and smell very gradually. Shake out your hay well and fill a net with a handful of hay then a handful of hayage, and so on. Do not put in a few slices of hay then a large chunk of hayage as the horse will find it very easy to select only what he wants.

It could be that he does not like the brand you have bought; if this is the case you could try a different brand, or if buying from a farm, try a different farm and therefore a different batch.

If you can find a type he likes and mix it with hay initially, I am sure you will find he takes to it. Most horses like hayage so much that they do not want to revert to hay once they are used to it.

Always Worm Regularly

Q *The livery yard where I keep my horse will not let us turn our horses out during the winter. I sympathise with their view that this will ruin the paddocks, but am worried by their advice that we do not need to worm our horses so often if they are not eating grass, thus enabling us to save money. Is this true?*

A Certainly not. Worms vary in their activities, and are more active at some times than others. Worms taken in while the horse has access to grass take time to mature inside his body and can certainly cause trouble all winter even if he is not on grass for a few months. You should continue to worm your horse according to your vet's advice all year round. Probably the recommended period will be every four to eight weeks, depending how densely stocked the paddocks are during the grazing season, and what drug is used.

Incidentally, do replace the grass missing from your horses' winter diet by leading them out to graze on any suitable spot you can find during this period, and by asking the yard to give ample succulents in the feeds, soaked sugar-beet pulp and carrots being the most common and popular; they should have these in each feed, not just once a day.

A Forage-based Diet

Q *We feed our cob only nice hay in winter (with winter grass) and just grass at other seasons. However, I now understand that hay alone is deficient in certain nutrients, although he seems healthy. Should we continue with this diet?*

A Many apparently nice hays are short of vitamins and minerals, but the only way of knowing is to have them analysed. You could feed a branded forage mix instead which has balanced nutrients added; it may be more expensive, but it could set your mind at rest. If your cob's condition seems good you probably need not worry, but consider having your grazing assessed, too.

Picking up droppings daily goes a long way to greatly reducing the worm burden on your paddocks

Exposure to natural light is important for the manufacture of Vitamin D in the body. In winter, horses stabled or wearing turnout clothing may need supplementing

Vitamin D from Sunlight

Q *A friend has told me that I should not turn my horse out using a rug as he will become deficient in vitamin D. He is finely bred and in winter I feel I want him to have a rug to keep him fairly warm and dry during the day whilst I am at work. He comes in every night. I have heard that vitamin D is made in humans through the action of sunlight on the skin, but as the horse's skin is covered by hair surely this cannot be true of horses?*

A Yes, it is true. Enough light seems to get through the short summer coat to allow the process to take place, and the practice of turning horses out in a light rug during the spring, summer and autumn months must significantly inhibit the production of vitamin D in such animals. As in so many things, following nature as much as is reasonably possible is often the best way, and I feel it best not to use turnout rugs more than necessary.

In winter, when quite justifiably you want to rug your horse in the field, you can ensure that his feeds contain vitamin D or, if feeding 'straights' in feeds you make up yourself, you can use a good broad-spectrum supplement with vitamin D in it. Good hay contains vitamin D, but a given year's hay will usually have lost much of its vitamin D about six or seven months after harvesting; for horses on such a diet, the latter half of winter is therefore the time to pay particular attention to vitamin D supplementation.

Organic Feeds

Q *I have a little boy who is badly affected by synthetic additives in food and have been advised to keep him on as natural and organic a diet as possible. He has greatly improved, and this has started me thinking about organic feeds for our horse and pony. I have made enquiries but have come up against a certain amount of derision and certainly a brick wall when I question merchants and manufacturers. I find this amazing when one considers the increasing interest in things natural, old-fashioned and 'wholesome'. Is there any organic horse feed produced, and how can I find out about it?*

A You may like to contact the British Association of Holistic Nutrition and Medicine, 8 Borough Court Road, Hartley Wintney, Basingstoke, Hampshire, RG27 8JA for information on their recommended horse feeds. Merchants and manufacturers will probably produce feeds approved by the various organic organisations in due course in accordance with public demand. The derision is short-sighted and rude, of course, but not uncommon in the face of anything which is going to cause inconvenience and expense.

The subject of organically produced feed is not going to go away, and some manufacturers are making a start by using conservation-grade ingredients in their feeds – not actually organic, but a good deal more natural in origin than we have been used to. Synthetic additives may certainly affect horses and other animals in ways similar to those experienced by some humans, and even if a horse shows no signs of adverse effects, it is good to be thinking along the lines of prevention rather than cure should adverse reactions occur.

Don't Overfeed the In-foal Mare

Q *Our mare has recently been confirmed by our vet as in foal, much to our delight. We wish to do our very best by her and have increased her feed so as to feed for two. I hasten to add we haven't doubled her rations but have increased the energy and protein levels of the feed. What else should we do to ensure correct nutrition for her and the foal?*

A Possibly the first thing you should do is revert to her previous diet! She should not really be treated as a special case until she is several months pregnant. If she is working – and her regular exercise and routine will certainly be of benefit to her, unless her work is hard – she should be fed as for light to moderate work only as her body can easily cope with early pregnancy plus normal light work. Only when she comes into the last three months of her pregnancy should she start receiving a special stud diet, probably in the form of feed from a good manufacturer.

Ladybird, a mare from the famous Shalbourne Stud, shown as a winning broodmare in the 1950s. She is in foal but is not being fed for two!

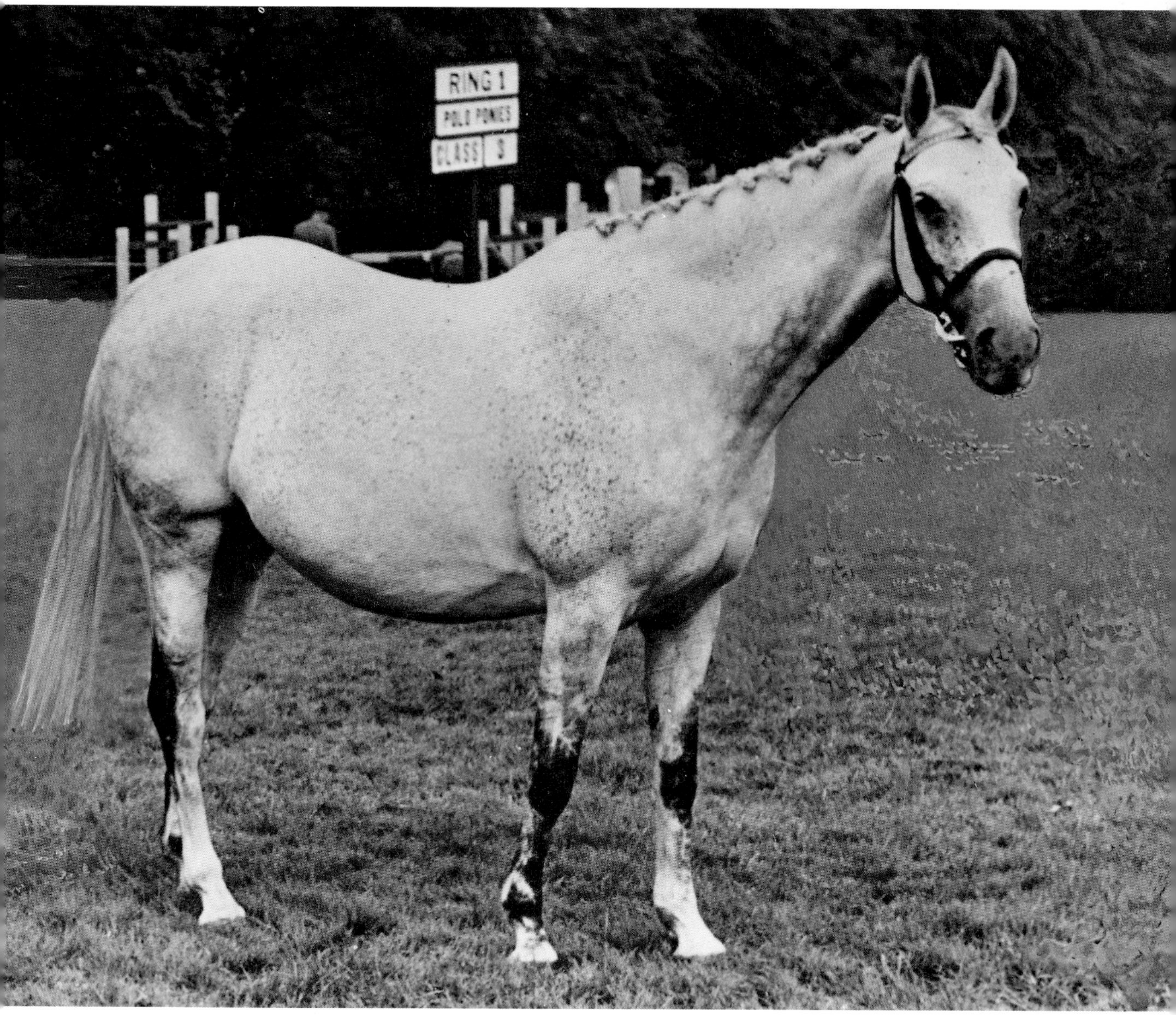

This Thoroughbred mare and foal on a top Thoroughbred stud are both correctly fed, *not* overweight. Fatness does not mean 'well-fed'

The Dangers of Overfeeding

Q *We have bred a lovely Thoroughbred foal from our elderly mare, and because he is rather special to us, we have been trying to do the very best by him. We have bred hunter and pony stock before, and we always take good care of our land without going over the top with fertilisers. However, we were advised that grass alone is not enough for a Thoroughbred even in spring, and so started supplementary feeding as soon as the foal showed interest in eating his dam's rations. Now, however, we are noticing various lumps and swellings around his fetlocks and knees and he seems generally sore on his legs. He does not have contracted tendons. What can be the problem?*

A It may well be that your grass is quite good enough to provide for all your foal's nutritional needs, and that it is not necessary to give him supplementary feed. Have you considered arranging for both a soil analysis to be done, and a herbage assessment so you can have a real idea of what he is eating? Why not contact your vet or an independent nutritionist and organise this, so you can see if the herbage he is eating is balanced for his needs? Meanwhile it would be safest to cut his concentrates by half, then half again and so on until he is getting only grass, and certainly consult your vet about the lumps and bumps.

Overfeeding is undoubtedly dangerous, and although youngstock need ample feed of the right sort, too much is in many ways worse than not enough. Take expert qualified advice on what extra feed, if any, to give your foal, remembering that he will need to be eating independently of his dam by weaning time.

Drinking Habits in Foals

Q *My mare foaled a few weeks ago and is feeding her foal very well. I realise that milk is all a young foal needs at first, but surely it should also be drinking water? Our foal has never been seen to drink water even when his dam does. We thought she would show him what to do, but he doesn't seem to be taking it on board. Will he be all right?*

A Your foal will surely start to drink very soon if he is not doing so already. You probably just have not noticed him doing so. Spend more time watching him, and as he develops you will surely see him drinking normally in due course.

Dunking Hay

Q *My horse is not broken-winded at all, and I feed her ordinary nice hay, but she insists on dunking it in her water before she eats – yet if I soak it for her she won't touch it! She makes an awful mess of her water doing this and I have to leave two buckets, one in a corner away from her haynet so she always has clean water to drink. Why does she do this, and how can I stop her?*

A It may annoy you that she does this, but she is obviously quite happy about it and I feel there is no real need to stop her. You could do what a friend of mine did and have the hay and water on opposite sides of the box in the hope that she will get tired of having to traipse to and fro across the box with each mouthful, and will eventually give up the habit. If she does not, however, or seems unhappy with the arrangement, perhaps it is not worth stopping her.

Feeding the Riding Club Horse

Q I am trying to get my horse fit for riding club hunter trials and events. He is my first horse and I have just brought him back to keep at home after a year of keeping him at livery. He has the company of a rescued pony and seems happy enough, but I don't know how to progress with his feeding as he gets fitter. He is currently on the diet he had at the livery stable, which is as much hay as he wants, with horse and pony nuts three times a day. He is 15.2hh and likes his food, but doesn't run to fat although he is not a poor doer. I need him to be fitter than he has been in the past, and am increasing his work carefully. What sort of diet should he be on?

A sensible diet and daily turnout will keep riding club-type horses physically well fed, with plenty of energy but no excess weight, and mentally relaxed

A If you wish to keep him on hay and cubes, be sure to get the best hay you can as far as quality goes. If he is half fit now, having been on moderate hacking work with a little schooling, meadow-type hay should suit him fine and should be all he needs for riding club and local event-type work. If you are more ambitious and aim at higher level work you could eventually and gradually change the hay for a seed hay of some sort.

As for cubes, use a type with a stated energy level of about 10 MJ of DE per kg for the present. If he progresses to quite hard work you can gradually change to one giving 12 MJ. You should not need more than this. With a good brand you need not worry about protein levels or vitamins and minerals as they should be properly balanced accordingly.

Feed ratios

For moderate work it would probably be advisable to split his daily hay and cubes into about two-thirds to three-quarters hay and one-third or one-quarter cubes, narrowing the ratio as he gets fitter. Current thinking, however, indicates that it is not a good plan to reduce the hay portion too much: in the past, hard-working horses (three-day eventers and suchlike) had their hay cut to only a quarter of their total daily ration, but nowadays this is often felt to be insufficient. Horses do need bulk and roughage in order for their digestive systems to work properly and digest the concentrate portion of their diet, so one-third hay would probably be the minimum he should ever have – and for riding club type work there is probably no need for it to be as little as this. A 50:50 ratio should be quite adequate for him, and it would probably be in order to keep his hay at about two-thirds of his ration and to increase the energy levels of hay and concentrates, if necessary.

Assessing his total daily feed

Use his bodyweight to calculate how much feed in total he needs per day, and work on feeding him 2.5 per cent of his bodyweight daily in total feed weight. You will have to see how he is on this sort of ration and adjust it according to his weight and energy. Feed him so that you feel his ribs fairly easily but cannot see them, and so that he has enough energy for his work.

With the increasing work of a fitness programme, you should find that the sort of ration and energy levels detailed above should be fine for him. Remember to cut down his concentrates and increase his hay if he is having time off, even if it is only a day; also to decrease the feed before the work and increase the work before the feed.

Avoid mashes

Do not follow the old practice of giving the horse a mash before a rest day: this constitutes a sudden change of feeding, even if the horse normally has bran. Instead, simply increase his hay and give him a very small concentrate feed bulked out with chop. You should add some chop to his nuts each feed, and add succulents, too, particularly if his grazing is curtailed for any reason. Lead him out in hand to graze, if necessary.

You say he likes his food, but you may find that if you increase his nuts and he has been having nuts for some months he may tire of them. If so, gradually change over to a coarse mix of the same energy level; horses often seem to continue to like these, whereas they sometimes go 'off' nuts or cubes.

Show Condition

The recent fashion for showing horses over-fat seems to have stemmed mainly from the 1960s.This lovely grey mare, Juniper, from the Shalbourne Stud, is in lean, well show condition and has won a championship. This picture was taken in the 1950s

Shalbourne Promised Land, with her breeder Miss Marguerite de Beaumont, shows excellent, lean but well-covered show condition. Few horses won more than the Shalbourne horses, which were always shown in correct, healthy condition. Another photograph taken in the 1950s

Q *I realise that there are moves afoot to persuade show exhibitors not to show their animals in what is nowadays considered to be an over-fat condition. However, I find that on showing my mare – an active hack as well as an amateur show horse – she is invariably placed well down the line despite having excellent conformation and going well for both me and the judge. A couple of judges have actually told me she would have been placed higher had she been in 'show condition'. I find this extremely frustrating. She is well covered but not fat and, I think, looks really well.*

A Old traditions and prejudices die hard! Try showing your mare in working classes such as working hunter and riding horse classes, or even potential competition horse classes, depending on her age. Pure showing classes (for hunters, hacks and so on) are the last bastions of old-fashioned ideas of what constitutes 'good' condition and otherwise, so if your horse has been correctly fed and is in *real* good condition she may look lean compared to her tubby fellow-competitors in such classes. Comfort yourself with the knowledge that she will be far healthier than they, all else being equal, and will probably have a longer, more comfortable working life. Your mare's wellbeing is surely far more important than any number of rosettes. Of course, if all competitors showed their animals in correct, healthy condition, the judges would have no choice but to put them up.

Rehabilitating a Two-year-old

Q *My wife and I have recently bought a two-year-old filly out of racing and she is in quite a poor state. Apparently she was raced early in her two-year-old season and did not stand up to it very well, being rather backward for her age and suffering from sore shins a good deal. She is not thin, yet she looks in poor health and depressed. As she is still growing should we be feeding her as stud stock, that is for growth, and will the sore shins have caused any permanent damage?*

A A two-year-old can, for practical feeding purposes, be treated almost as a mature horse in light work. Although she will still grow somewhat and fill out, she does not need excessive protein or energy. Feed her a good quality, balanced forage feed with the same company's recommended concentrate feeds as a back-up, to be sure of her intake, and speak to their nutritionist about her dietary requirements. Basically she needs about 10 to 11 per cent protein in her diet and 8.5 MJ of DE per kg. In spring and summer much depends on the quality of the grazing you have for her, but do not be tempted to overfeed her.

Rest and Dr Green

She may well be depressed and under par after her rough start, but a year off to let down and mature, and to get used to the fact that she will be kindly treated, will produce a vast improvement in her stature and general health. The sore shins should not have caused any permanent damage, although her joints, too, will have been subject to a good deal of stress. Arrange for your vet to check her over and possibly X-ray her legs so as to try and get more information on this. Although she has been ridden, I feel she should now be given a full year off before starting her again, to allow her back to mature and strengthen; youngsters generally mature from the ground up, the spine being one of the last body parts to mature. Correct nutrition, company, freedom and kind treatment will produce a big difference in her.

The Fussy Feeder

Q *My gelding is a very sporadic eater: sometimes he tucks into his food and at other times he doesn't want it, yet if I give him something different he will generally eat it happily. I have had my vet check his mouth, and all the feed is good: it just seems that he doesn't like the same thing all the time, yet this is how we are supposed to feed horses, to avoid sudden change. He has not had colic with these constant sudden changes, but I am a bit worried about the situation. Should I continue as I am doing now, or is there anything else I can do to improve his eating habits?*

A Fussy feeders can be a real head ache. You obviously know your horse well, but in addition to his mouth and the quality of the feed, have you checked the following points: his general health (he could have a sub-linical disorder), something so slight as to be unnoticeable); the cleanliness of his feed container, and also your storage and mixing equipment; the stabling arrangements – perhaps he is stabled next to an animal he does not like, or is stabled away from his friend, or in too noisy or quiet or boring an environment; maybe there is insufficient roughage/bulk in his whole diet; or his stable routine is inconsistent. These are all points which can affect eating habits.

As your horse has not actually had colic, presumably his digestive system is coping with his mental preferences; however, you could try a constant, gradual change to and from different feeds, never fully omitting one particular ingredient but constantly increasing and decreasing proportions, and see if he eats or seems any better. This could include a constantly changing mix of hay and hayage, perhaps, as well as other feeds.

As long as the horse seems content and healthy, I shouldn't worry too much about his eating habits, although a talk with a nutritionist (perhaps the one at the company whose feeds you use) may set your mind at rest.

A Régime for the Fat Pony

Q *We are having great difficulty in keeping our daughter's pony slim. We keep him with my wife's hunter mare at home on moderate grazing and with hay at night but no concentrates. When the mare receives a bucket feed the pony is given chop and carrots, but he is still too fat. He has not had laminitis but why, I do not know! What can we do?*

A Try to arrange some sort of grassless turnout for the pony. Depending on their individual temperaments, a grassless area next to the mare's paddock may be your answer, so the two are still together but the pony cannot get at the grass except possibly through the fence. It is far better to keep the pony like this where he is likely to walk around a bit, than to stable him away from the grass. Use your imagination about this area; most premises have some corner somewhere which could be converted, maybe with electric fencing. And if you have to turn him on grass most of the time, try to strip-graze the area, or fit him with the type of muzzle which enables him to get only a very few blades of grass at a time – though be very sure that the muzzle allows him to drink without trouble, as going short of water can obviously be very harmful. Your vet may be able to help you find a suitable muzzle if your saddler cannot.

If you can put him somewhere with no grass, he must nevertheless of course have some food; you could try feeding him a low-nutrient but clean hay, or a feeding straw such as oat or barley straw instead of the hay. Alternatively you could feed a special forage feed which is specially formulated for laminitic or native ponies: it doesn't matter that he has not had laminitis – this sort of feed is still what he needs in order to reduce his weight yet provide him with proper nutrition. The chop and carrots could be continued at feed times.

Exercise is essential

You must exercise the pony, but *not* by making him charge around on the lunge. He needs plenty of walking and gentle trotting, ideally two stints a day. If you do lunge him, take it steady, as fast work is damaging to a fat animal. Have you considered buying a small cart and driving him, maybe to the shops instead of taking the car? Driving can be great fun for pony and owners alike. It can be difficult for adults to exercise their children's ponies and driving is a good way to do it.

Keeping Weight on the Older Horse

Q *I have an old horse which I have owned since he was fifteen (sold to me cheaply as an 'old wreck and past it'). That was eight years ago and he is still going strong as my hack, apart from the fact that it is getting more and more difficult to keep weight on him although he only does the same work. He has the same strength and energy and I worm him regularly. I asked my vet to check his teeth but he said that if the horse is eating normally this is not necessary. Can you help?*

A First, I should contact your vet again and say you definitely want your gelding's teeth checking thoroughly. I prefer a vet to use a special gag which keeps the horse's teeth apart so that he can really check right to the back of the cheek teeth comparatively easily and without danger of being bitten. Not all vets use them, however, although this is perhaps not important as long as he really does a thorough job; just a quick look is not good enough – he must feel for sharp edges and hooks, and for missing, loose or damaged teeth.

A suitable worming régime

Second, check with your vet the suitability of your worming régime. He should be in the best position to know what species are more common in your area and what drug resistances, if any, the worms are developing, and he should be able to recommend different drugs to counteract this. Different drugs may also be recommended at different times of year to catch, for instance, bots and tapeworms as well as the more usual parasites, small redworm being the most dangerous.

Also be sure you are worming often enough. The general advice is still to worm, on average, every six weeks all year round to be quite sure of keeping burdens down. However, if you use the drug ivermectin (zimecterin in the USA) it is usually acceptable to leave a slightly longer time between doses as it kills migrating larvae as well as mature worms, so really giving the horse a good 'clear out'.

Changing dietary needs

With the teeth and worming régime in order, the horse can make the best of his food. Nevertheless, the digestive system and general metabolism in the older horse often do not work as well as in the younger animal, so even though the feed may be the same and his teeth are working properly and the food itself is not wasted by parasites, it may be that it is not being digested or used as effectively. Also, dietary needs often change when horses age, the most notable in older animals being for a higher level of digestible protein in the diet.

It would certainly be worth discussing your horse's changing needs with a nutritionist or vet interested in nutrition – they may well recommend that you increase the protein level of his diet to around 14 per cent. This could be achieved by giving feeds which are generally higher in protein; by feeding a special mix compounded for old horses, which should also take account of changing needs for vitamins and minerals; or simply by feeding a special protein supplement.

Probiotics and/or yeast

To help the digestive system it may be recommended that the horse is given a course of probiotics and/or that a yeast product is added to his feeds. The probiotics will enhance the population of gut micro-organisms in the hind gut, and the yeast will help maintain a favourable gut environment for them to thrive and breed: the healthier the gut micro-organisms, the more efficient the horse's digestion will be, so enabling him to make the best possible use of his feed.

This combined plan of action should ensure that your horse's condition improves and remains satisfactory – unless there is some other reason why he is losing weight, such as actual disease. If the problem is very worn teeth, a softer but highly nutritious diet may still do the trick, but only your vet can determine these factors.

ACKNOWLEDGEMENTS

I should like to offer sincere thanks to the following people and organisations for their help, advice and support in connection with this book, and for information and photographs provided.

Sue Hall, my editor, and the team at David & Charles for their constant patience, understanding, tact and skill in piecing everything together. There is never any clue from the finished article as to just how complex writing and publishing a book is, and without a competent team approach it is just not possible to do a good job.

Hilton Herbs Ltd
Downclose Farm, North Perrott, Crewkerne, Somerset TA18 7SH

Dengie Crops Ltd
Hall Road, Asheldham, Southminster, Essex CM0 7JF

Rumenco
Stretton House, Derby Road, Stretton, Burton-on-Trent, Staffordshire DE13 0DW

Stafford Saddlery (for Aquacrop/Natrafeed)
Woodings Yard, Bailey Street, Stafford ST17 4BG

The International League for the Protection of Horses
Anne Colvin House, Hall Farm, Snetterton, Norwich, Norfolk NR16 2LR

The Horses and Ponies Protection Association
HAPPA House, 64 Station Road, Padiham, Burnley, Lancashire BB12 8EF

Robert Eustace FRCVS
The Laminitis Clinic, Mead House Farm, Dauntsey, Wiltshire SN15 4JA

Ms Janet Ely BVSc, MRCVS
Hurstwood Cottage, All Stretton, Church Stretton, Shropshire SY6 6LA

Miss Gillian McCarthy
The Dairy, Millslade Farm, Station Road, Ashcott, Bridgwater, Somerset TA7 9QP

PICTURE ACKNOWLEDGEMENTS

Kit Houghton pp2–3, 6, 7, 8, 10, 11(btm), 12(both), 13, 16, 17, 18, 23, 35(both), 38–9, 43(all), 50(both), 54, 57(both), 66, 67, 71, 74, 78, 79, 80, 85(both), 86, 87, 89, 93, 94, 99(top left and right), 102(both), 104, 114, 118, 121, 123, 126, 129, 130(top), 131(btm rt), 132(btm), 134(btm), 137, 145, 150
Bob Langrish pp4–5, 20, 31, 48, 52, 63, 81(centre left), 106, 116, 122, 130(btm), 131(btm left), 132(top), 140, 141, 142, 143, 144, 153
HAPPA p11(top and centre)
ILPH p98(both)
Photonews pp151, 154(both)
David Duckett p19(both)
Gregory Enterprises p134(top)
Peter Sweet p152
Horse and Rider pp30, 95, 100
Main Ring p55
RASE pp81(except centre left), 112

INDEX